ST/ESA/STAT/SER.Y/4

Department of International Economic and Social Affairs **Statistical Office**

**Statistics on
Special Population Groups**

Series Y   No. 4

Disability
Statistics Compendium

United Nations   New York, 1990

Note

The designations employed and the presentation of material in this publication do not imply the expression of any opinion whatsoever on the part of the Secretariat of the United Nations concerning the legal status of any country, territory, city or area or of its authorities, or concerning the delimitation of its frontiers or boundaries.

The term "country" and "area" as used in the text of this publication also refer, as appropriate, to territories, cities or areas.

Symbols of United Nations documents are composed of capital letters combined with figures.

ST/ESA/STAT/SER.Y/4

This publication has been prepared by the Statistical Office, Department of International Economic and Social Affairs of the United Nations Secretariat, with financial assistance from the United Nations Voluntary Fund for the Decade of Disabled Persons.

UNITED NATIONS PUBLICATION

Sales No. E.90.XVII.17

Inquiries should be directed to:
PUBLISHING DIVISION
UNITED NATIONS
NEW YORK, NY 10017

PREFACE

The World Programme of Action concerning Disabled Persons[1] was adopted by the United Nations General Assembly by its resolution 37/52 of 3 December 1982. In paragraph 198 of the World Programme the Statistical Office, Department of International Economic and Social Affairs of the United Nations Secretariat, together with other units of the Secretariat, the specialized agencies and regional commissions, were urged to co-operate with the developing countries in evolving a realistic and practical system of data collection based either on total enumeration or on representative samples, as may be appropriate, in regard to various disabilities, and in particular, to prepare technical manuals/documents on how to use household surveys for the collection of such statistics, to be used as essential tools and frames of reference for launching action programmes to ameliorate the condition of disabled persons.

The United Nations was also requested in the World Programme to develop in the years following the International Year of Disabled Persons (1981) suitable systems for the regular collection and dissemination of information on disability for programme evaluation at all levels (paras. 194 and 195). In response to this request, the Statistical Office completed in 1988 a microcomputer data base called "United Nations Disability Statistics Data Base" (DISTAT, Version 1). DISTAT contains disability statistics from national household surveys, population censuses, and population or civil registration systems of 55 countries. It is the first international data base of its kind.

Based upon the national statistics available in DISTAT, the Statistical Office has prepared the present document, which is the first international compendium of disability statistics. It provides detailed national data on 12 major topics about disabled persons, including age, sex, residence, educational attainment, economic activity, marital status, household characteristics, causes of impairment and special aids used. A draft of a preliminary version of the *Disability Statistics Compendium* was presented to the Global Meeting of Experts to Review the Implementation of the World Programme of Action concerning Disabled Persons at the Mid-Point of the United Nations Decade of Disabled Persons, held at Stockholm from 17 to 22 August 1987. At that meeting it was recommended that the draft be expanded and published as a contribution to the World Programme of Action concerning Disabled Persons. The comments of the experts at the Stockholm meeting have been taken into account in preparing the *Compendium*. The Statistical Office has collaborated with the United Nations Centre for Social Development and Humanitarian Affairs of the United Nations Office at Vienna and the World Health Organization on the development of the conceptual framework for the *Compendium*. Some financial support for the *Compendium* was provided by the Voluntary Fund for the United Nations Decade of Disabled Persons (previously the International Year of Disabled Persons Trust Fund).

---

[1] A/37/351/Add.1 and Add.1/Corr.1, annex, sect.VIII, recommendation, (IV).

In addition to the compilation and dissemination of disability statistics, a major goal of this volume is to establish international statistical standards which reveal the commonalities of national work on disability while also pointing out their differences. Another goal is to identify the substantive and methodological links between the various disciplines which produce disability statistics and to work towards a common framework for their further development. This has not been a simple task. There are few guidelines or recommendations at this time for production and compilation of disability statistics. Much of the work has been exploratory. Nevertheless, The *Compendium* provides valuable information on various methodologies for the further production of disability statistics which may lead to increased comparability and broader use of the findings by policy makers, planners and researchers.

The statistics presented in The *Compendium* are compiled from a subset of national statistical reports contained in DISTAT. DISTAT consolidates the available census and survey statistics on disability through the use of spreadsheets on microcomputers. Users of The *Compendium* who are interested in having access to DISTAT may use forms given in annex II of the present publication to order copies of the of the DISTAT *Technical Manual*,[2] which provides documentation and illustrations of the data base structure. Governments, organizations and researchers obtaining copies of the data base will automatically receive a copy of the *Technical Manual*. All registered DISTAT users will be kept informed of new work on disability statistics and any changes and updates to the data base that may be made by the Statistical Office in the coming few years. Comments and suggestions concerning either the present *Disability Statistics Compendium* or DISTAT are welcome. They should be addressed to the Director, Statistical Office, United Nations, New York 10017.

---

[2] *United Nations Disability Statistics Data Base, 1975-1986: Technical Manual* Statistical Papers, Series Y, No.3 (United Nations publication, Sales No.E.88.XVII).

CONTENTS

Annexes

List of tables

List of Figures

Explanatory notes

Reference to "dollars" ($) indicates United States dollars, unless otherwise stated.

The term "billion" signifies a thousand million.

A hyphen (-) between years, e.g., 1984-1985, indicates the full period involved, including the beginning and end years; a slash (/) indicates a financial year, school year or crop year, e.g., 1984/85.

A point (.) is used to indicate decimals.

The following symbols have been used in the tables:

Two dots (..) indicate that data are not available or are not separately reported.

A dash (--) indicates that the amount is nil or negligible.

A hyphen (-) indicates that the term is not applicable.

A minus sign (-) before a number indicates a deficit or decrease, except as indicated.

Details and percentages in tables do not necessarily add to totals because of rounding.

I. INTRODUCTION

A. United Nations programme on global monitoring of disablement

The present publication is a compendium of national disability statistics available for monitoring the implementation of the World Programme of Action concerning Disabled Persons, pursuant to paragraphs 194-195 and 198 of that Programme.[1] It is based upon the national statistical work that has been compiled in the newly produced United Nations Disability Statistics Data Base (DISTAT), Version 1.[2]

Disability description is confounded by divergent use of terminology by Governments, professionals, legislators, by disabled persons and their representative groups. In this *Compendium*, the words "disability", "disabled persons", and "disablement" are used to describe the generic situation of being "disabled", implying that one is part of a special population group of persons broadly referred to in the World Programme of Action concerning Disabled Persons. All references to *impairments*, *disabilities* and *handicaps* specifically use the definitions and codes applied to these terms in the International Classification of Impairments, Disabilities and Handicaps (ICIDH) issued by the World Health Organization.[3] Briefly, using ICIDH terminology, these three concepts are defined below:

(*a*) *Impairment:* "any loss or abnormality of psychological, physiological, or anatomical structure or function"; Impairments are disturbances at the level of the organ which include defects or loss of limb, organ or other body structure, as well as defects or loss of mental function. Examples of impairments that have been asked about in censuses or surveys include: blindness; deafness; loss of sight in an eye; paralysis of limb; amputations of limb; mental retardation; partial sight; loss of speech; mutism.

(*b*) *Disability:* a "restriction or lack (resulting from an impairment) of ability to perform an activity in the manner or within the range considered normal for a human being"; It describes a functional limitation or activity restriction caused by an impairment. Disabilities are descriptions of disturbances in function at the level of the person. Examples of disabilities that have been asked about in censuses or surveys include: difficulty seeing; speaking; hearing; moving; climbing stairs; grasping; reaching; bathing; eating; toileting.

---

1 The World Programme of Action concerning Disabled Persons was adopted by the United Nations General Assembly at its thirty-seventh session on 3 December 1982 by its resolution 37/52. See *Official Records of the General Assembly, Thirty-seventh Session, Supplement No. 51* (A/37/51).

2 For a more detailed discussion of DISTAT, see *United Nations Disability Statistics Data Base, 1975-1986: Technical Manual,* Statistical papers, Series Y, No. 3 United Nations Publication, (Sales No. E.88.XVII.12).

3 World Health Organization, *International Classification of Impairments, Disabilities and Handicaps* (Geneva, 1980), pp. 27-29.

(c) *Handicap:* a "disadvantage for a given individual, resulting from an impairment or disability, that limits or prevents the fulfilment of a role that is normal (depending on age, sex and social and cultural factors) for that individual"; the term is also a classification of "circumstances in which disabled people are likely to find themselves". Handicap describes the social and economic roles of impaired or disabled persons that place them at a disadvantage compared to other persons. These disadvantages are brought about through the interaction of the person with specific environments and cultures. Examples of handicaps that have been asked about in censuses, surveys and registries include: bedridden; confined to home; unable to use public transport; not working; underemployed; socially isolated.

People are identified in censuses, surveys and registration systems as "disabled" through screening of their impairments and/or disabilities. "Handicap", as described in the above definition of ICIDH, is not being utilized as a concept for identifying and screening disabled persons into censuses, surveys and registration systems; it is instead used as an analytical tool for assessing the social and economic situation of disabled persons identified through reporting of impairments or disabilities.

The World Programme of Action concerning Disabled Persons laid out some of the major concepts proposed for the study of the general situation of disabled persons and for monitoring programme action. The concepts include: prevention; rehabilitation; equalization of opportunities for education, employment and social role; disability and the new international economic order; and the consequences in economic and social development to disabled persons.

The World Programme of Action provides for monitoring the implementation of national action in order to:

(a) Increase participation of disabled persons in decision-making;
(b) Prevent impairment, disability and handicap;
(c) Develop rehabilitation programmes;
(d) Equalize opportunities of disabled persons with other population groups;
(e) Increase community action and interaction with disabled persons;
(f) Improve staff training for special disability programmes;
(g) Provide information and public education.

Although there is room for improvement, censuses, surveys and registration systems are already addressing a number of these issues. Table I.1 shows the topics covered in 63 national censuses, surveys and registration systems of 55 countries that have collected data on topics pertinent to the monitoring of the World Programme of Action. In all, 17 major topics, including assessment of socio-economic opportunity and integration are presented in table I.1. The table demonstrates that statistical work has already been started by countries on the socio-economic opportunities and integration of disabled persons, as well as on their personal experiences with impairments and disabilities. Each country having data on any particular topic is marked with an X. The actual topics being covered can be compared with the illustrative classification of topics suggested by the Expert Group Meeting on Disability Statistics, discussed in section B below.

Table I.1. Topics covered in national publications and reports concerning disability by type of data collection programme

(a) Demographic, socio-economic, household and family formation

Country or area	Data collection programme/ year	Demographic		Socio-economic			Household and family formation			
		Age group/ sex	Urban/ Rural	Educa-tional attain-ment	Economic activity	Occupation, industry and employment	Marital status	Household characteristics	Family information	Household and personal income
Census										
Total population										
Bahrain	1981	X		X	X					
Comoros	1980	X								
Egypt	1976	X		X	X	X				
Hong Kong	1981	X		X	X	X	X	X		X
Indonesia	1980	X								
Kuwait	1980	X		X	X	X				
Mali	1976	X	X							
Mexico	1980	X								
Neth.Antilles	1981	X								
Pakistan	1981	X	X							
Panama	1980	X								
Peru	1981	X		X		X				
Poland	1978	X								
Sri Lanka	1981	X	X			X		X		
Saint Helena	1976	X						X		
Tunisia	1984	X	X		X					
Tunisia	1975	X	X	X	X					
Turkey	1975	X								
United States	1980	X	X							
Subtotal		19	6	6	6	5	1	3	0	1
Economically inactive										
Belize	1980	X								
Burma*	1983	X	X							
Cape Verde	1980	X								
Central African Rep.	1975	X	X							
Cuba	1981	X								
Guyana	1980	X								
Ireland	1981	X								
Kiribati	1978	X								
Philippines	1980	X	X							
Spain	1981	X								
Trinidad & Tobago	1980	X								
Venezuela	1981	X	X							
Subtotal		12	4	0	0	0	0	0	0	0
Agricultural										
Jordan	1983	X								
Subtotal		1	0	0	0	0	0	0	0	0
Surveys										
Health/medical										
Canada	1983	X		X	X	X	X	X		X
Egypt	1979-81	X	X	X	X	X				

* Now Myanmar

3

Table I.1 (a) (continued)

Country or area	Data collection programme/ year	Demographic		Socio-economic			Household and family formation			
		Age group/ sex	Urban/ Rural	Educa-tional attain-ment	Economic activity	Occupation, industry and employment	Marital status	Household characteristics	Family information	Household and personal income
United States	1982	X	X							X
Uruguay	1984	X								
Living conditions										
Denmark	1976	X			X					
Finland	1978	X	X		X	X				
New Zealand	1980-81	X								
Norway	1983	X	X	X	X		X	X		
Sweden	1980-81	X		X	X	X	X	X	X	
Thailand	1981	X	X							
Demographic and socio-economic										
Fiji	1982	X	X							
China	1983	X	X							
Ethiopia	1979-81	X								
India	1981	X	X							
Swaziland	1983	X								
Thailand	1983	X	X							
Zimbabwe	1981	X		X	X					
Disability										
Australia	1981	X		X	X	X		X		X
Austria	1976	X			X					
Germany,Fed.Rep.of	1983	X								
Japan	1980	X			X	X	X			X
Nepal	1980	X	X		X				X	
Philippines	1980	X		X	X	X	X			
Trinidad & Tobago	1982	X								
Subtotal		24	10	7	12	7	5	4	2	4

Registration and other types

Country or area	Data collection programme/ year	Age group/ sex	Urban/ Rural	Educa-tional attain-ment	Economic activity	Occupation, industry and employment	Marital status	Household characteristics	Family information	Household and personal income
Schools										
Jamaica	1978	X	X	X						
General non-probability survey										
Kenya	1981	X		X		X			X	
Registration campaign										
Ethiopia	1981	X		X					X	
Jordan	1979	X								
Lebanon	1981	X								
UK (N.Ireland)	1978	X								
Disability registration										
Singapore	1985	X								
Subtotal		7	1	3	0	1	0	0	2	0
Grand total		63	21	16	18	13	6	7	4	5

Table I.1. (*continued*)

(b) Disability experience and other

Country or area	Data collection programme/ year	Presence of an additional impairment	Age of onset	Cause of impairment	Disability status	Severity of impairment/ degree of disability	Aids used for reducing disability	Services/ treatment received	Special disability issues
Census									
Total population									
Bahrain	1981			X					
Comoros	1980								
Egypt	1976								
Hong Kong	1981								
Indonesia	1980								
Kuwait	1980								
Mali	1976								
Mexico	1980								
Neth.Antilles	1981						X		
Pakistan	1981								
Panama	1980			X					
Peru	1981								
Poland	1978								
Sri Lanka	1981	X	X	X					
Saint Helena	1976								
Tunisia	1984								
Tunisia	1975								
Turkey	1975			X					
United States	1980								
Subtotal		1	1	4	0	0	1	0	0
Economically inactive									
Belize	1980								
Burma*	1983								
Cape Verde	1980								
Central African Rep.	1975								
Cuba	1981								
Guyana	1980								
Ireland	1981								
Kiribati	1978								
Philippines	1980								
Spain	1981								
Trinidad & Tobago	1980								
Venezuela	1981								
Subtotal		0	0	0	0	0	0	0	0
Agricultural									
Jordan	1983								
Subtotal		0	0	0	0	0	0	0	0
Surveys									
Health/medical									
Canada	1983			X	X	X	X		X
Egypt	1979-81							X	

* Now Myanmar

5

Table I.1 (b) *(continued)*

Country or area	Data collection programme/ year	Disability experience							Other
		Presence of an additional impairment	Age of onset	Cause of impairment	Disability status	Severity of impairment/ degree of disability	Aids used for reducing disability	Services/ treatment received	Special disability issues
United States	1982								
Uruguay	1984			X					
Living conditions									
Denmark	1976				X				
Finland	1978								X
New Zealand	1980-81								X
Norway	1983								X
Sweden	1980-81								X
Thailand	1981								X
Demographic and socio-economic									
Fiji	1982								
China	1983								
Ethiopia	1979-81								
India	1981		X	X			X	X	
Swaziland	1983								
Thailand	1983								
Zimbabwe	1981	X	X	X				X	
Disability									
Australia	1981		X						
Austria	1976		X			X	X	X	X
Germany,Fed.Rep.of	1983	X		X	X	X		X	X
Japan	1980			X		X			X
Nepal	1980			X					
Philippines	1980			X	X				X
Trinidad & Tobago	1982							X	X
Subtotal		2	4	9	4	5	3	6	11

Registration and other types

Schools

Jamaica	1978					X			

General non-probability survey

Kenya	1981		X	X		X			

Registration campaign

Ethiopia	1981		X	X					
Jordan	1979							X	X
Lebanon	1981								
UK (N.Ireland)	1978								X

Disability registration

Singapore	1985								
Subtotal		0	2	2	0	2	0	1	2
Grand total		3	7	15	4	7	4	7	13

Source: United Nations Disability Statistics Data Base (DISTAT, 1988).

As already mentioned, the WHO/ICIDH classification conceptually outlines three major components of disablement and then provides a framework for their description and measurement. These three components of ICIDH are useful for designing assessment of the three major goals for policy formulation and programme planning expressed in the World Programme of Action concerning Disabled Persons, namely, prevention, rehabilitation and equalization of opportunity.

In the World Programme of Action the three goals are described as follows:

(a) *Prevention:* measures aimed at preventing the onset of mental, physical and sensory impairments (primary prevention) or at preventing impairment when it has occurred, from having negative physical, psychological and social consequences;

(b) *Rehabilitation:* means a goal-oriented and time-limited process aimed at enabling an impaired person to reach an optimal mental, physical and/or social functional level, thus providing her or him with the tools to change her or his own life. It can involve measures to compensate for a loss of function or a functional limitation (for example by technical aids) and other measures intended to facilitate social adjustment or readjustment;

(c) *Equalization of opportunities:* the process through which the general system of society, such as the physical and cultural environment, housing and transportation, social and health services, educational and work opportunities, cultural and social life, including sports and recreational facilities are made accessible to all.

The text table below indicates how the three WHO/ICIDH components and the three United Nations goals complement each other. Shaded cells show the orientation of main activities of prevention, rehabilitation and equalization of opportunity programmes.

WORLD PROGRAMME OF ACTION			
ICIDH	Prevention	Rehabilitation	Equalization of opportunities
Impairments	I_p	I_r	I_e
Disabilities	D_p	D_r	D_e
Handicaps	H_p	H_r	H_e

The table provides a simplified description of survey strategy for monitoring disability programmes. Essentially, disabled people are identified through description of *impairments* and *disabilities*. Programmes are planned and implemented which aim to reduce impairments through the prevention of disease and accidents and through the general study of the cause of impairments, as well as through medical and health care for reduction in loss of function (cells I_p and I_r). An innoculation campaign for the prevention of infectious diseases, such as polio, which aims to innoculate total populations regardless of ability to pay, is an example of a prevention programme in cell I_e; in other words, it is an equal opportunity programme aiming to increase access to preventive services for reduction of impairments. Programmes are also planned and implemented which aim to reduce disabilities through early intervention and physical therapy, or which attempt to reduce barriers for disabled persons through the production and distribution of special aids to increase mobility, or vision, or the communication possibilities of disabled persons (cells D_r and D_e).

Prevention of handicaps, as shown in cell H_p, would work to reduce factors which isolate disabled persons (lack of services, negative community attitudes, prejudice towards disabled persons), whereas rehabilitation goals (cell H_r) might be to increase opportunities for independent living, community-based rehabilitation programmes, modified transport arrangements, public media programmes etc., to reduce the above mentioned negative influences. Equalization of opportunity programmes addressing handicaps (cell H_e) would concentrate on organizing opportunities for full participation and integration of disabled persons as national and international citizens.

B. General socio-economic and demographic framework

The general conceptual framework used by the Statistical Office for the development of social and economic statistics of special population groups, including disabled persons, is the United Nations framework for integration of social, demographic and related statistics.[4] Statistical measures of social equality, economic opportunity, marginality and socio-economic status of special population groups are strongly interrelated in their methodological and conceptual development. The use of an integrated framework encourages the development of disability statistics, not to study solely the disabled, but also the comparative situation of women, men, children, youth, the elderly, displaced persons, new migrants, rural households and large metropolitan communities concerning disability.

The way the data are organized in DISTAT leads to the development of indicators measuring equalization of opportunity and social integration for various groups of disabled persons. Indicators of opportunity and integration will very often match indicators developed on these same topics for other population groups. It is imperative that these statistical indicators be similar, otherwise disabled persons will be mistakenly viewed in the analysis as so uniquely different that comparisons with other population groups cannot be made.

Disabled persons are unique with respect to how they are studied in national censuses, surveys and registration or administrative record systems primarily because their impairments or disabilities are identified and reported. In all other ways, the goals of surveys measuring the situation of disabled persons and that of other special population groups are similar; for example, assessing demographic characteristics, social and economic status, patterns of school attendance and occupational histories, migration patterns or current residence.

---

4 *Toward a System of Social and Demographic Statistics*, Statistical papers, Series F., No. 18 (United Nations Publication, Sales No. E.74.XVII.8).

Generally five subject areas have been developed for statistical coverage of disability issues in population censuses, surveys and registration systems. They are (*a*) presence of impairments; (*b*) presence of disabilities; (*c*) causes of impairment, (*d*) social, economic and environment characteristics; and (*e*) distribution and use of services and support. The full list of related topics is given below, compiled in accordance with the recommendations of the Expert Group on Development of Statistics on Disabled Persons, which met at Vienna from 2 to 6 April 1984.[5]

The Expert Group generally supported the concepts of impairments and disabilities set forth in the WHO/ICIDH classification and agreed that work was needed in order to make the concepts more operable for survey purposes. A recommendation of the Expert Group was to define handicaps in terms of social, economic and cultural loss attributable to the interaction between the disability characteristics of disabled persons and the characteristics of their environment. In other words, handicap is a measure of social and economic conditions of the disabled when compared with other population groups who are not disabled. The Group noted that the scope of topics in ICIDH required modification in order to take into account measurement of principal social, economic and environmental concepts and the goal of equalization of opportunity set out in the World Programme.

Drawing on ICIDH and other technical documentation, the Expert Group developed the list of areas given in the illustrative classification below, which it proposed as a basis for the study of disablement through the use of population censuses, surveys and registration systems.

---

5 "Report of the Expert Group on Development of Statistics on Disabled Persons" (ESA/STAT/AC.18/7).

FIVE BROAD DISABILITY ISSUES

I. Presence of impairments

1.1 PHYSICAL

Sensory

Aural	Auditory sensitivity
Language	Language functions and speech
Ocular	Visual acuity

Other physical

Visceral	Internal organs and impairments of other special functions such as sexual organs, mastication and swallowing
Skeletal	Head and trunk region, mechanical and motor impairments of limbs and deficiencies of limbs
Disfiguring	Disfigurements of head and trunk regions and of limbs

1.2 INTELLECTUAL AND PSYCHOLOGICAL

Intellectual and other psychological	Intelligence, memory, thinking, consciousness and wakefulness, perception and attention, emotive and volitional functions and behaviour patterns

1.2 GENERALIZED AND OTHER

Generalized sensory and others

2.1 PHYSICAL FUNCTIONING

Locomotor	Ambulation and confining disabilities
Communication	Speaking, listening
Personal care	Personal hygiene, dressing, feeding and excretion
Body disposition	Domestic disabilities, such as preparing and serving food and care of dependants, and disabilities of body movement, such as fingering, gripping and holding
Dexterity	Skill in bodily movements, including manipulative skills and the ability to regulate control mechanisms

2.2 SOCIAL FUNCTIONING

Behaviour	Awareness and disabilities in reactions
Situational	Dependence and endurance and environmental disabilities relating to tolerance of environmental factors

2.3 OTHER

Disabilities of particular skills and other activity restrictions

III. *Causes of impairment*

Infectious and parasitic diseases
Congenital anomalies and perinatal conditions
Injury:

> Motor vehicle accidents
> Other transport accidents
> Accidental poisoning
> Injury resulting from accidental falls, fire, and operations of war
> Other external causes including natural and environmental factors
> Other diseases and conditions

IV. *Social, economic and environment characteristics*

Sex, age
Marital status
Household and family characteristics, or institutional
    characteristics
Education and training
Employment and occupation
Income and consumption
Health and nutrition characteristics, may include variables
    such as height, weight and calorie intake
Geographical distribution, residence
Housing and environment
Leisure and culture
Social and political participation
Transport
Communication
Attitudes and norms
Legislation and civil rights

V. *Distribution and use of services and support*

Primary health care
Prevention
Treatment of accident or trauma
Maternal and child health and family planning
General health services
Education (general, special, vocational)
Employment
Rehabilitation (including vocational)
Compensatory economic measures, social security and pensions
Counselling and public education and information (community and
    family attitudes and behaviour)
Legal protection or equal and non-segregated opportunities
Provision of equal mobility opportunities
Elimination of environmental barriers
Provision of technical aids and equipment
Provision of services for independent living

Areas I and II, or the concepts of impairment and disability, have been discussed extensively at national and international meetings, and they pose a special challenge in the development of statistics on disabled persons using population censuses, surveys and registration systems. This is because these two concepts provide the data collection and programme strategy for the definition and identification of disabled persons. Area III, cause of disability, provides the needed health and medical explanation of disablement. Survey assessment of cause is particularly important for the study of disability prevention. Areas IV and V are analytically important to the study of handicap, because both social and economic characteristics of disabled persons and reports of services received are strong indicators of access to equal opportunity for medical care, educational training, public facilities etc.

C. International Disability Statistics Data Base (DISTAT)

Statistics for the description of disability are often overlooked, in part because knowledge about survey work in this area is lacking. The sources of published tabulations are not widely known or understood. Requests by ministries and disability programmes for a special survey on disability are often made in the absence of knowledge about existing recent censuses, surveys and registration systems in which disability data have been collected.

In order to increase the dissemination, evaluation and use of national statistics on disability, the Statistical Office of the United Nations Secretariat has developed a data base of national disability statistics. The goals of the data base are to:

(a) Inform policy-makers, programme planners, service providers and researchers of existing statistics on disability;

(b) Provide a standardized system for retrieving and compiling statistics that describe the situations of disabled persons, and which can be used to monitor community programmes and policies;

(c) Encourage the development of disability statistics within the existing framework of demographic, social and health statistics programmes; and

(d) Review statistical methods and concepts currently utilized by survey research work in this area so that new surveys build upon previous experience.

To date there is no intergovernmental data collection system that requests countries systematically to submit national disability statistics from censuses, surveys and registration systems, for international use. In the absence of such an international data collection system, the Statistical Office has initiated a world-wide review of published reports available in statistical libraries, as well as having communicated directly with national statistical offices and other government ministries in order to locate published national statistics.

Initial development of DISTAT was carried out by the Statistical Office in collaboration with the Research Institute of Gallaudet University, Washington D.C. In this work, 95 countries and areas are identified as having collected statistics on disabled persons in population censuses and surveys since 1975. Data from 55 of these countries and areas have now been systematically compiled in the micro-computer data base.

DISTAT provides a beginning for systematically documenting population census, household survey, and registration data on disability. Using modern data management and data base design technologies, national disability data have been consolidated, standardized and integrated from diverse sources, bringing together data from censuses, surveys and administrative reporting systems on selected issues of disablement. The tables presented in this publication, all of which are derived from DISTAT, are the first of their kind - internationally standardized tables of disability statistics based upon published national data sources.

The data base is organized into 22 sections; the first five describe the data sources and these, as well as the methods of collection used, are reviewed in chapter III, "Technical notes", of the present publication. The remaining sections present the statistics on impairment and disability conditions, social and economic characteristics of disabled persons and other related topics, such as special aids and services used. The content and organization of the data base are summarized below. A detailed explanation of the data base is available in the *United Nations Disability Statistics Data Base, 1975-1976: Technical Manual.*[2]

Other United Nations publications which review methodologies of disability statistics include the following:

Development of Statistics of Disabled Persons: Case Studies. Statistical papers, Series Y, No. 2. Sales No.86.XVII.17.

Development of Statistical Concepts and Methods on Disability for Household Surveys. Statistical papers, Series F, No. 38. Sales No. 88.XVII.4.

II. OVERVIEW

A. Data collection strategies

This *Compendium* assesses how disability concepts and definitions are used in countries to identify disabled persons and how this affects statistical findings. Statistics presented in the *Compendium* indicate that the percentage of disabled persons ranges from a low of 0.2 to a high of 20.9 per cent for the 63 surveys of the 55 countries, when including data from all types of definitions, age ranges and data collection systems and recognizing their lack of comparability. Because of the variability and lack of standards in presentation, table II.1 displays the percentage of disabled for each of the data sets of DISTAT, stratified by type of data collection procedure used, and documenting each of the age ranges and types of populations included in the data set.

The high degree of variability in disability rates is at least partly determined by the selection and use of impairment and disability definitions and codes. This study found, for example, that census, survey and registration estimates of the percentage of disabled are lower when impairment questions rather than disability questions are used to identify disabled persons. In addition, when impairment questions are used for screening purposes, the resultant disability rates for men are generally higher than those for women. In contrast, when disability screening questions are used, rates are similar for women and men, and in some cases disability rates for women are higher.

Another consequence of the different approaches to identification techniques is that there are notable regional differences in the percentage of disabled. The countries of Africa and Asia, which generally implement impairment screens in their censuses, surveys and registration systems in order to identify disabled persons, report lower rates than do the countries of Europe and North America, which generally use disability screens to identify disabled persons (with the exception of the Caribbean countries which, until now, are still using impairment screens). This suggests that regional comparisons of disability rates may be very misleading unless the methodological differences between data collection systems are clearly stated.

These findings emphasize the necessity for international guidelines and survey standards for data collection on disability, so that rates may be more comparable, and more meaningful, both within and across countries.

The Statistical Office has identified an aspect of survey-taking that is particularly problematic to the development of disability statistics. The problem is that there is no agreed strategy for identifying disabled persons in any data collection methods e.g., censuses, surveys, registration systems, in an acceptable and reasonably standardized fashion. The present section addresses the specific methodological problem of objectively identifying people who are disabled through the use of survey research methods. It offers suggestions for improved methods for screening of disabled persons into surveys through the use of standardized survey instruments.

15

Table II.1.   Percentage disabled by sex, year and type of data collection programme

Country or area/ Type of data	Year	Age group	Percentage disabled Both sexes	Male	Female	Comments*
I. Population census		*Total population*				
Bahrain	1981	All ages	1.0	1.1	0.9	
Comoros	1980	All ages	1.7	1.9	1.5	
Egypt	1976	All ages	0.3	0.4	0.2	
Hong Kong	1981	All ages	0.8	..	..	
Indonesia	1980	All ages	1.1	..	..	*(a)*
Kuwait	1980	All ages	0.4	0.5	0.4	
Mali	1976	All ages	3.0	3.1	3.0	
Neth.Antilles	1981	All ages	2.9	3.3	2.5	
Pakistan	1981	All ages	0.5	0.4	0.5	
Panama	1980	0-39	0.7	0.8	0.6	
Peru	1981	All ages	0.2	..	..	
Poland	1978	All ages	7.1	..	..	
Sri Lanka	1981	All ages	0.4	0.6	0.4	*(a)*
Saint Helena	1976	All ages	1.6	1.5	1.7	
Tunisia	1975	All ages	0.8	0.9	0.6	
Tunisia	1984	All ages	0.9	1.1	0.7	
Turkey	1975	All ages	1.5	1.7	1.2	
United States	1980	16-64	8.5	9.0	8.0	
II. Population census		*Population not economically active*				
Belize	1980	15 years and over	2.5	2.8	2.3	*(b)*
Burma*	1983	10 years and over	0.4	0.6	0.3	*(c)*
Cape Verde	1980	10 years and over	4.3	3.5	4.9	*(d)*
Central African Rep.	1975	10 years and over	1.1	1.2	2.0	*(d)*
Cuba	1981	15 years and over	1.7	3.7	0.8	*(c)*
Guyana	1980	15 years and over	2.3	2.3	2.2	*(b)*
Ireland	1981	15 years and over	3.5	4.3	2.6	*(d)*
Kiribati	1978	15 years and over	0.5	0.7	0.4	*(d)*
Mexico	1980	6-14	2.8	2.9	2.7	*(e)*
Philippines	1980	15 years and over	1.4	..	..	*(c)*
Spain	1981	All ages	5.1	6.3	4.8	*(c)*
Trinidad and Tobago	1980	15 years and over	1.1	1.3	0.9	*(d)*
Venezuela	1981	12 years and over	3.8	8.4	2.0	*(c)*

*   Now Myanmar

Table II.1 (*continued*)

Country or area/ Type of data	Year	Age group	Percentage disabled			Comments*
			Both sexes	Male	Female	
III. Survey		*Health and medical*				
Canada	1983	All ages	11.2	10.6	11.8	
Egypt	1979-81	All ages	1.5	1.8	1.2	
United States	1982	All ages	..	..	..	(g)
Uruguay	1984	45 years and over	11.3	11.2	11.4	(h)
IV. Survey		*Living conditions*				
Denmark	1976	20-69	..	..	..	(g)
Finland	1978	15 years and over	..	..	..	(g)
New Zealand	1980	15 years and over	..	..	..	(g)
Norway	1983	16-79		15.0	20.0	
Sweden	1980-81	16-84	..	..	..	(g)
Thailand	1981	All ages	0.8	0.9	0.7	
V. Survey		*Demographic and socio-economic*				
China	1983	0-14	1.4	1.5	1.4	
Ethiopia	1979-81	All ages	5.5	..	..	(k)
Fiji	1982	All ages	0.9	1.7	0.5	(c)
Swaziland	1983	All ages	2.5	..	..	(k)
Thailand	1983	6-24	2.2	2.3	2.2	(e)
VI. Survey		*Disability*				
Australia	1981	All ages	13.2	..	..	
Austria	1976	All ages	20.9	19.9	21.8	
Canada	1986	All ages	13.2	12.7	13.8	
China	1987	All ages	4.9	..	..	
Germany, Fed. Rep.	1983	All ages	..	11.8	9.8	
India	1981	All ages	..	..	..	(g)
Japan	1980	18 years and over	2.4	..	..	(i)
Kenya	1981	15 years and over	..	..	..	(f)(j)
Nepal	1980	All ages	3.0	..	..	
Philippines	1980	All ages	4.4	5.1	3.7	
Spain	1986	All ages	15.0	14.8	15.7	
Trinidad & Tobago	1982	3-16	..	..	..	(f)
United Kingdom	1985-86	0-15 years	3.2	3.7	2.6	
United Kingdom	1985-86	16 years and over	14.2	12.1	16.1	
Zimbabwe	1981	All ages	..	..	..	(f)

Table II.1 (continued)

Country or area/ Type of data	Year	Age group	Percentage disabled			Comments*
			Both sexes	Male	Female	

VII. Registration   *Schools*

| Jamaica | 1978 | 4-11 | .. | .. | .. | (f) |

VIII. Registration campaign   *Registration campaign*

Ethiopia	1981	0-14	0.2	..	..	
Jordan	1979	All ages	..	..	..	(f)
Lebanon	1980	3-60	..	..	..	(f)
United Kingdom (N. Ireland)	1978	All ages	..	..	..	(f)

IX. Registration   *Disability registration*

| Singapore | 1985 | All ages | .. | .. | .. | (f) |

X. Agricultural census

| Jordan | 1983 | All ages | .. | .. | .. | (f) |

Source: United Nations Disability Statistics Data Base (DISTAT, 1988).

Key:
.. Rates not available.
* The following survey results now available but not included in DISTAT.
    Canada, 1986. *The Health and Activity Limitation Survey.*
    China, 1987. *The National Sampling Survey of Handicapped.*
    Spain, 1986. *Encuesta Sobre Discapacidades Deviciencias y Minusvalias.*
    United Kingdom, 1985-86. *OPCS Surveys of Disability in Great Britain.*
(a) Based on number of disabilities, not on number of disabled persons: if a person has three different types of disabilities, the person is counted three times.
(b) Disabled persons not attending school and not economically active among total not economically active population.
(c) Disabled persons not economically active among total not economically active population.
(d) Disabled persons not economically active among total population.
(e) Disabled children among children not attending school.
(f) Number of disabled persons given: however rates not computed because total population figures unavailable.
(g) Percentage disabled available by type of disabilities, but not for total population or for specific age groups.
(h) Montevideo only: disabled persons who are chronically ill among the total chronically ill population.
(i) Disabled persons living at home.
(j) A non-probability survey.
(k) For rural areas only.

For all practical purposes, once disabled persons are identified, census, survey or registry interviews of people who are disabled are no different from survey interviews of any other population group. Questions of socio-economic status, school attendance, labour force participation, family and household status are the same for the disabled as they are for any other person being interviewed. The one major exception is that specific questions may be added when interviewing disabled persons and their families concerning questions about the cause of the disability, the age at onset of the impairment and special aids used to reduce disability, all of which are uniquely asked of disabled persons.

1. Three types of data collection programmes

The three major types of data collection systems used to collect disability data are: (a) population and housing census programmes; (b) household survey programmes; and (c) disability registration systems. Each of the three data collection systems is briefly described below.

(a) Population and housing censuses

Population and housing censuses have as their goal the coverage of entire populations of countries. When a question about disability is asked in a census programme, it is intended that every household in the country will be asked about the presence of persons with disability. This is a very large task, yet it has been done in 32 of 55 countries included in DISTAT. One way to ask about disability in a census is to record information on disability for each member of the household (e.g. Bahrain, 1981; Kuwait, 1980). An alternative way is to ask special questions about disability of a sample of households, e.g. every tenth or twentieth household, thereby reducing the amount of work required of enumerators during data collection.

In some cases, disability is asked only as part of a census question. For example, it may be offered as a reason for economic inactivity along with other possible reasons, such as being a homemaker, student or retired person (e.g. Burma, 1983; Central African Republic, 1975; Venezuela, 1981). Another possibility tried by some countries is to ask whether disability is a reason for not attending school among children and youth (e.g. Mexico, 1980; Belize, 1980 and Cuba, 1981).

(b) Sample surveys

Sample surveys, unlike censuses, are not intended to enumerate every household or individual in the country; however, they are designed to be representative of the total population. Using scientifically designed sample selection procedures, the response of selected households or individuals are intended to be statistically representative of the answers one would get from the total population, even though as few as one per 100 or even one per 1,000 of the population are actually contacted and interviewed during a survey. Surveys are often conducted annually, quarterly or even monthly by countries in order to take into account seasonal and other cyclical differences. They cover many different topics, such as health, welfare, labour force, agriculture, and other socio-economic issues.

Using the survey method to collect information on disability, questions of disability may be "piggy-backed", that is attached as a special module, on to sample surveys that are focused on some other specific topic, i.e., labour force, health and medical, living conditions surveys. In such cases, a national health, medical or labour force survey, for example, is used as an avenue for screening for disability (e.g. Canada Labour Force Survey, 1981; Egypt Health and Medical Profile Survey, 1979-1981). Once screened in as being disabled, an in-depth survey of disability is conducted in that household, thereby reducing the amount of detailed questions on disability required in the larger national household survey programme. This design offers the opportunity to train certain members of the team to interview households having a disabled person and to concentrate usually limited resources on fewer households or individuals. In some surveys, the person selected for the special interview on disability is a lay interviewer or a paramedic or social-worker who receives special training on how to conduct the interview. In some cases, a medically trained individual such as a nurse or physician conducts the interview. When the second alternative is used, survey costs increase substantially because of the costs of utilizing highly trained professionals as interviewers.

Additional design considerations include such issues as to whether to stratify the selection of households before sample selection thereby ensuring sufficient selection of households with certain characteristics necessary for the analysis: for example, rural, urban, living in certain unique environments such as mountain areas or plateaux, households with small children, households having an elderly person, and so on. Cluster techniques may also be used in the sample plan, grouping the sample selection of households so that interviewers have less distance to travel between interviews. Each of these decisions has statistical implications and the effects of the design on the statistical analysis are usually estimated by survey sampling techniques.

(c) Administrative reporting systems

Population registration systems, birth registration, social security systems, health reporting, industrial recording of occupational injuries and other registries do have potential for being utilized along with census and survey data for statistically assessing disablement. The development of a national disability registration system is another method whereby information on disablement may be collected.

In general, there are two major approaches to disability registration or administrative reporting. The first approach is to institute an *ad hoc* one-time national campaign where disabled persons and their families are registered and then interviewed for further information. For example, a door-to-door campaign and survey which canvassed houses in order to find disabled residents was conducted in the United Kingdom (Northern Ireland) in 1978. Once identified, all disabled persons or members of their families were interviewed. In several national examples, families were asked to come to the centre and register disabled family members (e.g. Lebanon, 1980; Jordan, 1979). A survey questionnaire was then filled out which described the situation of the identified disabled person. In another case, community leaders were asked to identify disabled persons known to them in the community. Then both community leaders and parents or guardians of disabled persons were interviewed (e.g. Ethiopia, 1981).

In the case of a one-time registration campaign, no attempt is made to continue the registry beyond the time period of data collection.

The second approach is through sampling an on-going civil registration system (e.g. Austria, Federal Republic of Germany and Singapore). In this case, disabled persons who were registered in the national registration system as disabled are selected into the survey through sample selection of registered persons, and then the data of the registry are analysed.

Strengths and weaknesses of censuses, surveys and registration systems as sources of statistical information on disability are discussed in detail in the *Case Studies*.[6]

2. Identifying disabled persons: screening techniques

One important distinction in the way that data collection programmes differ is according to whether disabled people were screened into the study through the use of a disability or an impairment screening question. In order to more clearly see the distinction, two national examples are provided below.

(a) Example of a disability (D code) survey screen

The example is Canada. Canada combined census and survey activities in order to assess disability. It implemented in the 1986 population census a question about activity limitations. The census question, which was very broad, was broken into four major parts; each person in the household was asked the questions shown in the following boxes.

Are you limited in the kind or amount of activity that you can do because of a long-term physical condition, mental condition or health problem:[a]
    (a) At home? (No I am not limited, Yes I am limited);
    (b) At school or at work?
    (c) In other activities, e.g., transportation to or from work work, leisure time activities? (No, I am not limited, Yes, I am limited);
    (d) Do you have any long-term disabilities or handicaps? (No, Yes)

---

    [a] Statistics Canada, 1986 *Census of Canada* (Ottawa), form 2B, question 20.

The above question was used to develop a sampling frame for the Canadian Health and Activity Limitations Survey (HALS), which was fielded immediately following the 1986 Census of Population. HALS was a national multi-stage stratified sample of Canada, which used geographic and other demographic information from the 1986 Census questionnaires for planning the sample. Personal interviews were

---

6 *Development of Statistics of Statistics of Disabled Persons: Case Studies* Statistical Papers, Series Y, No.2 (United Nations publication, Sales No.86.XVII.17).

21

completed with 120,000 persons who responded "Yes" to some part of the disability census question and with 80,000 persons who responded "No" to all parts of the census disability question.

This census question was followed up with detailed disability screening questions in HALS:

"I would like to ask you about your ability to do certain activities, even when using a special aid. Please report only those problems which you expect to last six months or more".[a]

1. *Do you have any trouble hearing what is said in a normal conversation with one other person? (At what age did you first have trouble doing this? Are you completely unable to do this? What is the main condition or health problem which causes you trouble hearing what is said in a normal conversation with one other person? Followed by a check-list of selections for best describing the condition, which lead to determining the underlying impairment associated with each disability reported.)*

2. *Do you have any trouble hearing what is said in a group conversation with at least three other people? (All the screening questions were followed by a series of questions similar to the ones shown in parenthesis in item 1, yet were modified to take the specific disability into consideration.)*

3. *Do you have any trouble seeing clearly the print on this page?*

4. *Do you have any trouble seeing clearly the face of someone from 12 feet/4 metres (example: across a room), with glasses if normally worn?*

5. *Do you have any trouble speaking and being understood because of a condition or health problem?*

6. *Do you have any trouble walking 400 yards/400 metres without resting (about a quarter of a mile)?*

7. *Do you have trouble walking up and down a flight of stairs, that is about 12 steps?*

8. *Do you have any trouble carrying an object of 10 pounds for 30 feet/5 kg for 10 metres (example: carrying a 10-pound bag flour)?*

9. *Do you have any trouble moving from one room to another or moving about in a room?*

10. *Do you have any trouble standing for long periods of time, that is, more than 20 minutes? Remember, I am asking about problems expected to last 6 months or more.*

11. *When standing, do you have any trouble bending down and picking up an object from the floor (example: a shoe)?*

12. *Do you have any trouble dressing and undressing yourself?*

13. *Do you have any trouble getting in and out of bed?*

14. *Do you have any trouble cutting your own toenails or tying your own shoelaces?*

15. *Do you have any trouble using your fingers to grasp or handle, for example using scissors or pliers?*

16. *Do you have any trouble reaching in any direction (example: above your head)?*

17. *Do you have any trouble cutting your own food?*

18. *Because of a long-term physical condition or health problem, that is, one that is expected to last 6 months or more, are you limited in the kind or amount of activity you can do at home?...at school?...at work?...or supporting yourself by such activities as fishing, trapping or crafts?...in other activities such as travel, sports, or leisure? (Yes or No to each question).*

19. *Has a school, or health professional ever told you that you have a learning disability?*

20. *From time to time, everyone has trouble remembering the name of a familiar person, or learning something new, or they experience moments of confusion. However, do you have any ongoing problems with your ability to remember or learn?*

21. *Because of a long-term emotional, psychological, nervous, or mental health condition, are you limited in the kind or amount of activity you can do?*

---

[a] Statistics Canada Disability Database Program. *The Health and Activity Limitation Survey: Selected Data for Canada. Provinces and Territories,* (1988).

The percentage of disabled of HALS was 13.3 per cent. Children were asked somewhat different questions from adults. There was also a second part of HALS, that was a survey of disabled persons who resided in institutions, and this part was conducted in 1987.[7]

The 21 disability screening questions were grouped according to seven broad disability categories in the analysis of the data, as shown below.

1. *Mobility*
    Limited in ability to walk, move from room to room, carry an object for 10 metres, or stand for long periods;
2. *Agility*
    Limited in ability to bend, dress or undress oneself, get in and out of bed, cut toenails, tie shoes, use fingers to grasp or handle objects, reach or cut own food;
3. *Seeing*
    Limited in ability to read ordinary newsprint or to see someone from 4 metres, even when wearing glasses;
4. *Hearing*
    Limited in ability to hear what is being said in a conversation with one other person or two or more persons, even when wearing a hearing aid;
5. *Speaking*
    Limited in ability to speak and be understood;
6. *Other*
    Limited because of learning disability or emotional or psychiatric disability, or because of developmental delay;
7. *Unknown*
    Limited, but nature not specified.

Multiple disabilities were estimated by producing cross-tabulations, which grouped two through six types of disabilities into multiple disability categories.

(b)   Example of an impairment screen

The second example is the Philippines. It is based upon the 1980 National Disability Survey of the Philippines conducted by the National Commission Concerning Disabled Persons in collaboration with the Ministry of Health.[8] The survey covered 33,278 persons, or 0.8 per cent of the 1975 Philippine population. One respondent was interviewed in each selected household; all information about the household, including data on impairments, was obtained

---

7 Details of the data collection programme on disability in Canada may be acquired by contacting the Program Manager, Health and Activity Limitation Survey, 2D9, Jean Talon Building, Tunney's Pasture, Ottawa, I1A OT6.

8 National Commission Concerning Disabled Persons, Philippines, *National Disability Survey, 1986.*

from this respondent by public health nurses. Of the 33,278 persons covered in the survey, 1,470 were found to have impairments, or 4.4 per cent of the population.

In this survey persons were screened according to their impairments. A respondent from each sampled household was asked to enumerate all members of the household and then to identify among them which person had an impairment. It asked a general question about the presence of an impairment, and then coded into the survey all persons who reported having one. Essentially the question asked was: "Impaired?" Yes or No. Once identified as impaired, a special interview of impaired persons was conducted.

The survey instrument used to interview impaired persons then followed up the general impairment question by asking details about the type of impairment, as listed below.

Physical handicap/disability:
  1. *Missing limbs*
  2. *Unequal length of limbs*
  3. *Deformity of limbs*
  4. *Deformity of spine*
  5. *Joint/muscle pain*
  6. *Weakness/paralysis of limbs*
  7. *Impairment of sensation*
  8. *Abnormality in limb tone*
  9. *Abnormal movement of limb*
  10. *Weakness/paralysis of face*
  11. *Impairment of bowel/urinary control*
  12. *Impotence*
  13. *Hearing disorders*
  14. *Speech disorders*
  15. *Visual disorders*
  16. *Disfigurement*
  17. *Chronic respiratory disorders*
  18. *Mental impairment (followed by a check-list of signs and symptoms)*

Additional sections of the questionnaire asked impaired persons about functional limitations of daily life activities, including feeding, dressing, bathing, toileting, sexual performance, household activities, communication, manual dexterity, mobility and endurance. These functional limitations or disability questions were not used, however, as screening devices. They were asked only of impaired persons who were screened into the survey.

The examples of Canada and the Philippines give two different ways to collect disability information. When people are screened into a national disability census, survey or registry according to their impairments, as listed in the *I codes* of ICIDH, impaired persons are usually followed-up in interviews for descriptions of their disabilities as listed in the *D codes* (e.g. Philippines, 1980). Likewise, disability surveys that screen persons according to their disabilities usually follow-up with specific impairment questions in order to understand the underlying problems influencing the reported disability (e.g. Canada, 1983). In population censuses, questions are usually either solely impairment-oriented (see the following population censuses: Bahrain, 1981; Egypt, 1976; Hong Kong, 1981; Mali, 1976; Pakistan, 1981; and Peru, 1981) or are solely disability-oriented (see the following population censuses: Canada, 1986; Mexico, 1980; Poland, 1978 and the United States, 1980). This is because of both time and space limitations in the questions asked at the census level.

In either case, in this *Compendium*, both impairments and disabilities are quantified through the use of coding schemes that conceptually group disabled persons into *I codes* and *D codes* of the WHO/ICIDH classification scheme for further statistical analysis. DISTAT was used as the analytic tool for organizing and standardizing disparate census and survey *I codes* and *D codes* into their logical location in the WHO/ICIDH classification scheme.

3. Survey estimates of disability

Screening strategies in censuses and surveys appear to influence the results in a number of important ways. The examples below discuss how screening strategies affect the percentage of disabled for males, females and total population.

(a) Percentage of disabled

Probably the most frequently asked question about disability, is "What percentage of the population is disabled?" Table II.1 and figure II.1 show the percentage of disabled as calculated among the 63 published national reports of the 55 countries of DISTAT. Although presented in one table and one figure, for a number of reasons the data are not comparable; i.e., variation in definitions of disability, divergent screening procedures, different age ranges covered, modifications in the types of persons covered (economically inactive population only, total population, population of children not attending school, chronically disabled population only). The percentage of the population that is disabled varies from 0.2 to 20.9 per cent of the surveyed populations included in DISTAT.[9] This very wide

---

9 The percentage of the population that is disabled is not the same as the crude disability rate. The percentage of disabled is simply the number of persons found to be disabled over the number of persons interviewed, without any specification of population types. The crude disability rate is the prevalence rate of disability per total population, or the total number of disabled persons identified expressed as per 100, per 1,000 or per 100,000 total population in various reports.

Figure II.1. Percentage disabled, by country or area and year of data collection

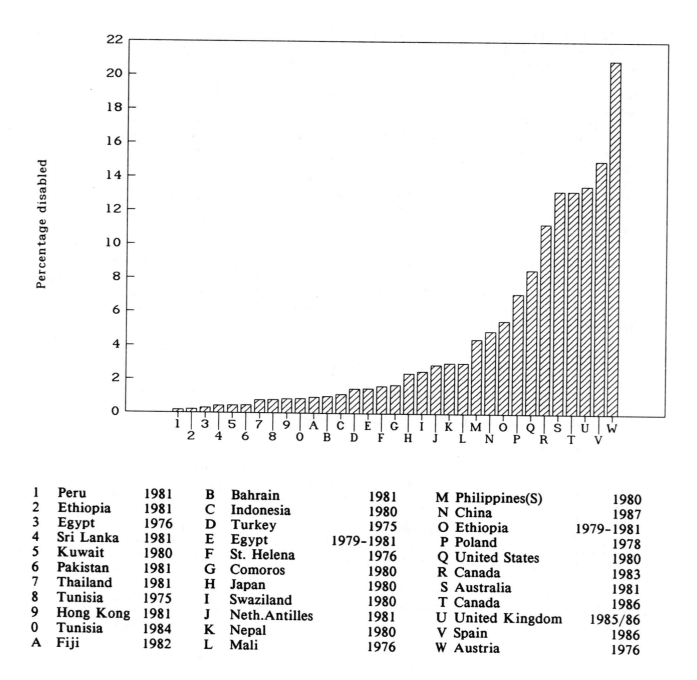

1	Peru	1981	B	Bahrain	1981	M	Philippines(S)	1980
2	Ethiopia	1981	C	Indonesia	1980	N	China	1987
3	Egypt	1976	D	Turkey	1975	O	Ethiopia	1979-1981
4	Sri Lanka	1981	E	Egypt	1979-1981	P	Poland	1978
5	Kuwait	1980	F	St. Helena	1976	Q	United States	1980
6	Pakistan	1981	G	Comoros	1980	R	Canada	1983
7	Thailand	1981	H	Japan	1980	S	Australia	1981
8	Tunisia	1975	I	Swaziland	1980	T	Canada	1986
9	Hong Kong	1981	J	Neth.Antilles	1981	U	United Kingdom	1985/86
0	Tunisia	1984	K	Nepal	1980	V	Spain	1986
A	Fiji	1982	L	Mali	1976	W	Austria	1976

Source: Table 1 (chap.IV).

range of disability rates reflects not only variations in the level of disability but also from a high degree of variability in the strategies for measurement of disability among countries.

Methods for calculating disability rates need greater standardization. In a number of cases, neither the rules for the numerator nor for the denominator of any disability rate are standardized. For example, the crude disability rate of impairment should by definition include all disabled persons for the total population in the numerator, and the denominator should include the number of the total population.

Age-specific disability rates need to maintain standard and comparable age ranges for their numerators and denominators.[10] Disability rates for special populations of disabled persons such as the economically inactive disabled population or the population of disabled children not attending school, should be tabulated and presented in a standardized way, if presented at all. In some cases national data were tabulated comparing total populations and special populations. In other cases national tabulations were prepared so that comparisons were made between total populations having special economic or educational characteristics and disabled populations with these same characteristics. For example, a comparison of disabled and total populations that were not economically active; or a comparison of total populations of children who did not attend school with disabled children who did not attend school (see table II.1 for examples). In any case, these population-specific rates should not be calculated in isolation of information for total populations. This is to ensure that proper comparisons may be made, for example between economically active disabled adults and economically active total populations. Even the most basic of instructions on methodology in this field would greatly improve data presentation and comparability of results.

Within nations, and even when using similar methods for estimating disability prevalence, disability estimates are found to vary widely in magnitude, primarily because they are sensitive to specific survey conditions. Work disability prevalence estimates in the United States of America, for example, have been shown to vary between 8.5 and 17 per cent of the population, depending upon differences in survey methods and data collection techniques used.[11] Surely, these widely varying conditions in survey applications could be reduced through international agreement on standards for the production and use of disability statistics in censuses, surveys and registration systems.

In addition to differences in methodology, it is also widely acknowledged that variations in the percentage of disabled are also partly attributable to such factors as differential chronic and infectious disease patterns; differential life expectancy; the age-structure of populations and population composition; differential nutritional status; differential rates of exposure to environmental, occupational and traffic hazards; and variations in public health practices.

---

10 For further discussion of this, see Y.C. Yu, "The demography of disability", paper presented at the United Nations International Workshop on Disability Statistics, 27 November - 6 December 1989, Malta.

11 Larry Haber, "Issues in the definition of disability and the use of disability survey data", paper presented at the Workshop on Disability Statistics of the Committee on National Statistics, National Research Council, 6-7 April 1989, Washington D.C. p.1.

(b)   Choosing between I codes or D codes for identifying disabled persons

Disability questions using *D codes* for identifying disabled persons in surveys lead to higher rates of disability than do impairment questions using *I codes* (see figure II.2).   This is because a single question assessing functional limitations, or disability, typically embraces behaviours associated with a broad range of impairment conditions. "Difficulty climbing stairs", for example, may be due to musculo-skeletal, visceral, disfigurement or other impairments.   Impairment screening questions, in contrast, are more directly related to specific conditions.   For example, "profound visual impairment of both eyes", or blindness, as well as "profound hearing loss in both ears", or deafness, are all highly specified descriptions of relatively unique impairment conditions.   It appears to be easier for individuals to initially discuss whether they have difficulty climbing stairs, or hearing conversations across a dining table, than it is to describe specific impairment conditions.   In addition, disability questions seem to throw out a wider net which captures more reports of mild and moderate disablement.   In order to cover the same ground that one or two disability questions can cover during a survey interview, a number of more detailed impairment questions must be utilized.

Nevertheless, both impairment and disability questions are needed in order to fully understand the dynamics of disablement.   It is insufficient, for example, to know only that a person has difficulty walking upstairs.   It is also imperative to ascertain the underlying reason that the person cannot walk upstairs.   Is it, for example, because the person has severely limited vision and cannot see where he or she is going, and has not been trained to be mobile with limited vision?   Or is it that the person is paralysed in both lower limbs, does not climb stairs and uses a wheelchair in order to be mobile?   Certainly, such distinctions are imperative for programme planning and also for comprehending the nature of the disability.   What is suggested by these findings, is that when screening for disabled persons through census and survey questions, one would begin by identifying disabled persons by using a disability question, followed by specific details about the underlying reason for the disability through the use of carefully selected impairment questions.

(c)   Consequences of screening techniques

The type of screening techniques used by countries appears to influence the findings in some unexpected ways.   For example, because of the way in which survey screens have been implemented, disability rates are usually higher in European and North American countries (e.g. Australia, 1981; Austria, 1976; Canada, 1983; Poland, 1978; Spain, 1981; United Kingdom (Northern Ireland), 1985-1986; United States, 1980) than in African and Asian countries (e.g. China, 1987; Egypt, 1979; Ethiopia, 1979-1981; Japan, 1980; Philippines, 1980; Sri Lanka, 1981).   The percentage of disabled ranges from 7.1 to 20.9 per cent for the European and North American countries mentioned above (see figure II.2).

Figure II.2. Percentage disabled by country or area, year of data collection and type of screen

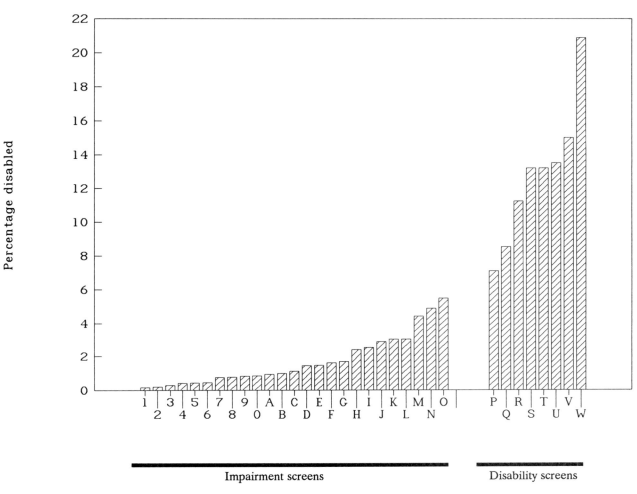

Impairment screens   Disability screens

1	Peru	1981	B	Bahrain	1981	M	Philippines(S)	1980
2	Ethiopia	1981	C	Indonesia	1980	N	China	1987
3	Egypt	1976	D	Turkey	1975	O	Ethiopia	1979-1981
4	Sri Lanka	1981	E	Egypt	1979-1981	P	Poland	1978
5	Kuwait	1980	F	St. Helena	1976	Q	United States	1980
6	Pakistan	1981	G	Comoros	1980	R	Canada	1983
7	Thailand	1981	H	Japan	1980	S	Australia	1981
8	Tunisia	1975	I	Swaziland	1983	T	Canada	1986
9	Hong Kong	1981	J	Neth.Antilles	1981	U	United Kingdom	1985/86
0	Tunisia	1984	K	Nepal	1980	V	Spain	1986
A	Fiji	1982	L	Mali	1976	W	Austria	1976

Source: Table 1 (chap.IV).

The countries of Africa, Asia, and South America have more often identified disabled persons through the use of impairment screens (e.g. China, 1987; Egypt, 1976; Ethiopia, 1979-1981; Japan, 1980; Peru, 1981; Philippines, 1980; Sri Lanka, 1981). The percentage of disabled among the countries using impairment screens range from 0.3 to 5.5 per cent. One exception is Uruguay, 1984, which used an impairment screen and found that 11.3 per cent of their studied population was disabled. This higher percentage of disabled is reached primarily because this study used a sample of adults over the age of 45 who were chronically ill.

Another unexpected consequence of survey screens is that differences in the percentage of disabled for males and females is partly determined by whether impairment I codes or disability D codes are initially used in screening questions to identify disabled persons in data collection systems (see table II.1).

This is shown graphically in figure II.3 where the ratio of male percentage of disabled to female percentage of disabled is plotted. In general, when a disability question is asked, the male to female ratios of the percentage disabled, are either slightly below or are very close to 1.0. This would indicate that when D codes are used, in general, for every man identified as disabled, a woman is also identified. In contrast, when I codes are used, they often result in male/female ratios of percentage disabled greater than 1.0, indicating a predominance of disabled males having been identified in the survey. Given the nature of I code questions, i.e., blind, deaf, leg amputated, mentally retarded etc., it might be concluded that severe impairments are male-dominated, whereas mild to moderate impairments are not. It might also be the case that survey reporting of impairments of women requires additional survey probes than those required for men.

Disability rates from diverse national data collection sources are not yet comparable, especially given all the differences in survey design, definitions, concepts and methods. However, it is important to note that when comparing disability rates within national data sets, according to age, or residence, for example, the relationships found between disability and other demographic and socio-economic variables are reasonably consistent, even though the magnitude of the relationships may vary from one survey to another. For example, a large proportion of surveys indicate that disabled persons are on the average less educated, and have lower socio-economic status and reside in rural or poor areas than do able-bodied persons.[12] In addition, it has been pointed out in several studies that survey data on disability is found to be reasonably internally consistent and reliable and competitive in quality with other types of survey data such as survey estimates of educational attainment data or marital status.[13]

---

[12] United Nations, ... *Case Studies;* also Haber, *op. cit.,* p. 14.

[13] Queen Alia Jordan Social Welfare Fund, *Evaluation Studies of Handicapped persons in Jordan* (Amman, 1983); United Nations, ... *Case Studies;* Haber, *op. cit.,* p. 14.

Figure II.3. Sex ratio of percentage disabled

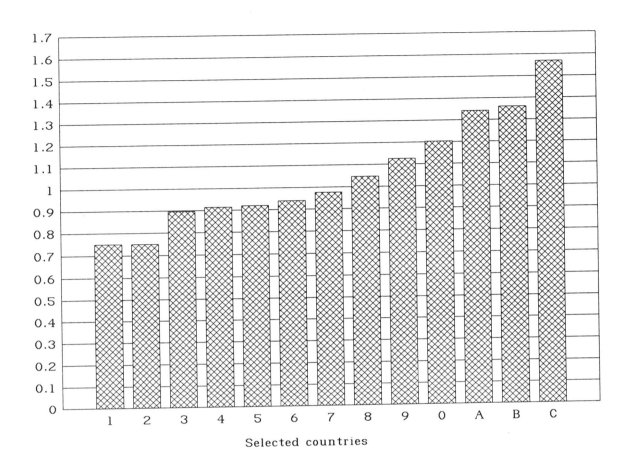

	Disability screens		Impairment screens
1 Norway	1983	8 Thailand	1983
2 United Kingdom*	1985/86	9 China	1983
3 Canada	1983	0 Germany, Fed.Rep.	1983
4 Austria	1976	A Thailand	1981
5 Canada*	1986	B Philippines	1980
6 Spain*	1986	C Egypt	1979-1981
7 Uruguay	1984		

Source: Table 1 (chap.IV).
* Survey results available but not yet included in DISTAT.

B. Illustrative examples

In the following sections, selected examples are given of the types of presentations that may be tried as a way of highlighting the data available in statistical tables 1-12 of the present publication. Examples are supported by graphs, summary text and tables indicating the purpose of the presentation.

1. Demographic characteristics

Analysis of disability data through the use of traditional demographic techniques has been presented in the United Nations *Case Studies*.[14] Presentation of numbers, percentages, rates and graphic production of age-sex pyramids of disablement, disability sex-ratios, and comparisons of disability rates according to age, sex, and geographic residence have elaborated clearly the national profile of disablement for countries included in the *Case Studies*. In this *Compendium* a similar presentation of basic statistical and demographic tables are given for 55 countries.

From these basic tables, the study of disablement among special population groups of disabled persons such as children, youth, women, men, adults and elderly may be initiated. It is possible to describe differences in urban and rural environents; to assess the potential for estimating disability-free life-expectancy, or to identify the proportion of the adult population that is disabled according to particular types of impairments and disabilities. In some respects, the results are crude. The age-groups are not always comparable. Under-enumeration of disabilities is a problem. Yet, with all their problems, the accumulation of information that can be acquired from these basic tables is remarkable. Selected examples are provided below.

(a) Population aging and disablement

As the proportion of the total population that is older gets larger, the influence of disablement is more visible (table II.2). Figures II.4(*a*) and (*b*) show graphically the proportion of the disabled population that is over age 60 and compare it to the proportion of the total population that is over age 60. The comparison suggests that the age-structure among disabled persons is predominantly elderly, while the total population age-structure is predominantly either youthful or middle-aged. This is further supported by the fact that rates of disablement are highest above the age of 50, world-wide. Graphic examples of the significant increase in prevalence rates of disability by age and sex for selected African countries are shown in figures II.5(*a*) and (*b*).

Illustrative examples of the influence of age upon particular impairments are offered in figures II.6(*a*), (*b*) and (*c*). In these examples, crude disability rates for African countries, and also mental impairment and blindness rates for selected Asian countries are shown according to age group and sex. Figure 6(*c*) specifically shows the accumulative effect of disability according to type of impairment and

---

14 United Nations, ... *Case Studies*, esp. pp. 20-87.

Table II.2. Population surveyed, and disabled persons by age group

(a) Censuses: Total population

Country or area	Census year	Age range		Age group (percentage)				
				0-14	*15-24*	*25-59*	*60+*	*n.a.*
Bahrain	1981	Total	*Population*	32.9	21.9	41.4	3.7	
			Disabled	14.2	15.5	36.7	33.7	
Comoros	1980	Total	*Population*	47.2	16.9	28.7	6.8	0.4
			Disabled	23.9	14.6	38.5	22.6	0.4
Egypt	1976	Total	*Population*	39.9	19.3	34.5	6.2	0.0
			Disabled	17.2	17.5	47.1	18.1	0.1
Kuwait	1980	Total	*Population*	40.2	18.0	39.6	2.3	
			Disabled	34.2	25.3	26.4	14.1	
Mali	1976	Total	*Population*	44.0	17.6	32.1	6.2	
			Disabled	10.0	10.4	50.9	28.6	
Neth.Antilles	1981	Total	*Population*	28.9	21.4	40.3	9.4	
			Disabled	17.8	17.3	33.3	31.5	
Pakistan	1981	Total	*Population*	44.5	17.1	31.5	7.0	
			Disabled	19.8	12.8	32.7	34.7	
Sri Lanka [a]	1981	Total	*Population*	35.3	21.0	37.1	6.6	
			Disabled	23.4	19.1	37.1	16.6	3.8
					(15-29)	*(30-39)*		
Tunisia	1975	Total	*Population*	43.7	25.6	24.7	5.8	0.1
			Disabled	15.1	20.7	31.7	32.4	0.2
						(15-59)		
Tunisia	1984	Total	*Population*	39.6		53.7	6.7	
			Disabled	12.2		59.1	28.6	
Turkey	1975	Total	*Population*	40.5	19.3	32.7	7.3	0.2
			Disabled	28.0	11.7	33.6	19.3	7.4

Table II.2 (continued)

(b) Not economically active

Country or area	Census year	Age range		0-14	15-24	25-59	60+	n.a.
					Age group (percentage)			
Belize	1980	15+	Population		34.8	51.9	12.6	0.7
			Disabled		8.9	22.5	68.3	0.3
				(10-14)				
Burma*	1983	10+	Population	29.2	27.4	34.0	9.3	
			Disabled	8.2	16.5	40.5	34.8	
				(10-14)				
Cape Verde	1980	10+	Population	20.1	30.3	31.1	11.1	7.5
			Disabled	2.0	4.7	11.8	64.7	16.8
Cuba	1981	15+	Population		38.2	35.3	26.5	
			Disabled		26.5	45.8	27.7	
Guyana	1980	15+	Population		34.7	54.7	10.2	0.4
			Disabled		9.3	30.1	60.3	0.2
Ireland	1981	15+	Population		25.1	53.7	21.2	
			Disabled		6.1	51.7	42.2	
Kiribati	1978	15+	Population		35.4	54.7	9.9	
			Disabled		21.7	52.0	26.3	
					(<30)	(30-64)	(65+)	
Spain	1981	Total	Population		22.2	49.2	28.6	
			Disabled		19.5	66.2	14.3	
Trinidad and Tobago	1980	15+	Population		35.0	52.9	12.1	
			Disabled		17.7	53.5	28.8	
				(12-14)				
Venezuela	1981	12+	Population	19.6	33.8	35.4	11.1	
			Disabled	2.8	11.3	27.4	58.5	

* Now Myanmar

Table II.2 (continued)

(c) Surveys

Country or area	Survey year	Age range		0-14	15-24	25-59	60+	n.a.
					(15-34)	(35-54)	(55+)	
Canada	1983	Total	*Population*	21.8	35.4	23.9	18.9	
			Disabled	11.0	14.4	21.1	53.5	
				(0-19)	(20-29)	(30-59)		
Egypt	1979-1981	Total	*Population*	54.9	12.4	24.8	7.3	0.6
			Disabled	28.0	11.0	29.3	30.2	1.4
						(45-64)	(65+)	
Uruguay b	1984	45+	*Population*			66.7	33.3	
			Disabled			54.5	45.5	
Thailand c	1981	Total	*Population*	40.2	21.0	33.8	5.0	
			Disabled	28.5	23.0	33.7	14.8	
						(25-64)	(65+)	
Fiji c,d	1982	Total	*Population*	57.9	15.7	23.8	2.8	
			Disabled	15.0	22.5	47.5	12.5	
					(15-29)	(30-59)		
Austria	1976	Total	*Population*	22.6	20.1	36.0	20.5	
			Disabled	3.5	6.2	37.3	53.1	
Philippines	1980	Total	*Population*	40.9	22.2	31.5	5.4	
			Disabled	22.0	13.4	43.1	23.5	
Ethiopia e	1979-1981	Total	*Population*	47.6	14.6	31.4	6.3	0.1
			Disabled	18.1	11.8	48.5	21.4	0.4

Source: Table 1.

a Disabilities, disabled persons not counted.

b Chronically ill population of Montevideo.

c Sum of age-specific numbers does not equal the total, as given by the country.

d Not economically active population.

e Rural.

Figure II.4. Percentage aged 60+ of total population and disabled population

(a) Censuses: total population

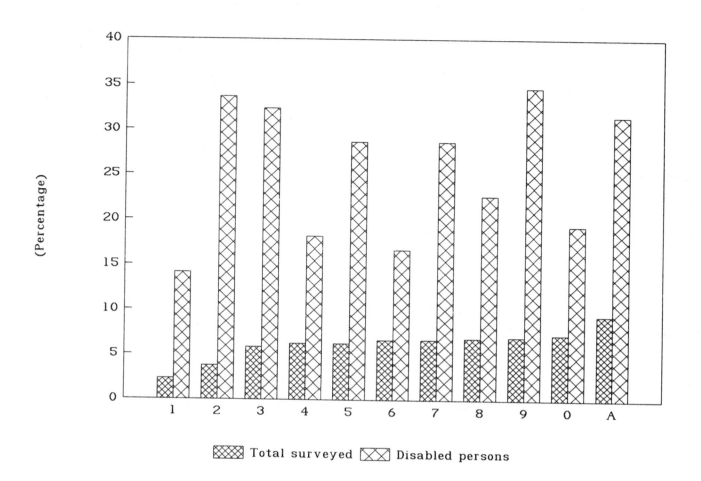

Total surveyed   Disabled persons

1	Kuwait	1980
2	Bahrain	1981
3	Tunisia	1975
4	Egypt	1976
5	Mali	1976
6	Sri Lanka	1981
7	Tunisia	1984
8	Comoros	1980
9	Pakistan	1981
0	Turkey	1975
A	Netherlands Antilles	1981

Figure II.4 *(continued)*

(b) Surveys

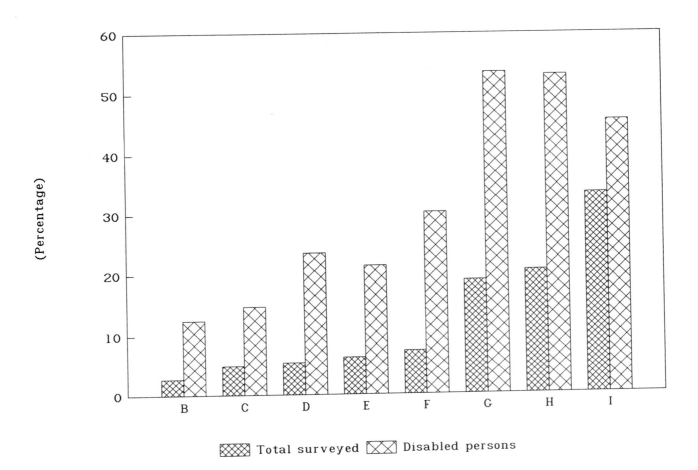

B	Fiji	1982
C	Thailand	1981
D	Philippines	1980
E	Ethiopia	1979–1981
F	Egypt	1979–1981
G	Canada	1983
H	Austria	1976
I	Uruguay	1984

Source: Table II.2 and table 1 (chap.IV).

Figure II.5. Age specific prevalence rates of disability per 100,000 population

(a) Africa: males

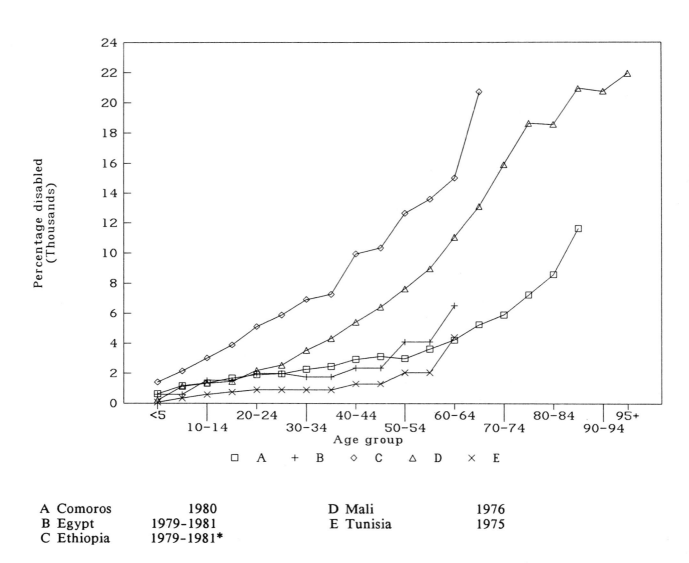

A Comoros	1980	D Mali	1976	
B Egypt	1979–1981	E Tunisia	1975	
C Ethiopia	1979–1981*			

* Rural population (both sexes)

Figure II.5 *(continued)*

(b) Africa: males and females

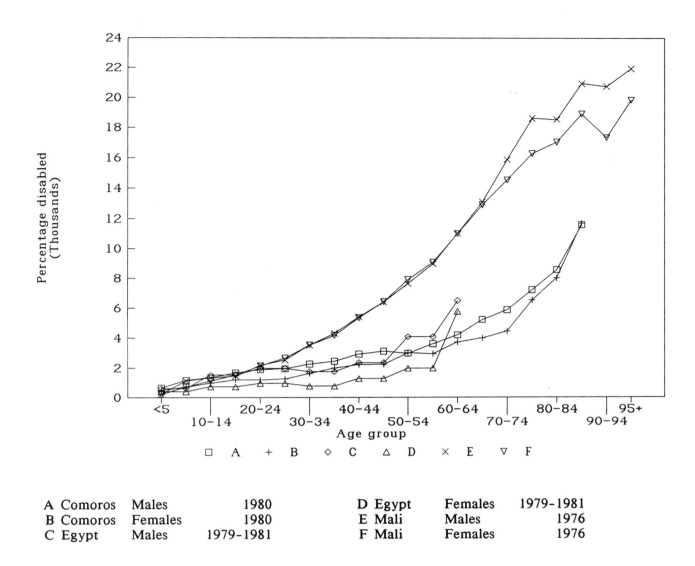

A Comoros	Males	1980	D Egypt	Females	1979-1981
B Comoros	Females	1980	E Mali	Males	1976
C Egypt	Males	1979-1981	F Mali	Females	1976

Source: Table 1 (chap.IV).

Figure II.6.   Illustrative prevalence rates per 100,000 population, by age and sex

(a) Blindness

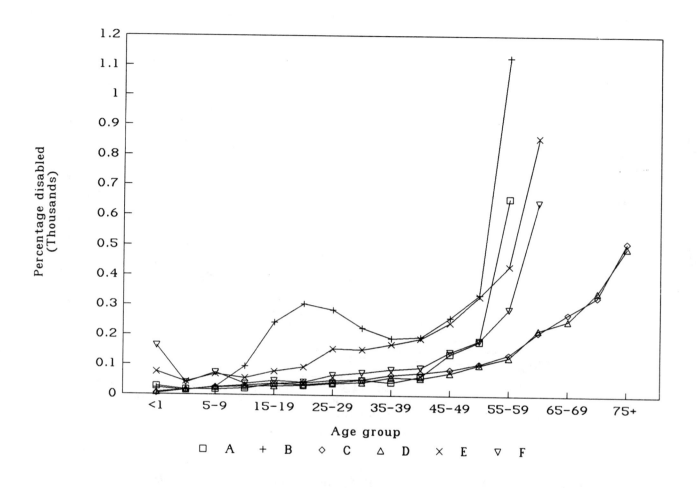

A Pakistan	Males	1981	D Sri Lanka	Females	1981
B Pakistan	Females	1981	E Turkey	Males	1975
C Sri Lanka	Males	1981	F Turkey	Females	1975

Figure II.6. *(continued)*

(b) Mental disabilities

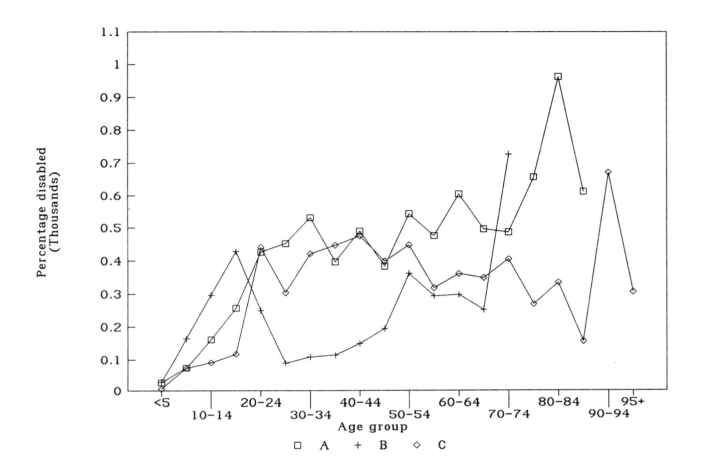

A   Comoros   Males   1980   Mentally handicapped
B   Bahrain   Males   1981   Mentally handicapped
C   Mali   Males   1976   Insanity

Figure II.6. *(continued)*

(c) *Various disabilities (Comoros, 1980)*

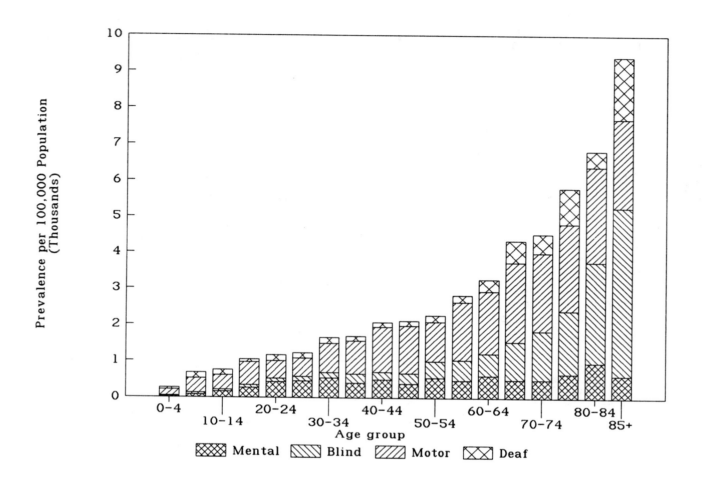

Source: Table 1 (chap.IV).

age group for one country, indicating that virtually all impairments and disabilities increase with age, although some appear to increase at faster rates according to age than do others. Regardless, the cumulative effect of disability and age is remarkable. Illustrative detailed statistics on populations, disabled persons, disabilities and prevalence rates of disability by age, sex and type of impairment or disability for 55 countries and areas, as available, are provided in detail in statistical tables 1-4 of this publication.

(b)   Geographical area, residence and disability

In addition to analysis of disability data by age and sex, geographical dis-aggregation of disability data is also being utilized to analyse disability data sets for differences in ecological, residential, and geographical characteristics. A recent article on pesticides and physical disability in India, for example, utilized the Indian national survey of disability and agricultural data on pesticide consumption per hectare of cropped area and found a significant and positive correlation between intensity of pesticide use and prevalence rates of deformity of limbs, dysfunction of joints, amputations and visual disabilities.[15] This type of areal analysis was possible because regional data were available from both the national survey of disability and from State-level data on pesticide use. Geographic disaggregation of disability data are available in a number of published tabulations of censuses and surveys (see table II.3 for geographical disaggregation available among the countries in DISTAT).

In addition to disaggregation by subnational areas, rural-urban residence is also distinguished (see table II.4). Higher disability rates are generally found among rural residents. A comparison of rates in table II.4, for example, indicates that in the Philippines in 1980, there are estimated to be 146 rural and 119 urban disabled people per 100,000 population. Likewise, in Venezuela, for every 478 rural disabled, there are 366 urban disabled persons per 100,000 economically inactive persons who are 12 years of age and older. This type of rural/urban ratio comparison per 100,000 population is summarized graphically in figure II.7. In figure II.7, a total of 10 national studies out of 13 had rural/urban ratios that were higher than 1.0, indicating a higher rate of disability among rural areas.

Detailed examination of table 6 in the statistical portion of this publication indicates that rates remain higher in rural areas even when controlling for age and sex of rural and urban populations. As was noted in the *Case Studies*, "The consistency with which rural/urban differences are reported leaves little doubt that impairment problems are more severe in rural areas, although rates in both areas are likely understated due to underenumeration of impairments in general".[16]

---

15 Dinesh Mohan, "Food vs. limbs: pesticides and physical disability in India", *Economic and Political Weekly*, vol. XXII, No. 13 (28 March 1987), pp. A23-A29.

16 United Nations ... *Case Studies*, p. 68.

Table II.3. Geographical disaggregation available in censuses and surveys covering disabled persons, selected countries and areas

Country or area	Year of data collection	Sub-level			
		First	Second	Third	Fourth
Australia	1981	8 states			
Austria	1976	9 regions			
Burma*	1983	Rangoon City			
Canada	1983	10 provinces	2 regions		
China	1983	29 districts			
Egypt	1976	4 regions	25 governorates		
Ethiopia	1979-81	16 regions	3 eritrean Awraja		
Ethiopia	1981	16 regions	3 eritrean Awraja		
India	1981	27 states			
Indonesia	1980	6 regions	27 provinces		
Ireland	1981	9 regions	4 provinces	27 counties	5 boroughs
Jordan	1979	5 governorates			
Jordan	1983	5 governorates			
Kenya	1981	8 provinces	17 districts		
Kiribati	1978	22 islands			
Mali	1976	7 regions	46 cercles	12 communes	1 district with 6 communes
Mexico	1980	32 entities			
Nepal	1980	2 regions			
Neth.Antilles	1981	6 eilandgebieds			
Pakistan	1981	4 provinces			
Panama	1980	10 provinces			
Peru	1981	25 departments			
Philippines	1980	13 health regions			
Swaziland	1983	4 districts	4 regions	3 Domains	
Trinidad & Tobago	1980	8 counties			
Trinidad & Tobago	1982	8 counties			
Tunisia	1975	18 governorates			
Tunisia	1984	4 regions	23 governorates		
United Kingdom (Northern Ireland)	1978	17 districts			
United States	1980	4 regions	9 divisions	50 States	1 district
United States	1982	4 regions	3 places		
Venezuela	1981	23 entities			

Source: United Nations Disability Statistics Data Base (DISTAT, 1988).

* Now Myanmar

Table II.4. Rural/Urban differences in disability prevalence rates

(Per 100,000)

Data collection type; Country or area	Year	Age group surveyed	Total surveyed urban population	Urban disabled	Total surveyed rural population	Rural disabled	Disability prevalence per 100 000 Urban	Rural	Ratio of rural to urban prevalence
Census: *Total population*									
Philippines	1980	15+	5 258 318	62 748	8 302 736	121 622	119.3	146.5	1.2
Pakistan	1981	Total	23 841 471	77 675	58 213 626	293 745	32.6	50.5	1.5
Mali	1976	Total	1 076 829	18 671	5 318 089	174 536	173.4	328.2	1.9
United States	1980	16-64	108 005 590	8 805 829	36 661 042	3 513 722	815.3	958.4	1.2
Tunisia	1984	Total	3 685 470	30 930	3 289 980	29 630	83.9	90.1	1.1
Tunisia	1975	Total	2 779 180	22 960	2 798 070	20 740	82.6	74.1	0.9
Census: *Economically inactive*									
Burma*	1983	10+	3 588 414	8 872	9 445 540	41 128	24.7	43.5	1.8
Central Afr.Rep. [a]	1975	10+	1 240 757	14 810	168 870	663	119.4	39.3	0.3
Venezuela [b]	1981	12+	4 285 706	156 961	796 801	38 099	366.2	478.1	1.3
Surveys									
Thailand	1981	Total	8 465 120	57 960	39 156 310	309 560	68.5	79.1	1.2
Fiji	1982	Total	162 500	1 500	259 400	2 500	92.3	96.4	1.0
China	1983	0-14	32 905	445	146 118	2 131	135.2	145.8	1.1
Thailand	1983	6-24	1 131 080	35 600	9 747 700	203 720	314.7	209.0	0.7

Source: United Nations Disability Statistics Data Base (DISTAT, 1988).

[a] Urban includes Banqui population.

[b] Urban includes "intermediate" population.

* Now Myanmar

Figure II.7. Ratio of rural/urban disability

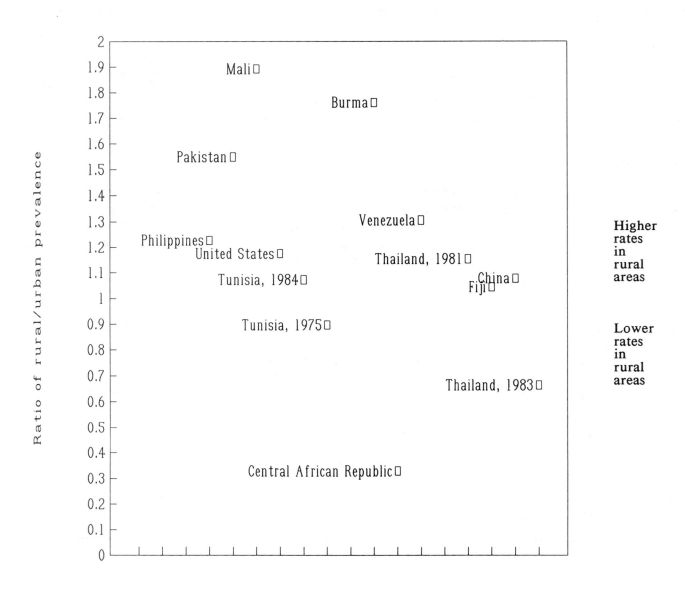

Source: Table 5 (chap.IV).

2. Socio-economic assessment of disablement

In many respects, the disability rate is a socio-economic indicator, a type of poverty index, or index of development. It is unique in that it estimates the quality of life of survivorship, or of persons who escape mortality and continue living with significant modifications of function. Lower socio-economic status and higher poverty levels are associated with higher disability rates, e.g., higher illiteracy rates, poor nutritional status, lower innoculation and immunization coverage of children, low birth weight of babies, higher unemployment rates, and lower occupational mobility.[17] As a development indicator, the study of disablement provides a unique perspective on the long-term consequences to individuals and their families of functional loss from disease, accident, trauma and deprivation. The study of disablement, in this perspective, goes beyond medical description and diagnosis and addresses questions of quality of life and socio-economic conditions.

(a) Educational attainment and school attendance

Perhaps one of the more devastating handicapping effects of disablement among children is the loss in opportunity to attend school. For example, based upon the more detailed statistics available in statistical table 8 (chap. IV) it may be noted that for the population of Hong Kong, based upon 1981 census data, the educational experience of disabled persons is substantially different than the experience of the total population of Hong Kong (figure II.8). In this example, a comparison is made between the percentage of persons who have never attended school for both the total population of Hong Kong and for the total population of persons reported to have a disability according to their age group. The graph indicates that fewer than 4 per cent of the population of youth, ages 15-24, in Hong Kong report that they have never attended school, whereas over 25 per cent of the total population of youth who are disabled report that they have never attended. Without a doubt, this ultimately results in a significant differential in occupational structure and employment status among young disabled adults when compared to the total population, since the disabled have been largely excluded from the educational system.

(b) Labour force participation and employment opportunities

Another area of serious concern to policy makers and planners are the financial and social implications of unemployment rates among disabled persons and the differential policies of payment of disability pensions to unemployed disabled people.[18] As an example of existing data available to study this issue, a comparison of employment status of Australians is presented in figure II.9. Comparisons are made for the total population of males and females, as well as for the population of disabled males and females, who are between the ages of 15 and 64. The

---

17 United Nations, ... *Case Studies*; Haber, *op. cit.*

18 A recent article discussing the relationship between definitions of disability, retirement, and unemployment, and the subsequent economic costs to the government of social security and disability benefits, has brought needed attention to concerns of labour force participation of disabled persons. See Barry A. Mirkin, "Early retirement: an international overview." *Monthly Labor Review*, vol.110, No.3 (March 1987), pp. 16-21.

Figure II.8. Persons having no schooling, by age group, total and disabled population: Hong Kong, 1981

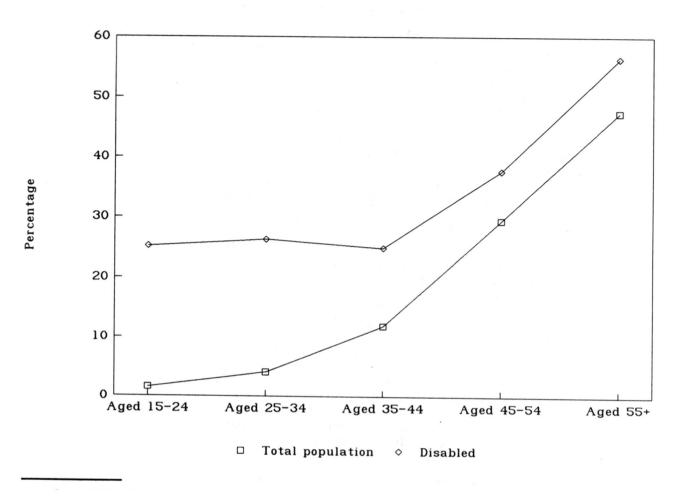

Source: Table 6 (chap.IV).

Figure II.9. Employment status: Australia, 1981

Percentage distribution

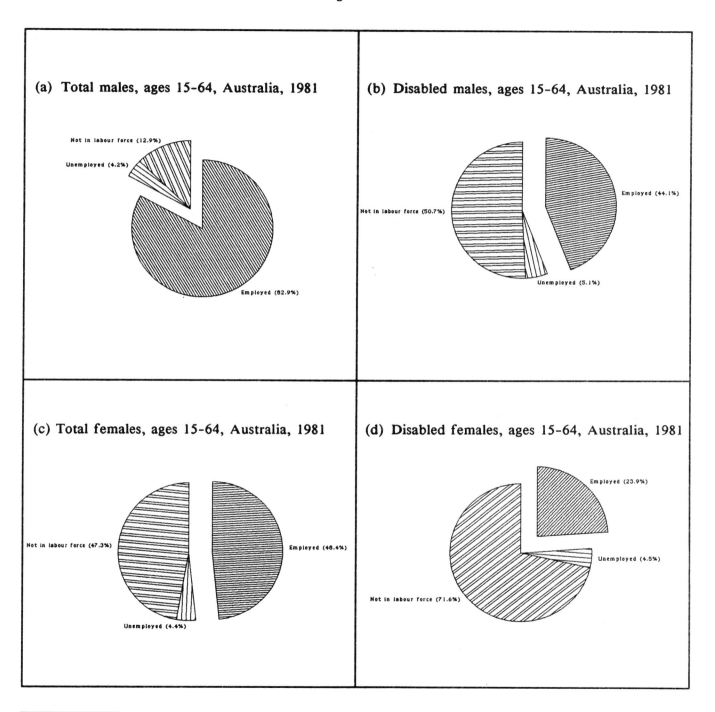

(a) Total males, ages 15-64, Australia, 1981

Not in labour force (12.9%)
Unemployed (4.2%)
Employed (82.9%)

(b) Disabled males, ages 15-64, Australia, 1981

Not in labour force (50.7%)
Employed (44.1%)
Unemployed (5.1%)

(c) Total females, ages 15-64, Australia, 1981

Not in labour force (47.3%)
Employed (48.4%)
Unemployed (4.4%)

(d) Disabled females, ages 15-64, Australia, 1981

Employed (23.9%)
Unemployed (4.5%)
Not in labour force (71.6%)

Source: Table 7 (chap.IV).

proportions of disabled males and females not in the labour force are substantially higher than are the proportions for the total population of Australian men and women. These low labour force participation rates of disabled persons are not unique to Australia. In general, statistics consistently show lower rates of labour force participation among disabled persons than among total populations (see detailed statistics in table 7, (chap. IV) for additional examples).

(c)   Marital status and family formation; living arrangements

Family formation and living arrangements are particularly important for assessing equal opportunity and social integration.

(i)   Marital status and family formation

In figure II.10(*a*), an example from Sweden highlights the rate of disability per 100 population by family cycle and marital status of persons who have limited hearing or eyesight. Figure II.10(*b*) shows the same relationship for persons who report having a work capacity limitation or a mobility limitation. In both cases, there are substantial differences in disability rates according to one's stage in the family cycle. For example, highest rates of hearing impairment were reported among pensioners aged 75-84 who were cohabitating, followed by single pensioners. Rates of visual disability were highest among single pensioners, followed by childless persons aged 45-64 who were single or cohabitating. Parents, ages 16-84, who had children 18 years of age or younger reported less disability, and single youth aged 16-24, reported the least.

Single persons in every stage of the family cycle indicated higher rates of mobility limitations than cohabitating persons. With the exception of pensioners aged 75-84, single persons also showed higher rates of work capacity limitation than did persons who were cohabitating.

(ii) Living arrangements

What is the role of institutions in providing living arrangements of disabled persons? Figure II.11 shows the number of institutionalized persons by age group and type of institution for Australia, 1981. In this example, both the type of institution, and also the numbers of persons who are reported as institutionalized are largely determined by the age of the disabled persons involved. Children aged 5-34 who are disabled and institutionalized are reported most often as living in special homes or psychiatric hospitals. Among adults aged 35-64 who live in institutions, most are found in nursing homes and in psychiatric hospitals or special homes. The greatest number of adults who live in institutions are aged 75 and older and they largely reside in nursing homes and homes for the aged.

3.   Disability description

This section describes disability specific experiences, such as reporting on the cause of the impairment, or on special aids used to reduce disability among persons reported as disabled. Unlike the previous socio-economic and family topics which were asked of total populations and of disabled persons, the questions asked below are only asked of persons who are reported to have disabilities.

Figure II.10.   Rate of disability, by family cycle and marital status: Sweden, 1980

(a) Hearing and eyesight
(Per 100 population)

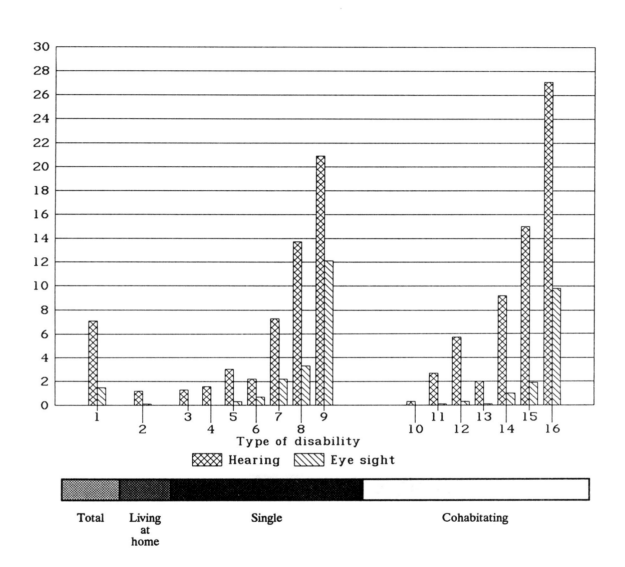

			Single	Cohabitating
1	Total ages 16-84	3	Aged 16-24	10
2	Living at home	4	Parents (ages 16-84) with child < 7 years of age	11
		5	Parents (ages 16-84) with child age 7-18 years	12
		6	Childless (ages 25-44)	13
		7	Childless (ages 45-64)	14
		8	Pensioners aged 65-74	15
		9	Pensioners aged 75-84	16

Figure II.10. *(continued)*

(b) Work capacity and mobility
(Per 100 population)

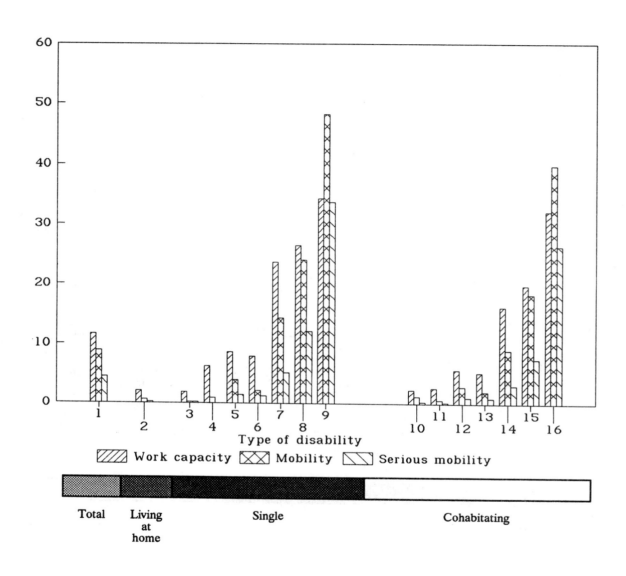

Work capacity Mobility Serious mobility

Total Living at home Single Cohabitating

			Single	Cohabitating
1	Total ages 16-84	3	Aged 16-24	10
2	Living at home	4	Parents (ages 16-84) with child < 7 years of age	11
		5	Parents (ages 16-84) with child age 7-18 years	12
		6	Childless (ages 25-44)	13
		7	Childless (ages 45-64)	14
		8	Pensioners aged 65-74	15
		9	Pensioners aged 75-84	16

Source: Table 8 (chap.IV).

Figure II.11. Institutionalized disabled persons, by age group and type of institution: Australia, 1981

(*In thousands*)

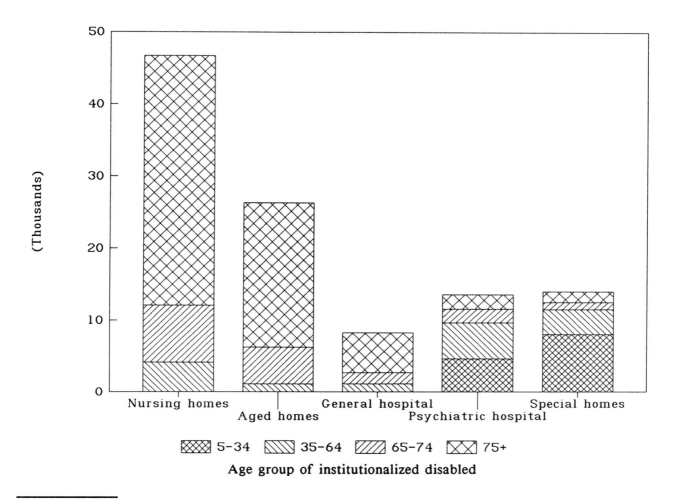

Age group of institutionalized disabled

Source: Table 10 (chap.IV).

(a)   Causes of impairment or reasons for disability

Figure II.12(*a*) displays stated reasons for limb deformity and paralysis among urban and rural disabled persons in India, 1981. Poliomyelitis, burns or injury, and other illnesses were reported by urban and rural areas as the major reason for limb deformity. However, polio was offered as the explanation in 43 per cent of the cases of limb deformity in urban areas and in only 29 per cent of rural cases. One possible explanation could be that the polio cases in rural areas were more likely to go undiagnosed and were therefore reported in the general category of "other" or "other illness" rather than with a specific diagnosis. In addition, another important distinction between urban and rural areas, is that leprosy was reported as the reason for limb deformity among 7.5 per cent of rural and 3.2 per cent of urban cases. This contributes substantially to the reported differences between the two geographical areas in the cause of limb deformity. Further comparisons of these groups might be improved were they to be presented according to type of cause per 100,000 population rather than as percentage distribution of causes among disabled persons. Then, the comparisons between reports of leprosy, polio and burns and injury could be more standardized.

Paralysis was also reported to be polio-related among 28 per cent of rural and 44 per cent of urban disabled. In this case, cerebral palsy was also noted among 10 per cent of paralysis. Again, the percentage of paralysis explained by the general categories of "other" and "other illness" is greater in rural than in urban areas.

Figure II.12(*b*) shows the reported cause of amputation and joint dysfunction for urban and rural India. The majority of amputations were reported as due to "other" or "other illness" for both rural and urban areas. Leprosy was reported as the reason in 12 per cent of rural and 8 per cent of urban areas. Burns and injury were also significant, with 22 per cent of rural and 28 per cent of reported amputations being due to them.

In contrast, joint dysfunction was largely reported as being due to burns and injuries for both rural and urban areas (42 per cent of all causes). Polio also remained an important cause, with 8 per cent of rural and 12 per cent of urban persons with joint dysfunction saying that it was due to polio.

(b)   Special aids used

Although relatively infrequently reported by these 55 countries and areas, the topic of special aids for disabled persons was included because of its importance for programme planning. There is a significant increase in the demand for information by Governments and industry about the potential use of special aids by disabled persons, primarily because of recently improved technology and effectiveness of special aids available for disabled persons, as well as because of increased innovation in the computer industry and also in architectural design of homes and transport systems as well as public buildings.

Examples of available statistics for the study of special aids used by disabled persons are available in figures II.13(*a*),(*b*),(*c*) and (*d*). In these figures, a comparison is made of special aids used for reducing disabilities in households and in institutions among Australians who are disabled. In households, special aids are primarily used to reduce mobility disability and communication limitations. Mobility limitations are reduced through the use of sticks and crutches or "other" means. The diversity

Figure II.12.　Causes of disability:　India, urban and rural

(Percentage distribution)

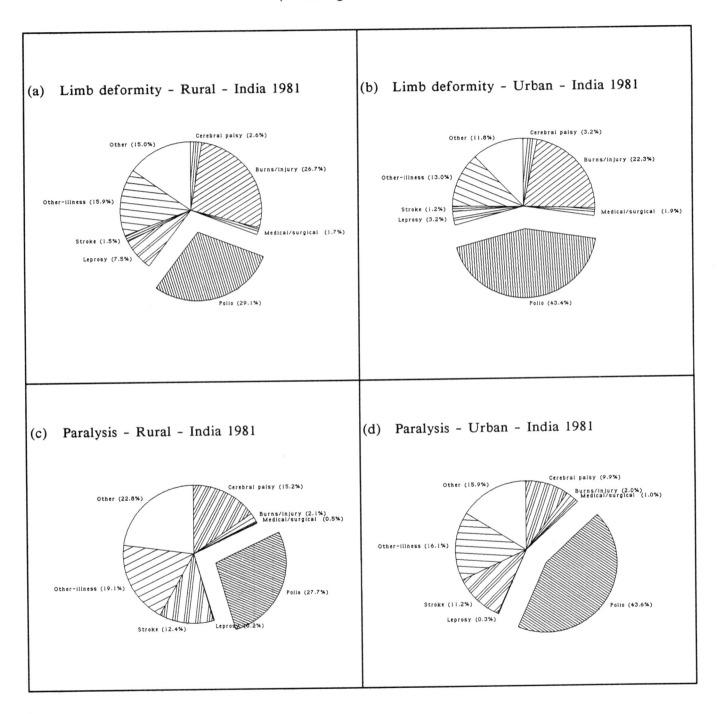

(a)　Limb deformity - Rural - India 1981

Other (15.0%)
Cerebral palsy (2.6%)
Burns/injury (26.7%)
Other-illness (15.9%)
Medical/surgical (1.7%)
Stroke (1.5%)
Leprosy (7.5%)
Polio (29.1%)

(b)　Limb deformity - Urban - India 1981

Other (11.8%)
Cerebral palsy (3.2%)
Burns/injury (22.3%)
Other-illness (13.0%)
Medical/surgical (1.9%)
Stroke (1.2%)
Leprosy (3.2%)
Polio (43.4%)

(c)　Paralysis - Rural - India 1981

Other (22.8%)
Cerebral palsy (15.2%)
Burns/injury (2.1%)
Medical/surgical (0.5%)
Other-illness (19.1%)
Polio (27.7%)
Stroke (12.4%)
Leprosy (0.2%)

(d)　Paralysis - Urban - India 1981

Other (15.9%)
Cerebral palsy (9.9%)
Burns/injury (2.0%)
Medical/surgical (1.0%)
Other-illness (16.1%)
Polio (43.6%)
Stroke (11.2%)
Leprosy (0.3%)

55

Figure II.12 *(continued)*

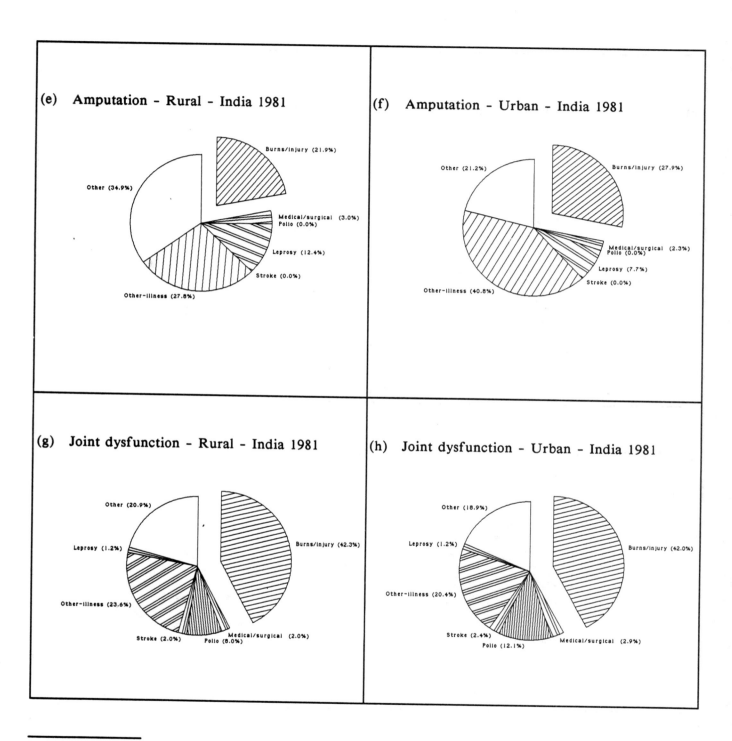

Source: Table 11(chap.IV).

Figure II.13   Special aids used: Australia, 1981

(a) For reducing disabilities, by residence

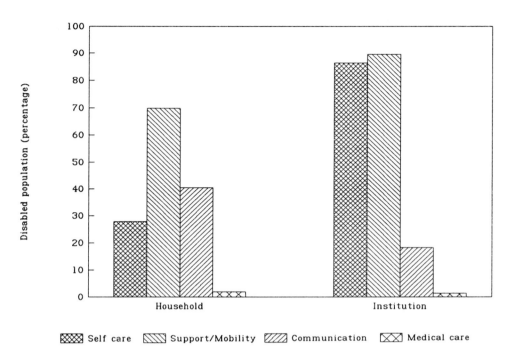

(b) By type of aid and, by residence

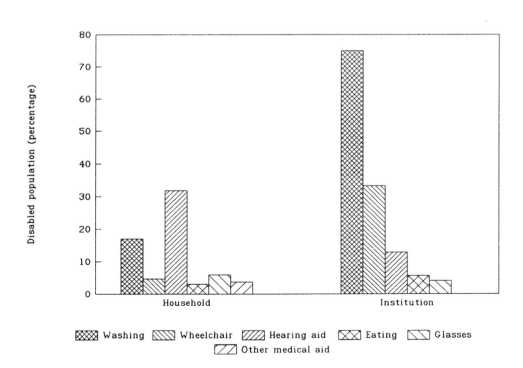

Figure II.13 *(continued)*

(c) For self care, by type of residence

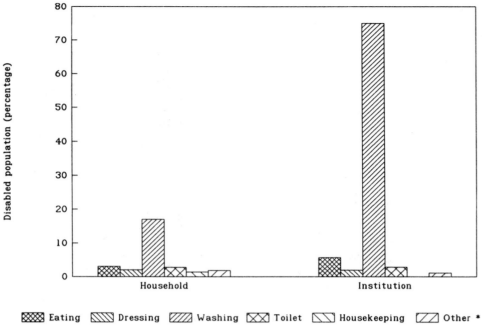

Eating   Dressing   Washing   Toilet   Housekeeping   Other *

(d) For mobility, by type of residence

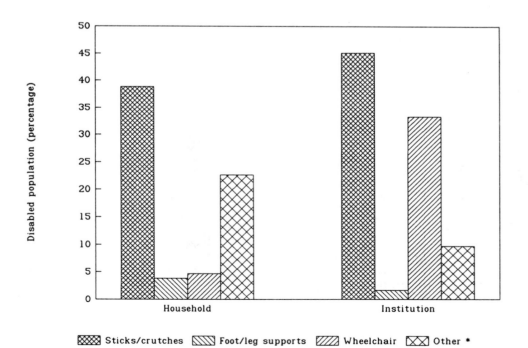

Sticks/crutches   Foot/leg supports   Wheelchair   Other *

Special aids

* Including artificial limb/s, calipers, braces, special chair, special bed, cane, rails/bars and other.

Source: Table 12 (chap.IV).

of mobility aids is much greater in households than in institutions, with "other" mobility aids, including artificial limbs, calipers, braces, special chairs, special beds, canes, rails/bars and the like. Communication barriers are reduced in households through greater use of hearing aids than in institutions.

In contrast, in institutions, special aids are heavily used to reduce self-care disabilities and also mobility limitations. Communication aids are less utilized in institutions than in households. Among disabled persons who live in institutions, self-care aids are often used to reduce washing and eating limitations, with washing aids used by approximately 75 per cent of disabled persons residing in institutions. Mobility limitations are reduced through the use of sticks or crutches. Wheelchairs are used by a substantially larger proportion of institutionalized disabled persons than by disabled persons who live in households. "Other" more diversified types of mobility aids are used less often in institutions than in households.

C. Conclusion

This completes the presentation of illustrative ways in which the statistics provided in tables 1-12 (chap. IV) of the *Compendium* may be highlighted and discussed through the use of graphics and summary tables. Further use of these statistics for analysis and presentation will contribute to the overall development of this field of statistics. It is only through exploratory development and use of statistics on disability that further refinements may be accomplished.

There has been a steady increase in the statistical study of disability by Governments and other organizations in the region, and a substantial increase in the application of national disability statistics for policy formulation and programme planning. Because of this, international methodological studies and guidelines are clearly needed to assist disparate national strategies.

In order to further develop this statistical field, support of national, regional and international work is needed in the following areas:

(*a*) Implementation of training workshops and international conferences to promote the policy-oriented scientific study of disablement through exchange of technical materials and survey research experience;

(*b*) Regular updating of DISTAT. The co-operation of national statistical offices and other organizations is needed in this area so that disability statistics can be submitted at regular intervals by Governments to the Statistical Office of the United Nations Secretariat in a comparable format;

(*c*) Monitoring national use of ICIDH in various data collection activities;

(*d*) Promoting the inclusion of disability topics in national surveys and national survey programmes;

(*e*) Achieving through systematic methodological monitoring and analysis of survey results general agreement on the underlying principles of survey screens used to identify persons with disabilities, ultimately resulting in methodological guidelines on the identification and assessment of disablement in censuses and surveys;

(*f*)   Expanding interregional technical advisory services to work with developing countries and other international and regional organizations in the production of disability statistics within the existing statistical systems and through appropriate Government offices and programmes, as requested in the World Programme of Action.

There are other activities that can be launched by various international and regional agencies, research institutes and interested organizations. For example, it would be very useful to generate a short list of impairments, disabilities and handicaps for more systematic and streamlined national and international application of ICIDH concepts and codes in survey work.

It is also important to ultimately design a university curriculum and training manuals for demographers, epidemiologists, statisticians and survey researchers interested in the study of disability, and a curriculum for training programmes to address the needs of professionals already working on national data collection, analysis and policy formulation in this area.

Finally, international and regional programmes should be encouraged to include at all times in training programmes and conferences on the development of disability statistics, opportunities for discussion and participation of disabled persons, their families, and programme staff concerned with disablement. This includes opportunities to observe the various dimensions of their environmental conditions so as to make survey methods more accommodating, appropriate and realistic to the needs of disabled persons and to the general description of disablement.

III. GENERAL TECHNICAL NOTES

These technical notes are designed to give the reader information for interpreting the data available in the 12 detailed statistical tables of this publication. The following sections refer to specific tables and include a description of the variables included under each statistical topic. When appropriate, details on computation of rates, ratios or percentages are presented.

A. Arrangement of tables

The tables are grouped into two major types: (a) disability tables by demographic characteristics, such as age and sex and urban and rural residence, by type of selected disability (tables 1-5); and (b) special topic tables (tables 6-12). Special topics are broken down into socio-economic status (tables 6-10) and disability description (tables 11 and 12). Each statistical table is preceded by some textual explanation or technical notes specific to that table.

B. Source of data

The primary source of statistics presented in this *Compendium* are the published reports of national censuses, household surveys and administrative registration systems, (see annex I), supplemented by information provided from correspondence with national statistical services. These national data sets were coded and placed in the United Nations International Disability Statistics Data Base (DISTAT, 1988). A full description of the international data base is provided in the United Nations 1988 publication, *United Nations Disability Statistics Data Base, 1975-1986: Technical Manual.*[2]

Age and sex-specific disability rates have been calculated by the Statistical Office of the United Nations Secretariat, using basic data from the national data sets, unless otherwise specified. There were some cases where countries published the rates without providing the figures used for their calculation. In these cases, the published rates were presented as given in the national reports. The methods used by the Statistical Office to calculate these rates and ratios are described in the technical notes for each table. The populations used for the computations are those described and published in the tables of the *Compendium*.

C. Geographical aspects

1. Coverage

Geographical coverage in the tables is as comprehensive as possible, given the exploratory nature of this first publication of a *Compendium* of disability statistics. Data are shown for as many individual countries or areas as could be identified during the Statistical Office search for national publications on disability statistics in selected libraries and official offices. Table 1 is the most comprehensive in national coverage, presenting data on numbers of disabled persons and age and sex-specific disability prevalence rates for every country or area included in DISTAT. Not all these countries or areas appear in subsequent tables. In many cases, the data required for a particular table are not available for a specific country. In general, the more detailed the data required for any table, the fewer the number of countries or areas that can provide them. Table I.1 in the Introduction provides a listing of all countries in DISTAT according to whether they have data on any particular topic covered in the *Compendium*. This table may be referred to for ascertaining the availability of national data on any particular disability topic.

To the extent possible, all data are presented at the national level. No global or regional estimates are provided. In some cases, when national level data have not been available, subnational statistics, i.e. for particular age groups, residence status, or for persons having particular labour force or educational characteristics, have been shown and footnoted accordingly. Because of the exploratory nature of this first *Compendium*, and owing to the general lack of knowledge about the quality and availability of disability statistics, the data here presented in the statistical tables are displayed as received, so that future work may benefit from full knowledge of previous experience.

2. Territorial composition

In so far as possible, all data relate to the territory within 1988 boundaries. Exceptions to this are footnoted in individual tables.

3. Nomenclature

Because of space limitations, the country or area names listed in the tables are generally the commonly employed short titles in use in the United Nations,[19] the full titles being used only when a short form is not available. Countries or areas are listed in English alphabetical order within the following continents: Africa, North America, South America, Asia, Europe, Oceania and the USSR.

The designations employed and the presentation of the material in this publication were adopted solely for the purpose of providing a convenient geographical basis for the accompanying statistical series. The same qualification applies to all notes and explanations concerning the geographical units for which data are presented.

4. Total populations

Population statistics, that is, those pertaining to the size, geographical distribution and demographic characteristics of the total population, are sometimes presented in a number of tables of the *Compendium*, especially when the source of disability data is a population and housing census. However, the primary purpose of the presentation of population statistics is for comparison of total population characteristics with disabled populations; it is not for the purpose of total population description. In some cases, the total number of persons surveyed nationally is significantly smaller than the total size of the population of a country, especially when sample surveys are utilized. For detailed population statistics describing the situation of total populations, see the United Nations series of *Demographic Yearbooks*. The primary purpose of presenting the total number of population surveyed in the present *Compendium* is so that prevalence rates of disability may

---

19 For a listing of the majority of these, see "Names of countries and adjectives of nationality" (United Nations document ST/CS/SER.F/317 and corrigenda).

be calculated, and also so that both numerators and denominators of derived disability rates are made available to the user thereby allowing other rates to be calculated as needed, e.g. percentage distributions of selected characteristics or other types of ratios.

5. Sources of variation in the data

The comparability of data is affected by several factors, including (*a*) definition of total population; (*b*) the definitions used to identify disabled persons; (*c*) definitions used to classify the population into its urban/rural components; (*d*) difficulties relating to age reporting; (*e*) extent of over-enumeration or under-enumeration in the most recent census or other source of bench-mark population statistics and of disabled persons; (*f*) quality of population estimates; and (*g*) the quality of disability estimates. Other relevant problems are discussed in the specific technical notes to the individual statistical tables. Readers interested in more detail, relating in particular to the sources of variation in disability data should consult some of the United Nations publications on this topic.[20]

(a) Variations in disabled population

One important impediment to comparability of disability statistics is the variation in census and survey definitions of disability. Because of its importance, there is a special chapter of this *Compendium* devoted to the discussion of variations in disability prevalence according to national differences in the definition of disability (see chapter II, section A.3 on Survey estimates of disability).

Confusion also occurs in the interpretation of data because some censuses and surveys count disabled people, others count numbers of disabilities found, and some count both. In the first case, the number of disabled people equals the total number of all disabled persons identified in the study. In the second case, for example,a disabled person may be counted once because of blindness, and then be counted again under hearing impairments. In the second case, the total number of disabilities counted is greater than the total number of disabled persons primarily because a certain proportion of the disabled population have multiple disabilities. Throughout the statistical tables, there are two columns available for presentation of total disability data in order to accommodate both types of national presentation: (*a*) the total number of disabled persons and (*b*) the total number of disabilities reported.

(b) Urban/rural classification

National classifications of urban/rural are presented according to the classifications used by each country. These definitions are available in the *Demographic Yearbook* and are therefore not presented here. In general, however, within national data sets, comparisons between urban/rural residence of total populations and disabled populations are comparable.

---

20 For example, see United Nations ... *Case Studies,* esp. pp. 24-65; also see *Development of Statistical Concepts and Methods on Disability for Household Surveys* (ST/ESA/STAT/Ser.F/38); and consult the *Principles and Recommendations for Population and Housing Censuses,* Statistical papers, Series M, No.67 (United Nations Publication, Sales No. E.80.XVII.8) for sources of variation in population data in general.

(c)   Collection and compilation of age data

Age is the estimated or calculated interval of time between the date of birth and the date of the census or survey, expressed in completed solar years.[21]   There are two methods of collecting age data. The first is to obtain the date of birth for each member of the population in a census or survey and then to calculate the completed age of the individual by subtracting the date of birth from the date of enumeration.[22]   The second method is to record the individual's completed age at the time of the census or survey, that is to say, age at last birthday.

(d)   Errors in age data

Errors in age data may be due to a variety of causes, including ignorance of correct age; reporting years of age in terms of a calendar concept other than completed solar years since birth; carelessness in reporting and recording age; a general tendency to state age in figures ending in certain digits (such as zero, two, five and eight); a tendency to exaggerate length of life at advanced ages; possibly subconscious aversion to a certain number, and wilful misrepresentations arising from motives of an economic, social, political or purely personal character. These reasons for errors in reported age data are common to most investigations of age and to most countries or areas, and they may impair comparability to a marked degree.

The classification of population by age is a core element of most analysis and estimation of disability statistics. Age data of disabled persons are, however, subject to a number of specific sources of error and non-comparability. It has been documented, for example, that in a number of cases, disabled children are seriously underenumerated, primarily because among pre-school children it is not yet known even to their parents that they have a disability, e.g. hearing impairment, difficulty seeing etc. Identifying pre-school-age children who are impaired or disabled is not an easy task, even when highly sophisticated equipment and medical techniques are used in the assessment. Although underenumeration of childhood disabilities is probably almost inevitable, that does not mean that survey reports of childhood disabilities cannot be improved through more explicit behavioural or functional questions on basic childhood developmental patterns.[23] In addition, the single-year estimates of age of persons over age 60 are also subject to a number of sources of error and non-comparability, primarily due to lack of precision among reporting of older persons, a general upward bias in the estimates of age, as well as a tendency among the elderly to round off their approximate age to the nearest decade. Given the significantly higher proportions of disabled persons among elderly groups, the problem of age-reporting takes on special significance in the study of disability. In general, because of the likelihood that people with disabilities have low status,

---

21 *Principles and Recommendations* ..., para. 2.88.

22 Alternatively if a population register is used, completed ages are calculated by subtracting the date of birth of individuals listed in the register from a reference data to which the age data pertain.

23 See a recent review of survey questions on childhood development by Lucille C. Atkin, "Analysis of instruments used in Latin America to measure psychosocial development in children from 0 to 6 years of age", (report of Instituto Nacional de Perinatologia, Mexico); also Lilian Belmont, *The International Pilot Study of Severe Childhood Disability: final report: Screening for severe mental retardation in developing countries* (Netherlands, Cahiers Geestelijk Gehandicapten, 1984).

In general, because of the likelihood that people with disabilities have low status, there is a propensity in some studies to have substantial proportions of the disabled population in the "age-unknown" categories. The "age-unknown" category should be monitored carefully when comparing age distributions of disabled populations with total populations of countries.

6. Quality of published statistics

With specific reference to the quality of disability statistics coming from censuses, this *Compendium* provides notes indicating deviations from full national coverage. The degree of underenumeration or overenumeration of disability estimates from censuses and surveys are not yet known. In general, however, internal consistency of national disability statistics are quite reasonable. It has been noted, for example in one case, that with respect to the United States Census and the national Survey of Income and Expenditure (SIE), "the data in the major surveys appear to be internally consistent and as reliable as other commonly used survey measures, such as years of education and marital status... The distribution of disability rates by states was also highly consistent over time. The correlation coefficients for state disability rates for the 1970 and 1980 Censuses and the 1976 SIE ranged from .93 to .95 for the three periods".[24] However, cross-national comparisons of statistics of disabled persons are currently a questionable activity, given the high diversity in data collection strategies and wide variations in definitions of disability utilized by countries resulting in a low level of comparability in the results. Because of the diversity, a special section has been prepared in this *Compendium* which reviews some of the problems confronted when making cross-national comparisons (see chapter II, section A.3). Further details of each of the census and survey designs are provided in the NOTES files of DISTAT, version 1.[25]

7. Disability statistics

For purposes of the *Compendium*, disability statistics have been defined as statistics concerning disabled persons, through presentation of findings on impairments, disabilities and handicaps of disabled persons. For survey research purposes, people who are disabled are essentially viewed as a special population group of individuals who have in common the fact that they live with long-term functional loss. The term "disabled persons" is used to indicate that one is part of a special population group of persons broadly referred to in the United Nations World Programme of Action concerning Disabled Persons.[1] This is the first time that the Statistical Office of the United Nations Secretariat has compiled national statistics in a systematic way on this topic.

(a) Statistical definitions of disability

The Compendium of Disability Statistics attempts to organize and group national disability statistics according to the standard definitions put forth in the World Health Organization's *International Classification of Impairments, Disabilities and Handicaps*. These are as follows:

---

24 Haber, *op. cit.*, p.18.

25 See the *Technical Manual* of DISTAT for complete details of these notes. Additional information is available in Mary Chamie, "Survey design strategies for the study of disability", *World Health Statistics Quarterly*, No. 3, 1989.

(i) Definition of impairment. *Impairment* is any loss or abnormality of psychological, physiological, or anatomical structure or function. The broad classification of impairments include the following nine coding categories available in the classification scheme at the one digit level: 1. Intellectual; 2. Other psychological; 3. Language; 4. Aural; 5. Ocular; 6. Visceral; 7. Skeletal; 8. Disfiguring; and 9. Generalized, sensory, and other impairments.

(ii) Definition of disability. *Disability* is any restriction or lack (resulting from an impairment) of ability to perform an activity in the manner or within the range considered normal for a human being. The broad classification of disabilities include the following nine coding categories available in the classification scheme at the one-digit level: 1. Behaviour; 2. Communication; 3. Personal care; 4. Locomotor; 5. Body disposition; 6. Dexterity; 7. Situational; 8. Particular skills; 9. Other activity restrictions.

(iii) Definition of handicap. *Handicap* is a disadvantage for a given individual, resulting from an impairment or a disability, that limits or prevents the fulfilment of a role that is normal (depending on age, sex and social and cultural factors) for that individual.[26] In every national data set, disabled persons were identified either through reporting of their impairments or their disabilities. Disabled persons were not identified as disabled through the reporting of their handicaps. The concept of handicap was utilized in a number of reports primarily as an avenue for describing situations of disabled persons after they had already been identified in the survey either as impaired or disabled.

The areas outlined in the general socio-economic and demographic framework shown in the Introduction, section B, are used for assessing the dimensions of handicap. "It is important to recognize that the handicap classification is neither a taxonomy of disadvantage nor a classification of individuals. Rather it is a classification of circumstances in which disabled people are likely to find themselves, circumstances that place such individuals at a disadvantage relative to their peers when viewed from the norms of society."[27] Statistical tables 6-10 specifically present information that may be used to describe their circumstances.

(b) Disability: incidence versus prevalence

Thus far, national data set of censuses, surveys and registries have concentrated on prevalence rather than incidence of disability. This means that reports are given of all people who are disabled in the community and not just newly disabled during any particular time period. There is some data available in selected countries on age-at-onset of disability, but these statistics are not presented in the *Compendium*. They are, however, available in DISTAT.

(c) Variations in the percentage of disabled

There are strong methodological implications to estimates of the percentage of disabled, depending upon whether impairment or disability questions are used to identify disabled persons. To summarize briefly, estimates of the percentage of

---

26 World Health Organization, *International Classification ...*, p. 207 (Guidance on assessment).
27 *Ibid.*, p. 183

persons who are disabled ranged from 0.2 to 20.9 per cent of the population for the 63 surveys of the 55 countries presented in this *Compendium*. The high degree of variability in disability rates are partly determined by what are perceived as impairment and disability and their degrees by various countries. It is also partly determined by whether impairments or disability definitions and codes are used to identify disabled persons.

Survey estimates of the percentage of disabled appear lower when impairment questions rather than disability questions are used to identify disabled persons. In addition, when impairment questions are used for screening purposes, the resultant disability rates of men are generally higher than those of women. In contrast, when disability screening questions are used, rates are similar for women and men, and in some cases disability rates for women are higher. This suggests that comparisons of disability rates may be very misleading unless the methodological differences between surveys are clearly stated.[28]

Variations in disability rates are also partly due to differences in age ranges and populations covered by surveys. Differences in population ages and special populations covered by the surveys presented in this *Compendium* are noted in the footnotes to the tables.

---

28 "International development of disability statistics: accomplishments and goals", report presented to the Conference on Capabilities and Needs of Disabled Persons in the ESCWA Region, Amman, 20-28 November 1989.

IV. STATISTICAL TABLES

Table 1. Population, disabled persons, disabilities reported and prevalence of disability, by age and sex

Statistical table 1 presents the number of disabled persons, disabilities, and total persons by age group and sex, and the prevalence of disability per 100,000.

Description of variables

Estimates of the total number of population surveyed, disabled persons and disabilities are presented, as provided by each available data set from surveys, censuses or administrative registrations systems conducted between the years 1975 and 1986.

All age and sex-specific prevalence rates produced in the table were prepared by the Statistical Office except in the case of countries where no numbers were published. Under those conditions, prevalence rates were taken from the published reports of the censuses and surveys, as available. *Disabled persons prevalence rates* are defined as the number of persons identified as disabled in the total population surveyed, divided by the total population surveyed and multiplied by 100,000. *Disabilities prevalence rates* are defined as the number of disabilities in the total population surveyed, divided by the total population surveyed and multiplied by 100,000. The reader is reminded that a person may have multiple disabilities. In cases where the total number of disabilities found is reported rather than the number of disabled persons, the disabilities rate is then calculated and published in the appropriate column in table 1. In order to reduce confusion, these two types of disability data were distinguished by presenting the number of disabled persons and numbers of disabilities in separate columns. The data are organized so that national data are presented in English alphabetical order within regions.

Not all total populations in table 1 are conceptually the same. In some cases, for example, total populations presented in the table are comprised only of persons in specific-age ranges, e.g. ages 10+, 15+, 6-24, or 20-69. In other cases, the total population is comprised of the total population that is not economically active, or the total population of persons who are not attending school or, in one case, the total chronically ill population. Certain surveys presented statistics on the rate of disability among the economically active population, and others presented statistics on the rate of economically inactive disability among the total population. These distinctions are noted through the use of population labels in the national tables of table 1. Another distinction is that in some surveys they have sampled the total population of children, of elderly persons, of rural areas or of city populations. In addition, national registration systems often provide no estimate of the total population of the registered area because disabled persons only were surveyed by the registry. In any case, each of these differences in definition and presentation of total populations are specified in the table itself through footnotes and label descriptions.

Data quality in table 1 is highly variable. Explanations of variation in quality of demographic data from population and household censuses are reported as available in the *Demographic Yearbook*. Several studies have been conducted of the validity and reliability of disability data from population and housing censuses.[a] There is a general understanding, however, based upon existing research, that census data underenumerates disability.[b] In table 1, data from sample surveys are sometimes presented along with estimates of their standard errors; however such presentations are still rare and are presented, when available, as footnotes of the table. Registration data presented in the table are complicated by the fact that in some cases, disabilities were registered by non-medical personnel and at other times by medical personnel, depending upon the type of registry. A major difficulty to be addressed is the design of suitable classification lists of impairments and disabilities for use in surveys, with due consideration for ICIDH and national differences in terminology, and considering also the training of persons collecting the data.[c]

---

[a] For example, see the following documents for examples of reports of validity and reliability checking that have been produced:

Australia,
Australian Bureau of Statistics, Canberra, "Technical note on sampling variability", *Handicapped Persons: Australia, 1981* (ABS Catalogue No. 4343.0), p. 185.

Canada,
Statistics Canada, Health and Activity Limitation Survey, *Comparison of the Results from the 1986 Census and the Health and Activity Limitation Survey for Persons with Disabilities Residing in Households*, paper prepared by Adele Furrie, (3 October 1989).

Hong Kong,
Census and Statistics Department, "Assessment of quality of disablement data", *Hong Kong 1981 Census: Disablement Characteristics*, pp. 7-19.

India,
National Sample Survey Organization (1983), "Comparison of survey results with the census figures", *Report on Survey of Disabled Persons*, (Thirty-sixth round, No. 305, July-December 1981), pp. A5-A14.

Jordan,
Queen Alia Jordan Social Welfare Fund, Amman (1983), *Evaluation Studies of Handicapped Persons in Jordan*.

United States,
Lawrence D. Haber, "Identifying the disabled: concepts and methods in the measurement of disability" *Social Security Bulletin*, No. 30(1967) pp. 17-34;
Barry Bye, and Evan Schecter, "Technical introduction" *Survey of Disability and Work* (Washington D.C., Social Security Administration).
Wendi Thelan, "Reinterview results for the 1978 disability survey" United States Bureau of the Census (unpublished report cited in Haber, L., "Issues in the definition of disability", April 1989.

[b] Hong Kong. *op. cit.*; India, *op. cit.*

[c] A short-list of impairment and disability codes for surveys has been proposed by Mary Chamie, "Survey design strategies", *World Health Statistics Quarterly*, No. 3.(1989), pp. 136-137.

71

Chapter II, section B.1. presents findings from statistical table 1 in a more graphic and analytic way, as illustrative examples of the kind of analysis that might be tried with these data sets.

1. Population, disabled persons and disabilities reported and prevalence of disability by age and sex

Age and sex	Population surveyed	Disabled persons	Disabilities	Prevalence rate per 100,000 population	
				Disabled persons	Disabilities

CAPE VERDE, population census 1980

Age and sex	Population surveyed	*Not economically active*	Disabilities	Disabled persons	Disabilities
Males	92 757	3 210	..	3 460.7	..
10-14	20 864	92	..	441.0	..
15-19	18 779	104	..	553.8	..
20-24	10 853	103	..	949.0	..
25-29	5 393	60	..	1 112.6	..
30-34	2 770	46	..	1 660.6	..
35-39	2 693	57	..	2 116.6	..
40-44	4 071	56	..	1 375.6	..
45-49	4 219	61	..	1 445.8	..
50-54	3 973	105	..	2 642.8	..
55-59	2 538	100	..	3 940.1	..
60-64	2 669	178	..	6 669.2	..
65-69	2 787	362	..	12 988.9	..
70-74	2 518	626	..	24 861.0	..
75+	2 054	903	..	43 963.0	..
Unknown	6 576	357	..	5 428.8	..
Females	116 152	5 700	..	4 907.4	..
10-14	21 158	85	..	401.7	..
15-19	19 310	95	..	492.0	..
20-24	14 372	117	..	814.1	..
25-29	8 824	72	..	816.0	..
30-34	4 326	32	..	739.7	..
35-39	4 755	69	..	1 451.1	..
40-44	6 839	84	..	1 228.2	..
45-49	6 132	79	..	1 288.3	..
50-54	5 236	113	..	2 158.1	..
55-59	3 104	117	..	3 769.3	..
60-64	3 292	354	..	10 753.3	..
65-69	3 328	644	..	19 351.0	..
70-74	2 949	899	..	30 484.9	..
75+	3 539	1 796	..	50 748.8	..
Unknown	8 988	1 144	..	12 728.1	..

Note. Column headings in italics show the national terminology.

Table 1 *(continued)*

Age and sex	Population surveyed	Disabled persons	Disabilities	Prevalence rate per 100,000 population	
				Disabled persons	Disabilities

CENTRAL AFRICAN REPUBLIC, population census 1975

Age and sex	Population surveyed	*Not economically active*	Disabilities	Disabled persons	Disabilities
Males 10+	675 010	8 332	..	1 234.4	..
Females 10+	734 617	7 141	..	972.1	..

Note. Column headings in italics show the national terminology.

Table 1 *(continued)*

Age and sex	Population surveyed	Disabled persons	Disabilities	Prevalence rate per 100,000 population	
				Disabled persons	Disabilities

COMOROS, population census 1980

Age and sex	Population surveyed	Disabled persons	Disabilities	Disabled persons	Disabilities
Males	167 089	3 247	..	1 943.3	..
0-4	28 034	178	..	634.9	..
5-9	30 027	348	..	1 159.0	..
10-14	23 041	312	..	1 354.1	..
15-19	15 218	258	..	1 695.4	..
20-24	11 484	219	..	1 907.0	..
25-29	9 519	187	..	1 964.5	..
30-34	8 848	202	..	2 283.0	..
35-39	7 313	180	..	2 461.4	..
40-44	7 969	234	..	2 936.4	..
45-49	4 956	155	..	3 127.5	..
50-54	5 526	165	..	2 985.9	..
55-59	2 735	99	..	3 619.7	..
60-64	4 305	181	..	4 204.4	..
65-59	1 815	95	..	5 234.2	..
70-74	2 672	157	..	5 875.7	..
75-79	915	66	..	7 213.1	..
80-84	1 143	98	..	8 573.9	..
85+	818	95	..	11 613.7	..
Not stated	751	18	..	2 396.8	..
Females	168 061	2 454	..	1 460.2	..
0-4	27 561	128	..	464.4	..
5-9	28 979	201	..	693.6	..
10-14	20 484	197	..	961.7	..
15-19	16 307	191	..	1 171.3	..
20-24	13 620	162	..	1 189.4	..
25-29	11 769	146	..	1 240.5	..
30-34	9 817	161	..	1 640.0	..
35-39	7 886	159	..	2 016.2	..
40-44	7 723	172	..	2 227.1	..
45-49	4 286	97	..	2 263.2	..
50-54	5 594	169	..	3 021.1	..
55-59	2 336	69	..	2 953.8	..
60-64	4 164	156	..	3 746.4	..
65-59	1 499	60	..	4 002.7	..
70-74	2 602	116	..	4 458.1	..
75-79	764	50	..	6 544.5	..
80-84	1 297	104	..	8 018.5	..
85+	939	110	..	11 714.6	..
Not stated	434	6	..	1 382.5	..

Table 1 *(continued)*

Age and sex	Population surveyed	Disabled persons	Disabilities	Prevalence rate per 100,000 population	
				Disabled persons	Disabilities

EGYPT, population census 1976

Age and sex	Population surveyed	Disabled persons	Disabilities	Disabled persons	Disabilities
Males	18 647 289	82 361	..	441.7	..
0-4	2 548 265	453	..	17.8	..
5-9	2 421 813	4 225	..	174.5	..
10-14	2 581 979	8 192	..	317.3	..
15-19	2 141 854	7 697	..	359.4	..
20-24	1 522 279	6 885	..	452.3	..
25-29	1 321 665	6 805	..	514.9	..
30-34	1 036 480	6 343	..	612.0	..
35-39	1 024 782	6 673	..	651.2	..
40-44	935 787	6 556	..	700.6	..
45-49	789 521	5 758	..	729.3	..
50-54	719 185	5 844	..	812.6	..
55-59	481 997	4 358	..	904.2	..
60-64	479 943	4 690	..	977.2	..
65-69	268 777	2 772	..	1 031.3	..
70-74	202 422	2 479	..	1 224.7	..
75+	167 962	2 570	..	1 530.1	..
Not stated	2 578	61	..	2 366.2	..
Females	17 978 915	28 257	..	157.2	..
0-4	2 493 905	285	..	11.4	..
5-9	2 259 889	2 442	..	108.1	..
10-14	2 323 544	3 442	..	148.1	..
15-19	1 849 952	2 730	..	147.6	..
20-24	1 561 698	2 061	..	132.0	..
25-29	1 362 916	1 511	..	110.9	..
30-34	1 092 173	1 420	..	130.0	..
35-39	1 030 090	1 313	..	127.5	..
40-44	946 904	1 532	..	161.8	..
'45-49	738 203	1 174	..	159.0	..
50-54	741 914	1 693	..	228.2	..
55-59	412 093	1 090	..	264.5	..
60-64	490 379	2 054	..	418.9	..
65-69	242 404	1 305	..	538.4	..
70-74	234 906	1 894	..	806.3	..
75+	194 769	2 294	..	1 177.8	..
Not stated	3 176	17	..	535.3	..

Table 1 *(continued)*

Age and sex	Population surveyed	Disabled persons	Disabilities	Prevalence rate per 100,000 population	
				Disabled persons	Disabilities

EGYPT, national survey 1979–1981 d/

Age and sex	Population surveyed	Disabled persons	Disabilities	Disabled persons	Disabilities
Both sexes	..	1 116	..	..	..
Males	33 211	611	..	1 839.8	..
<10	12 284	72	..	586.1	..
10–19	8 423	129	..	1 531.5	..
20–29	3 263	65	..	1 992.0	..
30–39	2 504	44	..	1 757.2	..
40–49	2 031	48	..	2 363.4	..
50–59	1 960	80	..	4 081.6	..
60+	2 554	166	..	6 499.6	..
Unknown	192	7	..	3 645.8	..
Females	40 684	477	..	1 172.5	..
<10	11 014	41	..	372.3	..
10–19	8 882	63	..	709.3	..
20–29	5 870	55	..	937.0	..
30–39	4 848	36	..	742.6	..
40–49	3 797	48	..	1 264.2	..
50–59	3 170	63	..	1 987.4	..
60+	2 819	163	..	5 782.2	..
Unknown	284	8	..	2 816.9	..

d/ These data were taken from a recent report published by A.R.E. Ministry of Health, dated February, 1987. *Report of the Health Interview Survey: Fourth Cycle,* part VI, Disability Survey, (publication) No. 35/6, tables 4 and 5, p.p. 12 and 13. These data will be entered into the data base during the next round of data entry.

Table 1 *(continued)*

Age and sex	Population surveyed	Disabled persons	Disabilities	Prevalence rate per 100,000 population	
				Disabled persons	Disabilities

ETHIOPIA, rural survey 1979-1981

Age and sex	Population surveyed	Disabled persons	Disabilities	Disabled persons	Disabilities
Both sexes	26 595 685	1 459 683	..	5 488.4	..
0-4	4 808 568	68 400	..	1 422.5	..
5-9	4 853 664	104 109	..	2 145.0	..
10-14	3 003 087	91 031	..	3 031.2	..
15-19	2 187 658	85 192	..	3 894.2	..
20-24	1 690 180	86 341	..	5 108.4	..
25-29	1 867 007	109 772	..	5 879.6	..
30-34	1 632 064	112 831	..	6 913.4	..
35-39	1 457 459	105 847	..	7 262.4	..
40-44	1 220 943	121 209	..	9 927.5	..
45-49	860 235	88 831	..	10 326.4	..
50-54	847 653	107 050	..	12 629.0	..
55-59	455 006	61 773	..	13 576.3	..
60-64	609 257	91 404	..	15 002.5	..
65+	1 064 574	220 699	..	20 731.2	..
Not stated	38 330	5 194	..	13 550.7	..

ETHIOPIA, survey of children 1981

Age and sex	Population surveyed	Disabled persons	Disabilities	Disabled persons	Disabilities
Males	..	17 867	..	..	..
0-4	..	1 925	..	..	..
5-9	..	6 399	..	..	..
10-14	..	9 178	..	..	..
Not stated	..	365	..	..	..
Females	..	11 764	..	..	..
0-4	..	1 469	..	..	..
5-9	..	4 461	..	..	..
10-14	..	5 651	..	..	..
Not stated	..	183	..	..	..
Both sexes	14 819 300	29 631	..	199.9	..

Table 1 *(continued)*

Age and sex	Population surveyed	Disabled persons	Disabilities	Prevalence rate per 100,000 population	
				Disabled persons	Disabilities
KENYA, national survey of disabled persons 1981					
Males 15+	..	1 163	..	..	..
Females 15+	..	569	..	..	..
Sex not stated 15+	..	22	..	..	..

Table 1 (continued)

Age and sex	Population surveyed	Disabled persons	Disabilities	Prevalence rate per 100,000 population	
				Disabled persons	Disabilities
MALI, population census 1976					
Males	3 123 733	96 318	..	3 083.4	..
0-4	587 015	1 181	..	201.2	..
5-9	492 272	5 545	..	1 126.4	..
10-14	342 807	4 534	..	1 322.6	..
15-19	308 607	4 492	..	1 455.6	..
20-24	218 391	4 784	..	2 190.6	..
25-29	200 095	5 083	..	2 540.3	..
30-34	185 729	6 540	..	3 521.3	..
35-39	161 383	6 957	..	4 310.9	..
40-44	139 426	7 528	..	5 399.3	..
45-49	111 330	7 151	..	6 423.2	..
50-54	104 619	7 973	..	7 621.0	..
55-59	77 578	6 950	..	8 958.7	..
60-64	76 620	8 453	..	11 032.4	..
65-69	40 279	5 270	..	13 083.7	..
70-74	31 890	5 065	..	15 882.7	..
75-79	17 149	3 194	..	18 625.0	..
80-84	14 091	2 615	..	18 557.9	..
85-89	4 493	941	..	20 943.7	..
90-94	4 326	898	..	20 758.2	..
95+	5 236	1 149	..	21 944.2	..
Not stated	397	15	..	3 778.3	..
Females	3 271 185	96 889	..	2 961.9	..
0-4	589 394	1 110	..	188.3	..
5-9	482 851	3 315	..	686.5	..
10-14	321 959	3 586	..	1 113.8	..
15-19	333 508	5 142	..	1 541.8	..
20-24	265 842	5 742	..	2 159.9	..
25-29	267 018	7 155	..	2 679.6	..
30-34	225 950	8 006	..	3 543.3	..
35-39	165 949	6 929	..	4 175.4	..
40-44	147 829	7 912	..	5 352.1	..
45-49	98 453	6 319	..	6 418.3	..
50-54	103 607	8 174	..	7 889.4	..
55-59	62 917	5 717	..	9 086.6	..
60-64	81 466	8 963	..	11 002.1	..
65-69	36 832	4 753	..	12 904.5	..
70-74	37 747	5 487	..	14 536.3	..
75-79	16 730	2 725	..	16 288.1	..
80-84	17 831	3 039	..	17 043.4	..
85-89	4 376	828	..	18 921.4	..
90-94	4 915	852	..	17 334.7	..
95+	5 637	1 119	..	19 851.0	..
Not stated	374	16	..	4 278.1	..

Table 1 *(continued)*

Age and sex	Population surveyed	Disabled persons	Disabilities	Prevalence rate per 100,000 population	
				Disabled persons	Disabilities
ST. HELENA, national survey 1976					
Males	2 514	37	..	1 471.8	..
Females	2 633	46	..	1 747.1	..
SWAZILAND, national survey 1983					
Males	..	..	1 531	..	..
0–4	..	..	64	..	..
5–14	..	..	322	..	..
15–29	..	..	351	..	..
30–44	..	..	251	..	..
45–59	..	..	234	..	..
60+	..	..	273	..	..
Unknown	..	..	36	..	..
Females	..	..	1 234	..	..
0–4	..	..	60	..	..
5–14	..	..	266	..	..
15–29	..	..	263	..	..
30–44	..	..	165	..	..
45–59	..	..	155	..	..
60+	..	..	286	..	..
Unknown	..	..	39	..	..
Both sexes	101 246	2 544	..	2 512.7	..

Table 1 *(continued)*

Age and sex	Population surveyed	Disabled persons	Disabilities	Prevalence rate per 100,000 population	
				Disabled persons	Disabilities
TUNISIA, population census 1975					
Males	2 827 540	26 800	..	947.8	..
0-4	455 250	300	..	65.9	..
5-9	417 000	1 410	..	338.1	..
10-14	376 380	2 190	..	581.9	..
15-19	320 960	2 390	..	744.6	..
20-29	386 280	3 420	..	885.4	..
30-39	264 430	2 360	..	892.5	..
40-49	249 220	3 220	..	1 292.0	..
50-59	172 770	3 550	..	2 054.8	..
60+	180 960	7 920	..	4 376.7	..
Not stated	4 290	40	..	932.4	..
Females	2 749 710	16 900	..	614.6	..
0-4	436 370	400	..	91.7	..
5-9	398 590	890	..	223.3	..
10-14	356 210	1 400	..	393.0	..
15-19	307 400	1 300	..	422.9	..
20-29	412 810	1 930	..	467.5	..
30-39	288 560	1 390	..	481.7	..
40-49	248 860	1 610	..	647.0	..
50-59	153 650	1 710	..	1 112.9	..
60+	143 500	6 230	..	4 341.5	..
Not stated	3 760	40	..	1 063.8	..
TUNISIA, population census 1984					
Males	3 546 040	37 850	..	1 067.4	..
<5	521 600	380	..	72.9	..
5-14	896 920	3 980	..	443.7	..
15-59	1 872 230	22 900	..	1 223.1	..
60+	255 290	10 590	..	4 148.2	..
Females	3 429 410	22 710	..	662.2	..
<5	493 730	390	..	79.0	..
5-14	853 280	2 660	..	311.7	..
15-59	1 871 710	12 910	..	689.7	..
60+	210 690	6 750	..	3 203.8	..

Table 1 *(continued)*

Age and sex	Population surveyed	Disabled persons	Disabilities	Prevalence rate per 100,000 population	
				Disabled persons	Disabilities
ZIMBABWE, national survey 1981					
Both sexes	..	..	276 300	..	..
0–4	..	..	15 000	..	..
5–15	..	..	54 900	..	..
16–59	..	..	139 800	..	..
60+	..	..	66 600	..	..

Table 1 *(continued)*

Age and sex	Population surveyed	Disabled persons	Disabilities	Prevalence rate per 100,000 population	
				Disabled persons	Disabilities

BELIZE, population census 1980
(not economically active population and not attending school)

Age and sex	Population surveyed	Disabled persons	Disabilities	Disabled persons	Disabilities
Males	36 595	1 019	..	2 784.5	..
15–19	6 438	64	..	994.1	..
20–24	6 308	45	..	713.4	..
25–29	4 446	46	..	1 034.6	..
30–34	3 378	36	..	1 065.7	..
35–39	2 617	31	..	1 184.6	..
40–44	2 562	35	..	1 366.1	..
45–49	2 307	39	..	1 690.5	..
50–54	2 209	49	..	2 218.2	..
55–59	1 601	40	..	2 498.4	..
60–64	1 343	58	..	4 318.7	..
65+	3 086	573	..	18 567.7	..
Unknown	300	3	..	1 000.0	..
Females	35 770	812	..	2 270.1	..
15–19	6 260	36	..	575.1	..
20–24	6 156	18	..	292.4	..
25–29	4 458	16	..	358.9	..
30–34	3 258	14	..	429.7	..
35–39	2 550	11	..	431.4	..
40–44	2 426	8	..	329.8	..
45–49	2 250	17	..	755.6	..
50–54	1 992	21	..	1 054.2	..
55–59	1 515	49	..	3 234.3	..
60–64	1 309	54	..	4 125.3	..
65+	3 357	566	..	16 860.3	..
Unknown	239	2	..	836.8	..

Table 1 *(continued)*

Age and sex	Population surveyed	Disabled persons	Disabilities	Prevalence rate per 100,000 population	
				Disabled persons	Disabilities

CANADA, health and disability survey 1983/1984

Age and sex	Population surveyed	Disabled persons	Disabilities	Disabled persons	Disabilities
Males	12 088 000	1 283 000	..	10 613.8	..
0-4	916 000	44 000	..	4 803.5	..
5-9	893 000	63 000	..	7 054.9	..
10-14	923 000	68 000	..	7 367.3	..
15-34	4 336 000	186 000	..	4 289.7	..
35-54	2 917 000	269 000	..	9 221.8	..
55-64	1 086 000	268 000	..	24 677.7	..
65+	1 017 000	385 000	..	37 856.4	..
Females	12 372 000	1 466 000	..	11 849.3	..
0-4	870 000	34 000	..	3 908.0	..
5-9	848 000	40 000	..	4 717.0	..
10-14	876 000	53 000	..	6 050.2	..
15-34	4 334 000	209 000	..	4 822.3	..
35-54	2 922 000	312 000	..	10 677.6	..
55-64	1 183 000	293 000	..	24 767.5	..
65+	1 339 000	525 000	..	39 208.4	..

Table 1 *(continued)*

Age and sex	Population surveyed	Disabled persons	Disabilities	Prevalence rate per 100,000 population	
				Disabled persons	Disabilities

CUBA, census of population and housing, 1981
(not economically active population)

Age and sex	Population surveyed	Disabled persons	Disabilities	Disabled persons	Disabilities
Males	970 312	35 517	..	3 660.4	..
15-19	421 110	5 472	..	1 299.4	..
20-24	86 356	4 450	..	5 153.1	..
25-29	21 452	3 391	..	15 807.4	..
30-34	11 674	2 927	..	25 072.8	..
35-39	9 630	2 359	..	24 496.4	..
40-44	9 974	2 187	..	21 927.0	..
45-49	10 747	1 936	..	18 014.3	..
50-54	15 789	2 009	..	12 724.0	..
55-59	24 161	1 967	..	8 141.2	..
60-64	62 070	1 842	..	2 967.6	..
65-69	89 095	1 767	..	1 983.3	..
70+	208 254	5 210	..	2 501.8	..
Females	2 264 331	17 999	..	794.9	..
15-19	499 116	2 367	..	474.2	..
20-24	228 077	1 913	..	838.8	..
25-29	177 882	1 336	..	751.1	..
30-34	165 805	1 263	..	761.7	..
35-39	150 635	1 238	..	821.9	..
40-44	137 160	1 102	..	803.4	..
45-49	131 427	996	..	757.8	..
50-54	135 476	969	..	715.3	..
55-59	140 314	834	..	594.4	..
60-64	142 186	791	..	556.3	..
65-69	128 162	821	..	640.6	..
70+	228 091	4 369	..	1 915.5	..

Table 1 *(continued)*

Age and sex	Population surveyed	Disabled persons	Disabilities	Prevalence rate per 100,000 population	
				Disabled persons	Disabilities

JAMAICA, survey of handicapped children in schools 1978

Age and sex	Population surveyed	Disabled persons	Disabilities	Disabled persons	Disabilities
Males 4-11	..	439	..	..	..
Females 4-11	..	288	..	..	..
Sex not stated 4-11	..	1	..	..	..

MEXICO, general census of population and housing 1980
(children not attending school)

Age and sex	Population surveyed	Disabled persons	Disabilities	Disabled persons	Disabilities
Males	2 314 005	66 025	..	2 853.3	..
6-8	698 191	32 855	..	4 705.7	..
9-11	267 633	16 645	..	6 219.3	..
12-14	1 348 181	16 525	..	1 225.7	..
Females	2 386 598	63 288	..	2 651.8	..
6-8	680 081	30 497	..	4 484.3	..
9-11	272 758	15 265	..	5 596.5	..
12-14	1 433 759	17 526	..	1 222.4	..

Table 1 *(continued)*

Age and sex	Population surveyed	Disabled persons	Disabilities	Prevalence rate per 100,000 population	
				Disabled persons	Disabilities

NETHERLANDS ANTILLES, general census of population and housing 1981

Age and sex	Population surveyed	Disabled persons	Disabilities	Disabled persons	Disabilities
Males	112 148	3 657	..	3 260.9	..
0-4	10 575	74	..	699.8	..
5-9	11 494	221	..	1 922.7	..
10-14	12 019	388	..	3 228.2	..
15-19	13 501	399	..	2 955.3	..
20-24	11 449	327	..	2 856.1	..
25-29	9 436	235	..	2 490.5	..
30-34	8 626	211	..	2 446.1	..
35-39	6 969	161	..	2 310.2	..
40-44	5 928	184	..	3 103.9	..
45-49	5 124	165	..	3 220.1	..
50-54	4 244	165	..	3 887.8	..
55-59	3 445	175	..	5 079.8	..
60-64	2 876	192	..	6 675.9	..
65-69	2 256	152	..	6 737.6	..
70-74	2 098	228	..	10 867.5	..
75-79	1 262	182	..	14 421.6	..
80-84	563	115	..	20 426.3	..
85+	283	83	..	29 328.6	..
Females	119 784	2 984	..	2 491.2	..
0-4	10 131	93	..	918.0	..
5-9	11 103	156	..	1 405.0	..
10-14	11 745	252	..	2 145.6	..
15-19	13 180	235	..	1 783.0	..
20-24	11 484	191	..	1 663.2	..
25-29	10 745	184	..	1 712.4	..
30-34	9 610	130	..	1 352.8	..
35-39	8 076	145	..	1 795.4	..
40-44	6 979	105	..	1 504.5	..
45-49	5 757	123	..	2 136.5	..
50-54	4 712	116	..	2 461.8	..
55-59	3 836	113	..	2 945.8	..
60-64	3 463	176	..	5 082.3	..
65-69	2 778	138	..	4 967.6	..
70-74	2 569	207	..	8 057.6	..
75-79	1 664	212	..	12 740.4	..
80-84	1 125	198	..	17 600.0	..
85+	827	210	..	25 393.0	..

Table 1 *(continued)*

Age and sex	Population surveyed	Disabled persons	Disabilities	Prevalence rate per 100,000 population	
				Disabled persons	Disabilities
PANAMA, general census of population and housing 1980					
Males 0-39	734 693	5 514	..	750.5	..
Females 0-39	720 030	4 256	..	591.1	..
TRINIDAD AND TOBAGO, population and housing census 1980					
		Not economically active			
Males	339 942	4 447	..	1 308.2	..
15-19	65 399	412	..	630.0	..
20-24	54 885	397	..	723.3	..
25-29	42 914	346	..	806.3	..
30-34	35 189	355	..	1 008.8	..
35-39	27 398	290	..	1 058.5	..
40-44	23 117	295	..	1 276.1	..
45-49	18 871	324	..	1 716.9	..
50-54	17 497	408	..	2 331.8	..
55-59	15 750	502	..	3 187.3	..
60-64	13 365	609	..	4 556.7	..
65+	25 557	509	..	1 991.6	..
Females	346 694	3 193	..	921.0	..
15-19	65 275	293	..	448.9	..
20-24	54 681	253	..	462.7	..
25-29	43 216	188	..	435.0	..
30-34	34 769	175	..	503.3	..
35-39	27 838	162	..	581.9	..
40-44	23 504	175	..	744.6	..
45-49	19 950	187	..	937.3	..
50-54	18 140	313	..	1 725.5	..
55-59	15 084	365	..	2 419.8	..
60-64	12 713	464	..	3 649.8	..
65+	31 524	618	..	1 960.4	..
TRINIDAD AND TOBAGO, Survey of children 1982					
Both sexes 3-16	..	603	..	..	..

Note. Column headings in italics show the national terminology.

Table 1 *(continued)*

Age and sex	Population surveyed	Disabled persons	Disabilities	Prevalence rate per 100,000 population	
				Disabled persons	Disabilities

UNITED STATES, census of population 1980

Work disabled

Males

Age and sex	Population surveyed	Disabled persons	Disabilities	Disabled persons	Disabilities
16-64	70 680 243	6 379 603	..	9 026.0	..

Females

16-64	73 986 389	5 939 948	..	8 028.4	..

Public transport disabled

Both sexes

16+	168 824 776	6 186 167	..	3 664.3	..
16-64	144 666 632	2 597 631	..	1 795.6	..
65+	24 158 144	3 588 536	..	14 854.4	..

Note. Column headings in italics show the national terminology.

Table 1 *(continued)*

Age and sex	Population surveyed	Disabled persons	Disabilities	Prevalence rate per 100,000 population	
				Disabled persons	Disabilities *

UNITED STATES, national health interview survey, 1982
(civilian and non-institutionalized population)

Age and sex	Population surveyed	Disabled persons	Disabilities	Disabled persons	Disabilities *
Males	109 535 000	..	40 387 000	..	36 871.3
Under 45	78 223 000	..	18 033 000	..	23 053.3
45-64	20 941 000	..	12 135 000	..	57 948.5
65-74	..	..	6 175 000	..	..
75+	..	..	4 044 000	..	..
65+	10 371 000	..	..	..	..
Females	117 578 000	..	34 538 000	..	29 374.5
Under 45	79 323 000	..	12 573 000	..	15 850.4
45-64	23 235 000	..	8 755 000	..	37 680.2
65-74	..	..	6 703 000	..	..
75+	..	..	6 507 000	..	..
65+	15 020 000	..	..	..	..
Both sexes	227 113 000	..	74 925 000	..	32 990.2
Under 45	157 546 000	..	30 606 000	..	19 426.7
45-64	44 176 000	..	20 890 000	..	47 288.1
65-74	15 832 000	..	12 878 000	..	81 341.6
75+	9 559 000	..	10 551 000	..	110 377.7

----

* Disability was based on a selection of impairments that were listed under chronic conditions in the survey and were aggregated for this presentation. Impairments included were speech, hearing, tinnitus, visual, cataracts, color blindness, glaucoma, back, upper extremities, lower extremities, paralysis of extremities, absence of extremities and epilepsy.

Table 1 *(continued)*

Age and sex	Population surveyed	Disabled persons	Disabilities	Prevalence rate per 100,000 population	
				Disabled persons	Disabilities

GUYANA, population census 1980
(population not economically active and not attending school)

Age and sex	Population surveyed	Disabled persons	Disabilities	Disabled persons	Disabilities
Males	206 189	4 783	..	2 319.7	..
15-19	34 178	310	..	907.0	..
20-24	37 030	249	..	672.4	..
25-29	28 356	187	..	659.5	..
30-34	21 514	195	..	906.4	..
35-39	16 333	190	..	1 163.3	..
40-44	13 876	203	..	1 463.0	..
45-49	12 637	271	..	2 144.5	..
50-54	11 461	388	..	3 385.4	..
55-59	9 247	439	..	4 747.5	..
60-64	6 712	437	..	6 510.7	..
65+	13 837	1 905	..	13 767.4	..
Not stated	1 008	9	..	892.9	..
Females	214 573	4 779	..	2 227.2	..
15-19	35 372	200	..	565.4	..
20-24	39 410	134	..	340.0	..
25-29	28 986	105	..	362.2	..
30-34	22 458	79	..	351.8	..
35-39	17 203	93	..	540.6	..
40-44	14 350	85	..	592.3	..
45-49	13 117	129	..	983.5	..
50-54	11 458	229	..	1 998.6	..
55-59	8 951	288	..	3 217.5	..
60-64	6 747	442	..	6 551.1	..
65+	15 778	2 981	..	18 893.4	..
Not stated	743	14	..	1 884.3	..

Table 1 *(continued)*

Age and sex	Population surveyed	Disabled persons	Disabilities	Prevalence rate per 100,000 population	
				Disabled persons	Disabilities

PERU, national census of population and housing 1981

Age and sex	Population surveyed	Disabled persons	Disabilities	Disabled persons	Disabilities
Both sexes	17 005 210	26 560	..	156.2	..

URUGUAY, 1984 survey of the chronically ill

Age and sex	Population surveyed	Disabled persons	Disabilities	Disabled persons	Disabilities
Males	376	42	..	11 170.2	..
45–54	99	10	..	10 101.0	..
55–64	145	16	..	11 034.5	..
65+	132	16	..	12 121.2	..
Females	594	68	..	11 447.8	..
45–54	190	12	..	6 315.8	..
55–64	213	22	..	10 328.6	..
65+	191	34	..	17 801.0	..

Table 1 *(continued)*

Age and sex	Population surveyed	Disabled persons	Disabilities	Prevalence rate per 100,000 population	
				Disabled persons	Disabilities

VENEZUELA, census of population and housing 1981
(not economically active population)

Age and sex	Population surveyed	Disabled persons	Disabilities	Disabled persons	Disabilities
Males	1 465 125	123 661	..	8 440.3	..
12-14	486 283	3 428	..	704.9	..
15-19	437 526	7 874	..	1 799.7	..
20-24	142 743	6 593	..	4 618.8	..
25-29	57 439	5 202	..	9 056.6	..
30-34	31 107	4 229	..	13 595.0	..
35-39	21 837	3 571	..	16 353.0	..
40-44	21 371	4 026	..	18 838.6	..
45-49	22 661	4 631	..	20 436.0	..
50-54	28 881	7 034	..	24 355.1	..
55-59	33 850	8 557	..	25 279.2	..
60-64	40 615	11 908	..	29 319.2	..
65+	140 812	56 608	..	40 201.1	..
Females	3 617 382	71 399	..	1 973.8	..
12-14	511 325	2 103	..	411.3	
15-19	670 054	4 149	..	619.2	..
20-24	468 089	3 509	..	749.6	..
25-29	376 098	2 456	..	653.0	..
30-34	296 069	2 033	..	686.7	..
35-39	223 612	1 746	..	780.8	..
40-44	193 369	1 895	..	980.0	..
45-49	181 550	2 077	..	1 144.0	..
50-54	170 178	2 847	..	1 673.0	..
55-59	141 869	3 052	..	2 151.3	..
60-64	118 854	4 786	..	4 026.8	..
65+	266 315	40 746	..	15 299.9	..
					..

Table 1 (continued)

Age and sex	Population surveyed	Disabled persons	Disabilities	Prevalence rate per 100,000 population	
				Disabled persons	Disabilities

BAHRAIN, population census 1981

Age and sex	Population surveyed	Disabled persons	Disabilities	Disabled persons	Disabilities
Males	204 793	2 205	..	1 076.7	..
0-4	22 174	43	..	193.9	..
5-9	18 899	118	..	624.4	..
10-14	17 206	135	..	784.6	..
15-19	17 768	194	..	1 091.9	..
20-24	24 838	160	..	644.2	..
25-29	30 492	116	..	380.4	..
30-34	22 098	101	..	457.1	..
35-39	14 114	80	..	566.8	..
40-44	11 425	116	..	1 015.3	..
45-49	8 225	137	..	1 665.7	..
50-54	6 368	171	..	2 685.3	..
55-59	4 092	155	..	3 787.9	..
60-64	3 029	214	..	7 065.0	..
65-69	1 589	139	..	8 747.6	..
70+	2 476	326	..	13 166.4	..
Females	146 005	1 273	..	871.9	..
0-4	21 588	25	..	115.8	..
5-9	18 588	69	..	371.2	..
10-14	17 007	104	..	611.5	..
15-19	17 642	112	..	634.8	..
20-24	16 705	72	..	431.0	..
25-29	13 676	37	..	270.5	..
30-34	9 088	39	..	429.1	..
35-39	7 157	44	..	614.8	..
40-44	6 417	45	..	701.3	..
45-49	5 175	50	..	966.2	..
50-54	4 255	108	..	2 538.2	..
55-59	2 701	76	..	2 813.8	..
60-64	2 307	113	..	4 898.1	..
65-69	1 278	74	..	5 790.3	..
70+	2 421	305	..	12 598.1	..

Table 1 *(continued)*

Age and sex	Population surveyed	Disabled persons	Disabilities	Prevalence rate per 100,000 population	
				Disabled persons	Disabilities

BURMA*, population census 1983
(not economically active population)

Age and sex	Population surveyed	Disabled persons	Disabilities	Disabled persons	Disabilities
Males	4 650 757	26 694	..	574.0	..
10–14	1 955 687	2 344	..	119.9	..
15–19	953 153	2 751	..	288.6	..
20–24	403 026	2 419	..	600.2	..
25–29	229 373	1 759	..	766.9	..
30–34	154 187	1 706	..	1 106.4	..
35–39	121 508	1 534	..	1 262.5	..
40–44	108 260	1 511	..	1 395.7	..
45–49	113 053	1 731	..	1 531.1	..
50–54	114 929	1 668	..	1 451.3	..
55–59	98 361	1 607	..	1 633.8	..
60–64	116 632	1 841	..	1 578.5	..
65+	282 588	5 823	..	2 060.6	..
Females	8 383 197	23 306	..	278.0	..
10–14	1 850 072	1 767	..	95.5	..
15–19	1 214 317	1 659	..	136.6	..
20–24	1 004 394	1 408	..	140.2	..
25–29	830 996	1 175	..	141.4	..
30–34	641 663	1 063	..	165.7	..
35–39	486 428	967	..	198.8	..
40–44	440 762	1 153	..	261.6	..
45–49	413 945	1 107	..	267.4	..
50–54	384 976	1 682	..	436.9	..
55–59	299 342	1 570	..	524.5	..
60–64	273 290	2 435	..	891.0	..
65+	543 012	7 320	..	1 348.0	..

* Now Myanmar

Table 1 *(continued)*

Age and sex	Population surveyed	Disabled persons	Disabilities	Prevalence rate per 100,000 population	
				Disabled persons	Disabilities

CHINA, *annual population survey 1983*
(special children's question on disability)

Age and sex	Population surveyed	Disabled persons	Disabilities	Disabled persons	Disabilities
Males	92 694	1 410	..	1 521.1	..
<1	5 155	26	..	504.4	..
1	5 837	68	..	1 165.0	..
2	5 579	70	..	1 254.7	..
3	4 856	69	..	1 420.9	..
4	5 540	93	..	1 678.7	..
5	5 340	80	..	1 498.1	..
6	5 268	84	..	1 594.5	..
7	5 532	85	..	1 536.5	..
8	5 822	96	..	1 648.9	..
9	6 431	113	..	1 757.1	..
10	6 767	110	..	1 625.5	..
11	7 310	111	..	1 518.5	..
12	7 729	119	..	1 539.7	..
13	7 890	152	..	1 926.5	..
14	7 638	134	..	1 754.4	..
Females	86 329	1 166	..	1 350.6	..
<1	4 939	42	..	850.4	..
1	5 353	64	..	1 195.6	..
2	5 129	52	..	1 013.8	..
3	4 521	73	..	1 614.7	..
4	5 177	76	..	1 468.0	..
5	4 863	52	..	1 069.3	..
6	4 826	73	..	1 512.6	..
7	5 209	72	..	1 382.2	..
8	5 442	72	..	1 323.0	..
9	5 995	84	..	1 401.2	..
10	6 476	97	..	1 497.8	..
11	6 645	94	..	1 414.6	..
12	7 136	101	..	1 415.4	..
13	7 480	110	..	1 470.6	..
14	7 138	104	..	1 457.0	..

Table 1 *(continued)*

Age and sex	Population surveyed	Disabled persons	Disabilities	Prevalence rate per 100,000 population	
				Disabled persons	Disabilities
HONG KONG, population census 1981					
Both sexes	..	41 738	..	837.0	..
0-14		4875			
15-19		3504			
20-24		4211			
25-29		3122			
30-34		2480			
35-39		1267			
40-44		1575			
45-49		1766			
50+		18938			
INDONESIA, population census 1980					
Both sexes	146 776 473	..	1 673 182 e/	..	1 140.0
0-14	59 893 050	..	254 134 e/	..	424.3
15+	86 883 423	..	1 419 048 e/	..	1 633.3
JAPAN, national survey of handicapped adults 1980					
Both sexes	..	2 030 000	..	..	..
18-19	..	11 000	..	351.0	..
20-29	..	86 000	..	494.0	..
30-39	..	135 000	..	696.0	..
40-49	..	260 000	..	1 603.0	..
50-59	..	417 000	..	3 369.0	..
60-69	..	508 000	..	12 457.0	..
70+	..	558 000	..	8 754.0	..
Total at home	..	1 977 000	..	2 379.0	..
In institution	..	53 000	..	..	..

e/ Sum of each impairment presented. It is uncertain whether these are the number of disabled people or the number of impairments reported by disabled people.

Table 1 *(continued)*

Age and sex	Population surveyed	Disabled persons	Disabilities	Prevalence rate per 100,000 population	
				Disabled persons	Disabilities

JORDAN, national registration campaign 1979

Both sexes	..	18 829	..	..	..

JORDAN, agricultural census 1983

Males	..	7 140	..	..	..
0-4	..	479	..	..	..
5-9	..	1 080	..	..	..
10-14	..	1 167	..	..	..
15-19	..	1 023	..	..	..
20-24	..	600	..	..	..
25-29	..	353	..	..	..
30-34	..	244	..	..	..
35-39	..	272	..	..	..
40-44	..	248	..	..	..
45-49	..	189	..	..	..
50-54	..	236	..	..	..
55-59	..	157	..	..	..
60-64	..	242	..	..	..
65+	..	850	..	..	..
Females	..	4 256	..	..	..
0-4	..	346	..	..	..
5-9	..	692	..	..	..
10-14	..	775	..	..	..
15-19	..	613	..	..	..
20-24	..	332	..	..	..
25-29	..	189	..	..	..
30-34	..	117	..	..	..
35-39	..	131	..	..	..
40-44	..	116	..	..	..
45-49	..	101	..	..	..
50-54	..	128	..	..	..
55-59	..	71	..	..	..
60-64	..	114	..	..	..
65+	..	531	..	..	..

Table 1 (continued)

Age and sex	Population surveyed	Disabled persons	Disabilities	Prevalence rate per 100,000 population	
				Disabled persons	Disabilities

KUWAIT, population census 1980

Age and sex	Population surveyed	Disabled persons	Disabilities	Disabled persons	Disabilities
Males	776 639	3 913	..	503.8	..
0-4	108 242	76	..	70.2	..
5-9	92 906	437	..	470.4	..
10-14	76 225	697	..	914.4	..
15-19	64 258	668	..	1 039.6	..
20-24	72 495	317	..	437.3	..
25-29	85 696	209	..	243.9	..
30-34	76 196	173	..	227.0	..
35-39	62 842	169	..	268.9	..
40-44	52 257	165	..	315.7	..
45-49	34 282	138	..	402.5	..
50-54	23 066	143	..	620.0	..
55-59	11 962	156	..	1 304.1	..
60-64	7 255	135	..	1 860.8	..
65-69	3 788	137	..	3 616.7	..
70-74	2 524	116	..	4 595.9	..
75-79	1 226	75	..	6 117.5	..
80-84	877	63	..	7 183.6	..
85+	542	39	..	7 195.6	..
Females	581 313	2 052	..	353.0	..
0-4	104 670	79	..	75.5	..
5-9	89 874	341	..	379.4	..
10-14	73 806	410	..	555.5	..
15-19	55 545	351	..	631.9	..
20-24	51 845	173	..	333.7	..
25-29	52 790	93	..	176.2	..
30-34	44 500	66	..	148.3	..
35-39	33 717	55	..	163.1	..
40-44	25 106	67	..	266.9	..
45-49	16 366	45	..	275.0	..
50-54	11 409	54	..	473.3	..
55-59	7 139	40	..	560.3	..
60-64	5 703	54	..	946.9	..
65-69	3 271	48	..	1 467.4	..
70-74	2 678	61	..	2 277.8	..
75-79	1 343	41	..	3 052.9	..
80-84	961	37	..	3 850.2	..
85+	590	37	..	6 271.2	..

Table 1 *(continued)*

Age and sex	Population surveyed	Disabled persons	Disabilities	Prevalence rate per 100,000 population	
				Disabled persons	Disabilities

LEBANON, *national survey of handicapped 1981*

Age and sex	Population surveyed	Disabled persons	Disabilities	Disabled persons	Disabilities
Both sexes 3-60	..	18 321	..	..	..

NEPAL, *national survey 1980*

Age and sex	Population surveyed	Disabled persons	Disabilities	Disabled persons	Disabilities
Males	..	853	982	..	..
<5	..	..	22	..	..
5-14	..	..	213	..	..
15-24	..	..	167	..	..
25-39	..	..	183	..	..
40-59	..	..	253	..	..
60-74	..	..	96	..	..
75+	..	..	48	..	..
					..
Females	..	509	582	..	..
<5	..	..	19	..	..
5-14	..	..	135	..	..
15-24	..	..	95	..	..
25-39	..	..	110	..	..
40-59	..	..	123	..	..
60-74	..	..	72	..	..
75+	..	..	28	..	..
					..
Both sexes	45 348	1 362	1 564	3 003.4	3 448.3
<5	..	..	41	..	592.0
5-14	..	..	348	..	3 141.0
15-24	..	..	262	..	2 940.0
25-39	..	..	293	..	3 403.0
40-59	..	..	376	..	5 151.0
60-74	..	..	168	..	7 992.0
75+	..	..	76	..	17 967.0

Table 1 *(continued)*

PAKISTAN, *population census 1981*

Age and sex	Population surveyed	Disabled persons	Disabilities	Prevalence rate per 100,000 population	
				Disabled persons	Disabilities
Males	43 089 811	165 407	..	383.9	..
0-4	6 200 434	6 982	..	112.6	..
5-9	6 811 487	19 339	..	283.9	..
10-14	5 856 744	16 827	..	287.3	..
15-19	4 192 513	10 727	..	255.9	..
20-24	3 269 776	8 523	..	260.7	..
25-29	2 891 427	6 904	..	238.8	..
30-34	2 388 124	6 489	..	271.7	..
35-39	2 120 580	5 719	..	269.7	..
40-44	1 937 256	6 055	..	312.6	..
45-49	1 610 303	4 860	..	301.8	..
50-54	1 637 892	7 528	..	459.6	..
55-59	859 488	5 636	..	655.7	..
60+	3 313 787	59 818	..	1 805.1	..
Females	38 965 286	206 013	..	528.7	..
0-4	6 373 470	5 581	..	87.6	..
5-9	6 330 850	11 316	..	178.7	..
10-14	4 946 304	13 373	..	270.4	..
15-19	3 570 574	13 807	..	386.7	..
20-24	2 957 980	14 647	..	495.2	..
25-29	2 587 731	16 422	..	634.6	..
30-34	2 229 204	14 710	..	659.9	..
35-39	2 076 657	11 653	..	561.1	..
40-44	1 927 768	10 361	..	537.5	..
45-49	1 465 779	8 225	..	561.1	..
50-54	1 327 725	10 342	..	778.9	..
55-59	751 369	6 643	..	884.1	..
60+	2 419 875	68 933	..	2 848.6	..

Table 1 *(continued)*

Age and sex	Population surveyed	Disabled persons	Disabilities	Prevalence rate per 100,000 population	
				Disabled persons	Disabilities

PHILIPPINES, census 1980
(not economically active population)

Age and sex	Population surveyed	Disabled persons	Disabilities	Disabled persons	Disabilities
Males 15+	2 756 622	100 249	..	3 636.7	..
Females 15+	10 804 432	84 121	..	778.6	..

PHILIPPINES, national survey 1980

Age and sex	Population surveyed	Disabled persons	Disabilities	Disabled persons	Disabilities
Males	16 487	841 f/	..	5 101.0	..
Under 1	26	0	..	0.0	..
1-4	2 213	37	..	1 671.9	..
5-9	2 351	64	..	2 722.2	..
10-14	2 265	80	..	3 532.0	..
15-19	1 976	55	..	2 783.4	..
20-24	1 640	60	..	3 658.5	..
25-29	1 156	53	..	4 584.8	..
30-34	995	44	..	4 422.1	..
35-39	735	37	..	5 034.0	..
40-44	733	84	..	11 459.8	..
45-49	544	49	..	9 007.4	..
50-54	537	53	..	9 869.6	..
55-59	393	60	..	15 267.2	..
60-64	341	59	..	17 302.1	..
65-69	246	49	..	19 918.7	..
70-74	165	44	..	26 666.7	..
75+	171	43	..	25 146.2	..
Females	16 791	629	..	3 746.1	..
Under 1	25	0	..	0.0	..
1-4	2 055	21	..	1 021.9	..
5-9	2 314	54	..	2 333.6	..
10-14	2 351	68	..	2 892.4	..
15-19	2 114	39	..	1 844.8	..
20-24	1 665	43	..	2 582.6	..
25-29	1 232	29	..	2 353.9	..
30-34	1 007	33	..	3 277.1	..
35-39	813	30	..	3 690.0	..
40-44	721	38	..	5 270.5	..
45-49	630	42	..	6 666.7	..
50-54	565	45	..	7 964.6	..
55-59	409	36	..	8 802.0	..
60-64	327	40	..	12 232.4	..
65-69	247	27	..	10 931.2	..
70-74	159	33	..	20 754.7	..
75+	157	51	..	32 484.1	..

f/ Sum of age specific data does not equal total for males.

Table 1 *(continued)*

Age and sex	Population surveyed	Disabled persons	Disabilities	Prevalence rate per 100,000 population	
				Disabled persons	Disabilities

SINGAPORE, continuous registration system of disabled persons 1985

Age and sex	Population surveyed	Disabled persons	Disabilities	Disabled persons	Disabilities
Both sexes	..	9 952	..	..	..
0-4	..	71	..	..	..
5-13	..	1 365	..	..	..
14-19	..	1 488	..	..	..
20-29	..	3 174	..	..	..
30-39	..	1 743	..	..	..
40-49	..	731	..	..	..
50-59	..	529	..	..	..
60-69	..	377	..	..	..
70-79	..	329	..	..	..
80+	..	145	..	..	..

Table 1 *(continued)*

Age and sex	Population surveyed	Disabled persons	Disabilities	Prevalence rate per 100,000 population	
				Disabled persons	Disabilities

SRI LANKA, population census 1981

Age and sex	Population surveyed	Disabled persons	Disabilities	Disabled persons	Disabilities
Males	7 568 092	..	43 869	..	579.7
<1	207 323	..	42	..	20.3
1–4	741 807	..	1 791	..	241.4
5–9	857 907	..	3 513	..	409.5
10–14	863 911	..	4 337	..	502.0
15–19	815 199	..	4 444	..	545.1
20–24	753 338	..	3 795	..	503.8
25–29	637 547	..	3 191	..	500.5
30–34	569 523	..	2 894	..	508.1
35–39	423 003	..	2 315	..	547.3
40–44	360 922	..	2 067	..	572.7
45–49	309 159	..	2 022	..	654.0
50–54	284 167	..	2 227	..	783.7
55–59	221 528	..	2 053	..	926.7
60–64	183 903	..	2 131	..	1 158.8
65–69	133 823	..	1 761	..	1 315.9
70–74	97 564	..	1 491	..	1 528.2
75+	107 473	..	2 117	..	1 969.8
Not stated	..	..	1 678	..	..
Females	7 280 269	..	29 244	..	401.7
<1	198 727	..	43	..	21.6
1–4	709 407	..	1 373	..	193.5
5–9	831 549	..	2 834	..	340.8
10–14	826 344	..	3 179	..	384.7
15–19	792 336	..	3 101	..	391.4
20–24	756 461	..	2 624	..	346.9
25–29	635 830	..	2 222	..	349.5
30–34	553 334	..	2 002	..	361.8
35–39	415 722	..	1 510	..	363.2
40–44	337 577	..	1 193	..	353.4
45–49	300 991	..	1 181	..	392.4
50–54	258 390	..	1 200	..	464.4
55–59	200 682	..	1 037	..	516.7
60–64	157 822	..	1 142	..	723.6
65–69	121 759	..	1 001	..	822.1
70–74	83 047	..	926	..	1 115.0
75+	100 301	..	1 593	..	1 588.2
Not stated	..	..	1 083	..	..
Both sexes	14 848 364	61 824	73 113	416.4	492.4

Table 1 *(continued)*

Age and sex	Population surveyed	Disabled persons	Disabilities	Prevalence rate per 100,000 population	
				Disabled persons	Disabilities

THAILAND, national survey 1981

Age and sex	Population surveyed	Disabled persons	Disabilities	Disabled persons	Disabilities
Males	23 934 660	211 540	..	883.8	..
0–6	4 226 930	15 640	..	370.0	..
7–10	2 971 450	19 440	..	654.2	..
11–14	2 564 860	21 120	..	823.4	..
15–19	2 758 720	24 070	..	872.5	..
20–24	2 315 130	24 000	..	1 036.7	..
25–29	1 986 540	13 020	..	655.4	..
30–34	1 681 480	13 450	..	799.9	..
35–39	1 254 680	12 910	..	1 028.9	..
40–49	1 806 230	22 720	..	1 257.9	..
50–59	1 290 980	19 510	..	1 511.3	..
60+	1 077 660	25 660	..	2 381.1	..
Females	23 686 770	155 990	..	658.6	..
0–6	4 171 920	21 240	..	509.1	..
7–10	2 742 800	11 990	..	437.1	..
11–14	2 467 830	15 410	..	624.4	..
15–19	2 686 990	21 890	..	814.7	..
20–24	2 247 330	14 720	..	655.0	..
25–29	1 934 790	4 850	..	250.7	..
30–34	1 622 290	9 010	..	555.4	..
35–39	1 233 790	6 110	..	495.2	..
40–49	1 902 170	7 770	..	408.5	..
50–59	1 390 210	14 380	..	1 034.4	..
60+	1 286 640	28 620	..	2 224.4	..

THAILAND, national survey of children and young adults (not in school) 1983

Age and sex	Population surveyed	Disabled persons	Disabilities	Disabled persons	Disabilities
Males	5 354 190	120 520	..	2 250.9	..
6–11	469 960	22 820	..	4 855.7	..
12–14	482 160	13 610	..	2 822.7	..
15–19	2 144 650	44 580	..	2 078.7	..
20–24	2 257 410	39 510	..	1 750.2	..
Females	5 524 590	118 800	..	2 150.4	..
6–11	449 440	16 990	..	3 780.3	..
12–14	595 360	17 470	..	2 934.4	..
15–19	2 242 740	30 830	..	1 374.7	..
20–24	2 237 040	53 510	..	2 392.0	..

Table 1 *(continued)*

Age and sex	Population surveyed	Disabled persons	Disabilities	Prevalence rate per 100,000 population	
				Disabled persons	Disabilities

TURKEY, population census 1975

Age and sex	Population surveyed	Disabled persons	Disabilities	Disabled persons	Disabilities
Males	20 744 730	355 557	..	1 714.0	..
0–4	2 917 451	17 843	..	611.6	..
5–9	2 759 820	20 724	..	750.9	..
10–14	2 800 002	29 842	..	1 065.8	..
15–19	2 232 561	21 657	..	970.1	..
20–24	1 857 634	22 230	..	1 196.7	..
25–29	1 486 652	18 523	..	1 246.0	..
30–34	1 178 669	25 273	..	2 144.2	..
35–39	1 040 829	19 488	..	1 872.4	..
40–44	1 091 915	22 498	..	2 060.4	..
45–49	881 215	20 078	..	2 278.4	..
50–54	676 681	17 856	..	2 638.8	..
55–59	382 853	12 946	..	3 381.5	..
60–64	535 532	20 916	..	3 905.6	..
65+	850 652	46 000	..	5 407.6	..
Unknown	52 264	39 683	..	75 928.0	..
Females	19 602 989	232 710	..	1 187.1	..
0–4	2 783 798	57 822	..	2 077.1	..
5–9	2 620 295	16 597	..	633.4	..
10–14	2 448 837	21 818	..	891.0	..
15–19	2 031 938	13 871	..	682.6	..
20–24	1 674 510	11 294	..	674.5	..
25–29	1 346 030	8 886	..	660.2	..
30–34	1 116 102	8 934	..	800.5	..
35–39	1 098 730	9 438	..	859.0	..
40–44	1 054 284	9 976	..	946.2	..
45–49	802 470	8 136	..	1 013.9	..
50–54	664 996	8 980	..	1 350.4	..
55–59	384 295	6 538	..	1 701.3	..
60–64	548 341	11 838	..	2 158.9	..
65+	1 002 599	34 681	..	3 459.1	..
Unknown	25 764	3 901	..	15 141.3	..

Table 1 *(continued)*

Age and sex	Population surveyed	Disabled persons	Disabilities	Prevalence rate per 100,000 population	
				Disabled persons	Disabilities

AUSTRIA, sample survey on physical disabilities 1976

Age and sex	Population surveyed	Disabled persons	Disabilities	Disabled persons	Disabilities
Both sexes	7 424 000	1 550 200	..	20 880.9	..
0-5	515 800	8 300	..	1 609.2	..
6-9	481 800	16 300	..	3 383.1	..
10-14	679 200	29 600	..	4 358.1	..
15-19	607 900	31 000	..	5 099.5	..
20-29	884 900	64 500	..	7 289.0	..
30-39	919 900	117 600	..	12 784.0	..
40-49	881 500	165 100	..	18 729.4	..
50-59	868 200	294 900	..	33 966.8	..
60-69	782 100	354 600	..	45 339.5	..
70-79	580 100	347 800	..	59 955.2	..
80+	162 600	120 500	..	74 108.2	..
Males total	3 489 300	693 900	..	19 886.5	..
Females total	3 934 700	856 300	..	21 762.8	..

Table 1 *(continued)*

Age and sex	Population surveyed	Disabled persons	Disabilities	Prevalence rate per 100,000 population	
				Disabled persons	Disabilities

FEDERAL REPUBLIC OF GERMANY, biannual survey of 1983
(sample survey of State registration system of disabled persons)

Age and sex	Population surveyed	Disabled persons	Disabilities	Disabled persons	Disabilities
Males	..	3 472 731	..	11 800.0	..
<4	..	6 593	..	500.0	..
4–5	..	6 427	..	1 100.0	..
6–14	..	49 484	..	1 600.0	..
15–17	..	28 904	..	1 800.0	..
18–24	..	96 300	..	2 600.0	..
25–34	..	155 136	..	3 400.0	..
35–44	..	293 683	..	6 800.0	..
45–54	..	662 304	..	16 000.0	..
55–59	..	593 892	..	36 700.0	..
60–61	..	274 081	..	50 500.0	..
62–64	..	318 363	..	41 500.0	..
65+	..	987 564	..	31 700.0	..
Females	..	3 135 558	..	9 800.0	..
<4	..	5 557	..	500.0	..
4–5	..	5 059	..	900.0	..
6–14	..	36 545	..	1 200.0	..
15–17	..	21 461	..	1 400.0	..
18–24	..	66 642	..	1 900.0	..
25–34	..	110 136	..	2 600.0	..
35–44	..	225 313	..	5 500.0	..
45–54	..	479 491	..	11 900.0	..
55–59	..	404 892	..	20 900.0	..
60–61	..	186 487	..	23 100.0	..
62–64	..	226 236	..	18 900.0	..
65+	..	1 367 739	..	23 300.0	..

Table 1 *(continued)*

Age and sex	Population surveyed	Disabled persons	Disabilities	Prevalence rate per 100,000 population	
				Disabled persons	Disabilities

IRELAND, population census 1981

Age and sex	Population surveyed	*Not economically active*	Disabilities	Disabled persons	Disabilities
Males	1 193 945	50 931	..	4 265.8	..
15–19	166 677	1 121	..	672.6	..
20–24	140 446	1 733	..	1 233.9	..
25–29	124 378	2 068	..	1 662.7	..
30–34	118 287	2 585	..	2 185.4	..
35–39	99 286	2 762	..	2 781.9	..
40–44	85 320	3 455	..	4 049.5	..
45–49	77 781	4 221	..	5 426.8	..
50–54	75 320	5 882	..	7 809.3	..
55–59	73 289	7 950	..	10 847.5	..
60–64	67 978	9 348	..	13 751.5	..
65+	165 183	9 806	..	5 936.4	..
Females	1 205 731	31 951	..	2 649.9	..
15–19	159 752	820	..	513.3	..
20–24	135 681	1 404	..	1 034.8	..
25–29	121 675	1 420	..	1 167.0	..
30–34	113 671	1 493	..	1 313.4	..
35–39	94 543	1 379	..	1 458.6	..
40–44	80 604	1 595	..	1 978.8	..
45–49	74 069	1 927	..	2 601.6	..
50–54	74 360	2 616	..	3 518.0	..
55–59	76 317	3 465	..	4 540.3	..
60–64	71 288	3 780	..	5 302.4	..
65+	203 771	12 052	..	5 914.5	..

Note. Column headings in italics show the national terminology.

Table 1 *(continued)*

Age and sex	Population surveyed	Disabled persons	Disabilities	Prevalence rate per 100,000 population	
				Disabled persons	Disabilities
NORWAY, level of living survey 1983					
Males	1 966	..	..	15 000.0	..
16-24	385	..	..	6 000.0	..
25-44	752	..	..	5 000.0	..
45-66	603	..	..	23 000.0	..
67-79	226	..	..	44 000.0	..
Females	1 963	..	..	20 000.0	..
16-24	346	..	..	6 000.0	..
25-44	755	..	..	9 000.0	..
45-66	595	..	..	29 000.0	..
67-79	267	..	..	53 000.0	..
POLAND, population census 1978					
Both sexes	..	2 485 001	..	7 100.0	..

Table 1 *(continued)*

Age and sex	Population surveyed	Disabled persons	Disabilities	Prevalence rate per 100,000 population	
				Disabled persons	Disabilities

SPAIN, population census 1981
(not economically active population)

Age and sex	Population surveyed	Disabled persons	Disabilities	Disabled persons	Disabilities
Males	3 274 352	207 342	..	6 332.3	..
<30	844 331	39 870	..	4 722.1	..
30–44	117 340	38 482	..	32 795.3	..
45–64	684 729	108 076	..	15 783.8	..
65+	1 627 952	20 914	..	1 284.7	..
Females	11 046 119	525 340	..	4 755.9	..
<30	2 336 604	103 199	..	4 416.6	..
30–44	2 657 715	146 866	..	5 526.0	..
45–64	3 582 487	191 360	..	5 341.5	..
65+	2 469 313	83 915	..	3 398.3	..

SWEDEN, living conditions survey 1980/1981

Age and sex	Population surveyed	Disabled persons	Disabilities	Disabled persons	Disabilities
Males	..	3 187 000	..	..	..
16–44	..	1 701 000	..	..	..
45–64	..	919 000	..	..	..
65–74	..	382 000	..	..	..
75–84	..	184 000	..	..	..
Females	..	3 277 000	..	..	..
16–44	..	1 623 000	..	..	..
45–64	..	940 000	..	..	..
65–74	..	446 000	..	..	..
75–84	..	268 000	..	..	..

Table 1 *(continued)*

Age and sex	Population surveyed	Disabled persons	Disabilities	Prevalence rate per 100,000 population	
				Disabled persons	Disabilities

UNITED KINGDOM (NORTHERN IRELAND),
survey of handicapped persons 1978

Age and sex	Population surveyed	Disabled persons	Disabilities	Disabled persons	Disabilities
Both sexes	..	41 212	..	..	..
0–4	..	396	..	..	..
5–14	..	2 402	..	..	..
15–24	..	2 158	..	..	..
25–34	..	2 126	..	..	..
35–44	..	2 538	..	..	..
45–54	..	4 207	..	..	..
55–64	..	7 865	..	..	..
65–74	..	10 688	..	..	..
75+	..	8 832	..	..	..

Table 1 *(continued)*

Age and Sex	Population surveyed	Disabled persons	Disabilities	Prevalence rate per 100,000 population	
				Disabled persons	Disabilities

AUSTRALIA, national survey of handicapped persons 1981

Age and Sex	Population surveyed	Disabled persons	Disabilities	Disabled persons	Disabilities
Both sexes	..	1 942 200	..	13 240.0	..
0–4	..	39 500	..	3 500.0	..
5–14	..	156 700	..	6 100.0	..
15–24	..	145 500	..	5 770.0	..
25–34	..	188 800	..	7 980.0	..
35–44	..	195 400	..	10 820.0	..
45–54	..	255 100	..	16 870.0	..
55–64	..	367 100	..	27 450.0	..
65–74	..	324 800	..	35 460.0	..
75+	..	269 300	..	53 140.0	..

FIJI, employment/unemployment survey 1982
(not economically active population)

Age and Sex	Population surveyed	Disabled persons	Disabilities	Disabled persons	Disabilities
Males	153 500	2 600	..	1 693.8	..
0–14	127 000	300	..	236.2	..
15–24	16 000	700	..	4 375.0	..
25–44	1 300	400	..	30 769.2	..
45–64	4 100	800	..	19 512.2	..
65+	5 200	300	..	5 769.2	..
Females	268 300	1 400	..	521.8	..
0–14	117 100	300	..	256.2	..
15–24	50 100	200	..	399.2	..
25–44	66 400	300	..	451.8	..
45–64	28 400	400	..	1 408.5	..
65+	6 400	200	..	3 125.0	..

Table 1 *(continued)*

Age and Sex	Population surveyed	Disabled persons	Disabilities	Prevalence rate per 100,000 population	
				Disabled persons	Disabilities

KIRIBATI, census of population and housing 1978

Age and Sex	Population surveyed	*Not economically active*	Disabilities	Disabled persons	Disabilities
Males	15 776	108	..	684.6	..
15–19	3 336	11	..	329.7	..
20–24	2 312	10	..	432.5	..
25–29	1 955	12	..	613.8	..
30–34	1 593	5	..	313.9	..
35–39	1 421	6	..	422.2	..
40–44	1 037	9	..	867.9	..
45–49	1 180	18	..	1 525.4	..
50–54	852	7	..	821.6	..
55–59	683	6	..	878.5	..
60–64	545	9	..	1 651.4	..
65–69	390	10	..	2 564.1	..
70+	472	5	..	1 059.3	..
Females	17 082	67	..	392.2	..
15–19	3 396	9	..	265.0	..
20–24	2 597	8	..	308.0	..
25–29	2 147	5	..	232.9	..
30–34	1 594	3	..	188.2	..
35–39	1 489	0	..	0.0	..
40–44	1 172	3	..	256.0	..
45–49	1 123	7	..	623.3	..
50–54	977	4	..	409.4	..
55–59	741	6	..	809.7	..
60–64	682	8	..	1 173.0	..
65–69	485	6	..	1 237.1	..
70+	679	8	..	1 178.2	..

Note. Column headings in italics show the national terminology.

**Table 2. Disabled persons per 100,000 population by age and sex and by
selected intellectual, other psychological, language and
aural impairments**

This table provides the number of disabled persons per 100,000 population
according to age group and sex for mental; intellectual; other psychological;
language; severe communication; aural; and speech and hearing impairments.

Description of variables

The type of impairments reported are based upon the codes of ICIDH codes
1-4. In each case, the impairment reported by the national report was coded into
ICIDH by the Statistical Office, so that reasonably comparable data would be located
in the same column. Only selected impairments reported by countries are presented
here. A complete list of impairments that were reported on, among the 63 surveys
recorded in DISTAT, is provided below according to the number of surveys of
DISTAT that utilized the code. It may be noted that the shaded codes are the ones
selected for presentation in table 2. In addition to the above-mentioned ICIDH
codes, the original descriptions of an impairment utilized by the country, or their
translation into English, are also provided in the body of the table. This is done
so that the reader may evaluate to a certain extent, the appropriateness of the
placement by the Statistical Office of the impairment into the ICIDH coding scheme.
This is the first trial by the Statistical Office to utilize ICIDH as a coding scheme
for organizing national impairment data into reasonably comparable and meaningful
groups.

Statistical definition

To the extent possible, the *Compendium* attempts to collect data on
impairments using the standard definitions set forth in pages 53-78 of the
WHO/ICIDH. These are shown below.

Mental impairments (M1.1). This code was devised by the Statistical Office for
placing impairments described as either intellectual or psychological impairment,
without distinction between the two categories. No such combination code was
provided in ICIDH.

Intellectual (1). Intellectual impairments include those of intelligence, memory and
thought. (Impairments of language and learning [30-34] are excluded).

Impairment description	ICIDH code	Number of surveys coded into this category
CODE 1: INTELLECTUAL		
Mental handicap	1.1*	17
Intellectual	1	12
Intelligence: Profound mental retardation	10	1
Intelligence: severe mental retardation	11	2
Intelligence: moderate mental retardation	12	3
Intelligence: global dementia	14.0	1
Other intellectual	19	2
CODE 2: OTHER PSYCHOLOGICAL		
Other psychological	2	14
Retardation and other psychological	2.1*	1
Intermittent impairment of consciousness	21	1
Drives: sexual performance	25.4	1
Drives: drug dependence	25.6	1
Emotion, affect and mood	26	2
Other: emotion, affect and mood	26.88	2
Behaviour pattern	29	1
Unspecified: behaviour pattern	29.9	4
CODE 3: LANGUAGE		
Language	3	9
Severe communication	30	13
Unspecified severe communication	30.9	1
Voice production	35	1
Voice quality	36.6	1
Speech fluency	37.0	1
CODE 4: AURAL		
Aural	4	18
Total or profound hearing loss	40	18
Speech and hearing	40.1*	17
Deaf and/or mute	40.2*	2
Deaf and blind	40.3*	2
Multiple: deaf and mute and blind	40.4*	3
Total hearing loss in one ear, mild loss in other	44.1	2
Moderately severe hearing loss, one ear other not known	45.3	2
Moderately bilateral hearing	45.4	3
Mild bilateral hearing	45.7	1
Tinnitus	47.2	2
Vestibular and balance function	48	1

*Not an ICIDH code, but devised to accommodate items not readily coded within ICIDH categories.

Other psychological (2). Psychological impairments have been interpreted so as to include interference with the basic functions constituting mental life. For the purposes of this scheme, the functions listed as being impaired are those that normally indicate the presence of basic neurophysiological and psychological mechanisms. The level of organization of these functions is usually recorded in a clinical examination of the central nervous system and in the examination of "mental status". In addition, some more complex psychological functions to do with drives, emotional control and reality testing have also been included.

Language (3). Language impairments relate to the comprehension and use of language and its associated functions, including learning.

Severe impairment of communication (30). Severe impairments of communciation include mutism, autism, severe dysphasia, and other severe interference with communication.

Aural (4). Aural impairments relate not only to the ear, but also to its associated structures and functions. The most important subclass of aural impairment is made up of impairments relating to the function of hearing.

Total or profound hearing (40). An individual who has lost or never had the ability to hear and understand speech, even when amplified.

Speech and hearing (M40.1). According to ICIDH, deaf mutism should be coded as 40 above. However, because the two categories in the surveys did not distinguish between total or profound hearing according to the age at which the hearing was lost, the speech and hearing category was formed by the Statistical Office to cover the reporting of "deaf mutism" by censuses and surveys, as separate from people who were reported as "deaf". It is possible that in the future, in non-medical descriptions of hearing loss, it may be useful to consider three groups of persons with hearing impairments: persons who have difficulty hearing, persons who cannot hear at all or who are profoundly hard of hearing and who *can* communicate with speech, and persons who cannot hear at all or who are profoundly hard of hearing and who *cannot* communicate with speech. The use of sign language as a form of communication would have to be considered separately, under the Disability and Handicap descriptions.

Limitations

Being derived in part from subsets of numbers presented in table 1, the estimated prevalence rates are subject to all the basic limitations set forth in table 1. Table 2 has the additional problem of differential variation in the ability of households to identify specific impairments through household survey lay reporting. In cases of impairments reported, however, i.e. blindness, deafness, deaf mutism etc., the impairments, typically, are severe and highly noticeable.

2. Disabled persons per 100,000 population by age and sex and by selected intellectual, other psychological, language and aural impairments

Age and sex	Mental	Intellec-tual	Other psycho-logical	Language	Severe communi-cation	Aural	Total or profound hearing	Speech and hearing
ICIDH	M1.1	1	2	3	30	4	40	M40.1

COMOROS, population census 1980

	Mental handicap				*Mute*		*Deaf*	
Males	266.3	..	..	..	43.7	..	158.0	..
0-4	25.0	..	..	..	7.1	..	57.1	..
5-9	73.3	..	..	..	40.0	..	146.5	..
10-14	160.6	..	..	..	69.4	..	151.9	..
15-19	256.3	..	..	..	72.3	..	85.4	..
20-24	426.7	..	..	..	87.1	..	156.7	..
25-29	451.7	..	..	..	63.0	..	147.1	..
30-34	531.2	..	..	..	22.6	..	169.5	..
35-39	396.6	..	..	..	41.0	..	136.7	..
40-44	489.4	..	..	..	25.1	..	125.5	..
45-49	383.4	..	..	..	20.2	..	141.2	..
50-54	542.9	..	..	..	0.0	..	181.0	..
55-59	475.3	..	..	..	0.0	..	182.8	..
60-64	603.9	..	..	..	69.7	..	325.2	..
65-59	495.9	..	..	..	55.1	..	606.1	..
70-74	486.5	..	..	..	0.0	..	524.0	..
75-79	655.7	..	..	..	0.0	..	983.6	..
80-84	962.4	..	..	..	175.0	..	437.4	..
85+	611.2	..	..	..	122.2	..	1 711.5	..
Not stated	133.2	..	..	..	133.2	..	0.0	..
Females	235.6	..	..	..	34.5	..	147.0	..
0-4	14.5	..	..	..	0.0	..	25.4	..
5-9	55.2	..	..	..	27.6	..	31.1	..
10-14	102.5	..	..	..	68.3	..	107.4	..
15-19	239.2	..	..	..	42.9	..	110.4	..
20-24	249.6	..	..	..	51.4	..	73.4	..
25-29	237.9	..	..	..	59.5	..	119.0	..
30-34	417.6	..	..	..	40.7	..	213.9	..
35-39	405.8	..	..	..	25.4	..	190.2	..
40-44	517.9	..	..	..	38.8	..	142.4	..
45-49	606.6	..	..	..	46.7	..	280.0	..
50-54	607.8	..	..	..	0.0	..	214.5	..
55-59	428.1	..	..	..	0.0	..	214.0	..
60-64	696.4	..	..	..	24.0	..	408.3	..
65-59	467.0	..	..	..	0.0	..	467.0	..
70-74	538.0	..	..	..	0.0	..	345.9	..
75-79	654.5	..	..	..	0.0	..	916.2	..
80-84	539.7	..	..	..	154.2	..	2 081.7	..
85+	958.5	..	..	..	106.5	..	2 555.9	..
Not stated	0.0	..	..	..	0.0	..	0.0	..

Note. Column headings in italics show the national terminology.

Table 2 *(continued)*

Age and sex	Mental	Intellec- tual	Other psycho- logical	Language	Severe communi- cation	Aural	Total or profound hearing	Speech and hearing
ICIDH	**M1.1**	**1**	**2**	**3**	**30**	**4**	**40**	**M40.1**

EGYPT, population census 1976

	Mentally disabled				*Mute*		*Deaf*	*Deaf and mute*
Males	30.8	..	..	..	13.1	..	20.1	46.0
0–4	2.2	..	..	..	0.8	..	0.8	6.6
5–9	17.5	..	..	..	10.6	..	6.2	32.5
10–14	35.4	..	..	..	16.6	..	12.0	41.3
15–19	34.7	..	..	..	19.8	..	11.5	46.5
20–24	41.4	..	..	..	18.9	..	20.6	50.8
25–29	47.2	..	..	..	17.4	..	22.8	54.5
30–34	48.3	..	..	..	16.3	..	32.3	75.8
35–39	51.5	..	..	..	13.0	..	32.0	77.0
40–44	43.3	..	..	..	15.7	..	34.3	71.1
45–49	39.5	..	..	..	14.2	..	37.0	66.0
50–54	31.8	..	..	..	9.5	..	39.8	63.7
55–59	24.9	..	..	..	10.0	..	44.8	66.8
60–64	20.4	..	..	..	9.8	..	47.3	50.4
65–69	23.4	..	..	..	8.9	..	55.8	41.7
70–74	30.1	..	..	..	11.4	..	58.3	46.4
75+	23.8	..	..	..	9.5	..	82.8	51.2
Not stated	116.4	..	..	..	0.0	..	0.0	0.0
Females	9.8	..	..	..	4.8	..	7.3	20.4
0–4	0.5	..	..	..	0.7	..	0.5	5.3
5–9	7.7	..	..	..	5.2	..	6.9	20.2
10–14	13.8	..	..	..	6.5	..	9.2	29.2
15–19	14.3	..	..	..	7.5	..	7.2	29.6
20–24	13.0	..	..	..	5.9	..	3.8	23.4
25–29	10.1	..	..	..	6.8	..	4.0	19.7
30–34	11.6	..	..	..	5.4	..	4.5	21.7
35–39	8.4	..	..	..	5.8	..	5.0	20.7
40–44	11.9	..	..	..	4.0	..	6.9	17.7
45–49	10.0	..	..	..	1.9	..	7.9	16.8
50–54	11.5	..	..	..	2.6	..	9.8	15.9
55–59	10.7	..	..	..	1.9	..	12.4	19.2
60–64	8.4	..	..	..	4.5	..	16.9	17.1
65–69	11.1	..	..	..	3.7	..	22.7	31.4
70–74	11.9	..	..	..	5.1	..	37.5	23.0
75+	16.4	..	..	..	7.7	..	57.0	28.8
Not stated	0.0	..	..	..	0.0	..	31.5	0.0

ETHIOPIA, survey of children 1981

		Mentally ill		*Mute*		*Hearing (deaf)*	*Deaf and mute*
Both sexes 0–14	..	..	11.0	..	8.0	..	17.9	28.0

Note. Column headings in italics show the national terminology.

Table 2 *(continued)*

Age and sex	Mental	Intellec-tual	Other psycho-logical	Language	Severe communi-cation	Aural	Total or profound hearing	Speech and hearing
ICIDH	M1.1	1	2	3	30	4	40	M40.1

MALI, population census 1976
Insanity

Age and sex	Mental	Intellec-tual	Other psycho-logical	Language	Severe communi-cation	Aural	Total or profound hearing	Speech and hearing
Males	..	..	212.8	..	..	..	..	..
0-4	..	..	5.3	..	..	..	..	..
5-9	..	..	72.3	..	..	..	..	..
10-14	..	..	90.4	..	..	..	..	..
15-19	..	..	117.3	..	..	..	..	..
20-24	..	..	441.0	..	..	..	..	..
25-29	..	..	303.9	..	..	..	..	..
30-34	..	..	421.0	..	..	..	..	..
35-39	..	..	446.8	..	..	..	..	..
40-44	..	..	474.8	..	..	..	..	..
45-49	..	..	397.9	..	..	..	..	..
50-54	..	..	447.3	..	..	..	..	..
55-59	..	..	317.1	..	..	..	..	..
60-64	..	..	360.2	..	..	..	..	..
65-69	..	..	347.6	..	..	..	..	..
70-74	..	..	404.5	..	..	..	..	..
75-79	..	..	268.2	..	..	..	..	..
80-84	..	..	333.5	..	..	..	..	..
85-89	..	..	155.8	..	..	..	..	..
90-94	..	..	670.4	..	..	..	..	..
95+	..	..	305.6	..	..	..	..	..
Not stated	..	..	1 511.3	..	..	..	..	..
Females	..	..	168.3	..	..	..	..	..
0-4	..	..	3.7	..	..	..	..	..
5-9	..	..	33.1	..	..	..	..	..
10-14	..	..	70.8	..	..	..	..	..
15-19	..	..	97.7	..	..	..	..	..
20-24	..	..	140.3	..	..	..	..	..
25-29	..	..	165.5	..	..	..	..	..
30-34	..	..	243.9	..	..	..	..	..
35-39	..	..	283.8	..	..	..	..	..
40-44	..	..	409.3	..	..	..	..	..
45-49	..	..	450.0	..	..	..	..	..
50-54	..	..	508.7	..	..	..	..	..
55-59	..	..	537.2	..	..	..	..	..
60-64	..	..	526.6	..	..	..	..	..
65-69	..	..	529.4	..	..	..	..	..
70-74	..	..	543.1	..	..	..	..	..
75-79	..	..	352.7	..	..	..	..	..
80-84	..	..	398.2	..	..	..	..	..
85-89	..	..	342.8	..	..	..	..	..
90-94	..	..	305.2	..	..	..	..	..
95+	..	..	479.0	..	..	..	..	..
Not stated	..	..	534.8	..	..	..	..	..

Note. Column headings in italics show the national terminology.

Table 2 *(continued)*

Age and sex	Mental	Intellec-tual	Other psycho-logical	Language	Severe communi-cation	Aural	Total or profound hearing	Speech and hearing
ICIDH	**M1.1**	**1**	**2**	**3**	**30**	**4**	**40**	**M40.1**

ST. HELENA, national survey 1976

	Mentally infirm							*Deaf and mute*
Males	318.2	..	..	..	..	..	..	159.1
Females	607.7	..	..	..	..	..	..	303.8

SWAZILAND, national survey 1983

	Mentally retarded						*Deaf*	..
Both sexes	324.0	..	..	..	..	..	378.3	..

Note. Column headings in italics show the national terminology.

Table 2 *(continued)*

Age and sex	Mental	Intellec-tual	Other psycho-logical	Language	Severe communi-cation	Aural	Total or profound hearing	Speech and hearing
ICIDH	**M1.1**	**1**	**2**	**3**	**30**	**4**	**40**	**M40.1**

TUNISIA, population census 1975

	Mental handicap							*Deaf and mute*
Males	157.4	..	..	..	..	..	..	102.6
0–4	0.0	..	..	..	..	..	..	11.0
5–9	48.0	..	..	..	..	..	..	107.9
10–14	124.9	..	..	..	..	..	..	140.8
15–19	218.1	..	..	..	..	..	..	112.2
20–29	245.9	..	..	..	..	..	..	108.7
30–39	215.6	..	..	..	..	..	..	87.0
40–49	288.9	..	..	..	..	..	..	88.3
50–59	248.9	..	..	..	..	..	..	98.4
60+	221.0	..	..	..	..	..	..	259.7
Not stated	233.1	..	..	..	..	..	..	0.0
Females	92.7	..	..	..	..	..	..	73.8
0–4	2.3	..	..	..	..	..	..	4.6
5–9	22.6	..	..	..	..	..	..	62.7
10–14	75.8	..	..	..	..	..	..	117.9
15–19	94.3	..	..	..	..	..	..	78.1
20–29	150.2	..	..	..	..	..	..	63.0
30–39	135.2	..	..	..	..	..	..	34.7
40–49	124.6	..	..	..	..	..	..	64.3
50–59	162.7	..	..	..	..	..	..	65.1
60+	223.0	..	..	..	..	..	..	327.5
Not stated	0.0	..	..	..	..	..	..	266.0

TUNISIA, population census 1984

Males	257.2	..	..	..	..	..	..	138.2
<5	11.5	..	..	..	..	..	..	30.7
5–14	140.5	..	..	..	..	..	..	134.9
15–59	363.7	..	..	..	..	..	..	141.5
60+	387.8	..	..	..	..	..	..	344.7
Females	144.3	..	..	..	..	..	..	108.8
<5	6.1	..	..	..	..	..	..	24.3
5–14	86.7	..	..	..	..	..	..	85.6
15–59	179.5	..	..	..	..	..	..	113.3
60+	389.2	..	..	..	..	..	..	360.7

Note. Column headings in italics show the national terminology.

Table 2 *(continued)*

Age and sex	Mental	Intellec-tual	Other psycho-logical	Language	Severe communi-cation	Aural	Total or profound hearing	Speech and hearing
ICIDH	**M1.1**	**1**	**2**	**3**	**30**	**4**	**40**	**M40.1**

CANADA, *health and disability survey 1983/84*

	Mental			*Speaking*		*Hearing*		
Males 15+	534.4	..	..	705.4		3 644.3	..	..
15–34	553.5	..	..	530.4		714.9	..	..
35–54	514.2	..	..	479.9		2 159.8	..	..
55–64	a/	..	..	736.6		7 274.4	..	..
65+	688.3	..	..	2 064.9		16 519.2	..	..
Females 15+	337.5	..	..	511.3		2 996.2	..	..
15–34	392.2	..	..	438.4		830.6	..	..
35–54	a/	..	..	308.0		1 676.9	..	..
55–64	a/	..	..	a/		4 564.7	..	..
65+	a/	..	..	1 269.6		11 501.1	..	..
Both sexes 15+	433.7	..	..	606.2		3 313.1	..	..
15–34	472.9	..	..	484.4		772.8	..	..
35–54	325.3	..	..	393.8		1 917.8	..	..
55–64	396.5	..	..	572.7		5 859.0	..	..
65+	594.2	..	..	1 570.5		13 667.2	..	..

JAMAICA, *survey of handicapped children (aged 4-11) in schools 1978* b/

	Mental		*Emotional*	*Speech*		*Auditory*		
Males 4-11	172	..	44	27	..	59	..	..
Females 4-11	84	..	52	14	..	43	..	..

----

a/ Quantity estimated has a coefficent of variation greater than 25 per cent and is therefore not reported.

b/ Figures for this country show actual number of disabled persons by age and sex and by selected intellectual, other psychological, language and aural impairments.

Note. Column headings in italics show the national terminology.

Table 2 *(continued)*

Age and sex	Mental	Intellec-tual	Other psycho-logical	Language	Severe communi-cation	Aural	Total or profound hearing	Speech and hearing
ICIDH	**M1.1**	**1**	**2**	**3**	**30**	**4**	**40**	**M40.1**

NETHERLANDS ANTILLES, general census of population and housing 1981

	Mental						*Deaf*	
Males	1 182.4	..	..	..	..	..	272.9	..
0-4	179.7	..	..	..	..	..	94.6	..
5-9	661.2	..	..	..	..	..	321.9	..
10-14	1 930.3	..	..	..	..	..	183.0	..
15-19	1 540.6	..	..	..	..	..	192.6	..
20-24	1 458.6	..	..	..	..	..	87.3	..
25-29	1 282.3	..	..	..	..	..	148.4	..
30-34	1 263.6	..	..	..	..	..	127.5	..
35-39	1 018.8	..	..	..	..	..	143.5	..
40-44	1 248.3	..	..	..	..	..	185.6	..
45-49	819.7	..	..	..	..	..	312.3	..
50-54	1 154.6	..	..	..	..	..	117.8	..
55-59	1 074.0	..	..	..	..	..	348.3	..
60-64	1 112.7	..	..	..	..	..	486.8	..
65-69	975.2	..	..	..	..	..	620.6	..
70-74	1 382.3	..	..	..	..	..	1 668.3	..
75-79	1 347.1	..	..	..	..	..	2 535.7	..
80-84	2 131.4	..	..	..	..	..	2 486.7	..
85+	3 180.2	..	..	..	..	..	4 593.6	..
Females	789.8	..	..	..	..	..	278.0	..
0-4	118.4	..	..	..	..	..	177.7	..
5-9	378.3	..	..	..	..	..	351.3	..
10-14	1 081.3	..	..	..	..	..	187.3	..
15-19	880.1	..	..	..	..	..	182.1	..
20-24	940.4	..	..	..	..	..	87.1	..
25-29	763.1	..	..	..	..	..	121.0	..
30-34	582.7	..	..	..	..	..	41.6	..
35-39	619.1	..	..	..	..	..	309.6	..
40-44	630.5	..	..	..	..	..	114.6	..
45-49	642.7	..	..	..	..	..	139.0	..
50-54	806.5	..	..	..	..	..	382.0	..
55-59	938.5	..	..	..	..	..	260.7	..
60-64	1 068.4	..	..	..	..	..	635.3	..
65-69	971.9	..	..	..	..	..	791.9	..
70-74	1 518.1	..	..	..	..	..	817.4	..
75-79	2 403.8	..	..	..	..	..	1 141.8	..
80-84	2 755.6	..	..	..	..	..	1 777.8	..
85+	2 902.1	..	..	..	..	..	3 627.6	..

Note. Column headings in italics show the national terminology.

Table 2 *(continued)*

Age and sex	Mental	Intellec- tual	Other psycho- logical	Language	Severe communi- cation	Aural	Total or profound hearing	Speech and hearing
ICIDH	**M1.1**	**1**	**2**	**3**	**30**	**4**	**40**	**M40.1**

PANAMA, general census of population and housing 1980

Age and sex	Mental	*Mentally retarded*	Other psycho- logical	Language	Severe communi- cation	Aural	Total or profound hearing	*Deaf/ mute*
Males 0-39	..	393.2	..	..	..	..	..	124.8
Females 0-39	..	307.5	..	..	..	..	..	120.6

TRINIDAD AND TOBAGO, survey of children 1982 c/

Age and sex				*Speech and language*	*Hearing*			
Both sexes 3-16	..	..	..	139	104		..	..

UNITED STATES, national health interview survey 1982
(Survey of civilian and non-institutionalized population.)

Age and sex				*Speech*	*Hearing*			
Males								
< 45	..	..	..	1 590.0	4 620.0		..	..
45-64	..	..	..	*280.0	19 570.0		..	..
65-74	..	..	..	*760.0	32 040.0		..	..
75+	..	..	..	*1 680.0	41 520.0		..	..
Females								
< 45	..	..	..	970.0	2 840.0		..	..
45-64	..	..	..	*330.0	9 490.0		..	..
65-74	..	..	..	*880.0	21 730.0		..	..
75+	..	..	..	*380.0	33 150.0		..	..

c/ Figures for this country show actual number of disabled children ages 3-16 in population surveyed by selected intellectual, other psychological, language and aural impairments. Non-response rates were significant (each about 50 per cent) at the two stages of screening and examination of the children.

* Refers to an estimate for which numerator has a relative standard error greater than 30 per cent.

Note. Column headings in italics show the national terminology.

Table 2 (continued)

Age and sex	Mental	Intellec-tual	Other psycho-logical	Language	Severe communi-cation	Aural	Total or profound hearing	Speech and hearing
ICIDH	M1.1	1	2	3	30	4	40	M40.1

PERU, national census of population and housing 1981

					Mute		Deaf	Deaf and mute
Both sexes	..	..	..	..	23.0	..	28.7	7.9

Note. Column headings in italics show the national terminology.

Table 2 *(continued)*

Age and sex	Mental	Intellec-tual	Other psycho-logical	Language	Severe communi-cation	Aural	Total or profound hearing	Speech and hearing
ICIDH	M1.1	1	2	3	30	4	40	M40.1

BAHRAIN, population census 1981

	Mentally handi-capped						*Deaf*	*Deaf and mute*
Males	191.4	..	..	..	..	..	70.3	73.2
0-4	27.1						9.0	54.1
5-9	164.0	..	..	..	..	..	42.3	116.4
10-14	296.4	..	..	..	..	..	29.1	122.1
15-19	427.7	..	..	..	..	..	28.1	152.0
20-24	249.6	..	..	..	..	..	40.3	64.4
25-29	88.5	..	..	..	..	..	26.2	23.0
30-34	108.6	..	..	..	..	..	4.5	40.7
35-39	113.4	..	..	..	..	..	42.5	28.3
40-44	148.8	..	..	..	..	..	70.0	52.5
45-49	194.5	..	..	..	..	..	133.7	60.8
50-54	361.2	..	..	..	..	..	172.7	15.7
55-59	293.3	..	..	..	..	..	415.4	73.3
60-64	297.1	..	..	..	..	..	462.2	165.1
65-69	251.7	..	..	..	..	..	566.4	314.7
70+	727.0	..	..	..	..	..	1 171.2	282.7
Females	135.6	..	..	..	..	..	58.2	54.8
0-4	23.2						0.0	13.9
5-9	75.3	..	..	..	..	..	26.9	69.9
10-14	241.1	..	..	..	..	..	11.8	58.8
15-19	215.4	..	..	..	..	..	45.3	90.7
20-24	137.7	..	..	..	..	..	18.0	53.9
25-29	65.8	..	..	..	..	..	29.2	29.2
30-34	143.0	..	..	..	..	..	0.0	44.0
35-39	111.8	..	..	..	..	..	41.9	55.9
40-44	93.5	..	..	..	..	..	46.8	15.6
45-49	173.9	..	..	..	..	..	58.0	0.0
50-54	235.0	..	..	..	..	..	141.0	94.0
55-59	185.1	..	..	..	..	..	111.1	0.0
60-64	130.0	..	..	..	..	..	476.8	43.3
65-69	78.2	..	..	..	..	..	469.5	156.5
70+	537.0	..	..	..	..	..	1 156.5	371.7

Note. Column headings in italics show the national terminology.

Table 2 *(continued)*

Age and sex	Mental	Intellec-tual	Other psycho-logical	Language	Severe communi-cation	Aural	Total or profound hearing	Speech and hearing
ICIDH	**M1.1**	**1**	**2**	**3**	**30**	**4**	**40**	**M40.1**

CHINA, annual population survey 1983
(special children's question on disability)

								Deaf and mute
Males 0-14	..	..	..	..	..	..	..	146.7
0	..	..	..	..	..	..	..	0.0
1	..	..	..	..	..	..	..	51.4
2	..	..	..	..	..	..	..	71.7
3	..	..	..	..	..	..	..	103.0
4	..	..	..	..	..	..	..	180.5
5	..	..	..	..	..	..	..	187.3
6	..	..	..	..	..	..	..	94.9
7	..	..	..	..	..	..	..	198.8
8	..	..	..	..	..	..	..	188.9
9	..	..	..	..	..	..	..	217.7
10	..	..	..	..	..	..	..	162.6
11	..	..	..	..	..	..	..	164.2
12	..	..	..	..	..	..	..	142.3
13	..	..	..	..	..	..	..	202.8
14	..	..	..	..	..	..	..	170.2
Females 0-14	..	..	..	..	..	..	..	142.5
0	..	..	..	..	..	..	..	20.2
1	..	..	..	..	..	..	..	18.7
2	..	..	..	..	..	..	..	58.5
3	..	..	..	..	..	..	..	110.6
4	..	..	..	..	..	..	..	38.6
5	..	..	..	..	..	..	..	20.6
6	..	..	..	..	..	..	..	165.8
7	..	..	..	..	..	..	..	134.4
8	..	..	..	..	..	..	..	183.8
9	..	..	..	..	..	..	..	116.8
10	..	..	..	..	..	..	..	247.1
11	..	..	..	..	..	..	..	285.9
12	..	..	..	..	..	..	..	182.2
13	..	..	..	..	..	..	..	240.6
14	..	..	..	..	..	..	..	168.1

Note. Column headings in italics show the national terminology.

Table 2 *(continued)*

Age and sex	Mental	Intellec- tual	Other psycho- logical	Language	Severe communi- cation	Aural	Total or profound hearing	Speech and hearing
ICIDH	M1.1	1	2	3	30	4	40	M40.1

HONG KONG, population census 1981

Age and sex	Mental	*Mentally retarded*	*Mentally ill*	Language	Severe communi- cation	Aural	*Severely deaf*	Speech and hearing
Both sexes	..	1 850.0	127.0	..	..	..	127.0	..
0-4	..	104.0	..	..	..	..	31.0	..
5-9	..	336.0	..	..	..	..	39.0	..
10-14	..	409.0	..	..	..	..	53.0	..
0-14	..	..	5.0	..	..	..	..	..
15-19	..	355.0	43.0	..	..	..	72.0	..
20-24	..	298.0	122.0	..	..	..	81.0	..
25-29	..	182.0	162.0	..	..	..	79.0	..
30-34	..	131.0	193.0	..	..	..	92.0	..
35-39	..	52.0	229.0	..	..	..	69.0	..
40-44	..	48.0	257.0	..	..	..	81.0	..
45-49	..	33.0	231.0	..	..	..	91.0	..
50+	..	17.0	..	..	..	..	..	..
50-54	..	..	216.0	..	..	..	113.0	..
55-59	..	..	193.0	..	..	..	164.0	..
60-64	..	..	196.0	..	..	..	219.0	..
65+	..	..	209.0	..	..	..	789.0	..

Note. Column headings in italics show the national terminology.

Table 2 (continued)

Age and sex	Mental	Intellec-tual	Other psycho-logical	Language	Severe communi-cation	Aural	Total or profound hearing	Speech and hearing
ICIDH	M1.1	1	2	3	30	4	40	M40.1

INDIA, national survey of handicapped 1981

				Speech		Hearing		
Urban males								
	..	..	..	342.0	..	386.0	..	..
0-4	..	..	..	..	..	..	..	..
5-14	..	..	..	506.0	..	266.0	..	..
15-39	..	..	..	304.0	..	216.0	..	..
40-59	..	..	..	203.0	..	386.0	..	..
60+	..	..	..	360.0	..	2 432.0	..	..
Urban females ..		..	..	207.0	..	395.0	..	..
0-4	..	..	..	..	..	..	..	..
5-14	..	..	..	345.0	..	220.0	..	..
15-39	..	..	..	159.0	..	198.0	..	..
40-59	..	..	..	122.0	..	468.0	..	..
60+	..	..	..	209.0	..	2 305.0	..	..
Rural males								
	..	..	..	379.0	..	595.0	..	..
0-4	..	..	..	..	..	..	..	..
5-14	..	..	..	486.0	..	343.0	..	..
15-39	..	..	..	359.0	..	386.0	..	..
40-59	..	..	..	262.0	..	647.0	..	..
60+	..	..	..	345.0	..	2 660.0	..	..
Rural females ..		..	..	228.0	..	510.0	..	..
0-4	..	..	..	..	..	..	..	..
5-14	..	..	..	324.0	..	283.0	..	..
15-39	..	..	..	189.0	..	250.0	..	..
40-59	..	..	..	175.0	..	579.0	..	..
60+	..	..	..	225.0	..	2 597.0	..	..

Note. Column headings in italics show the national terminology.

Table 2 *(continued)*

Age and sex	Mental	Intellec-tual	Other psycho-logical	Language	Severe communi-cation	Aural	Total or profound hearing	Speech and hearing
ICIDH	M1.1	1	2	3	30	4	40	M40.1

INDONESIA, population census 1980

	Mental handicap							
Both sexes	115.4	..	..	..	..	..	..	..
0-14	67.5	..	..	..	..	..	..	..
15+	148.4	..	..	..	..	..	..	..

JAPAN, national survey of handicapped adults 1980 b/

					Auditory disability			
Both sexes	..	..	..	..	..	317 000	..	..

JORDAN, national registration campaign 1979 b/

		Emotional disturbance						*Deaf and mute*
Both sexes	..	..	457	..	..	..	..	3 193

b/ Figures for this country show actual number of disabled persons, by age and sex and by selected intellectual, other psycho-logical, language and aural impairments.

Note. Column headings in italics show the national terminology.

Table 2 *(continued)*

Age and sex	Mental	Intellec- tual	Other psycho- logical	Language	Severe communi- cation	Aural	Total or profound hearing	Speech and hearing
ICIDH	**M1.1**	**1**	**2**	**3**	**30**	**4**	**40**	**M40.1**

JORDAN, agricultural census 1983 b/

	Mental							*Deaf and mute*
Males	1 473	..	..	..	..	..	..	1 334
0-4	59	..	..	..	..	..	..	111
5-9	207	..	..	..	..	..	..	300
10-14	280	..	..	..	..	..	..	275
15-19	309	..	..	..	..	..	..	211
20-24	174	..	..	..	..	..	..	116
25-29	110	..	..	..	..	..	..	53
30-34	77	..	..	..	..	..	..	33
35-39	76	..	..	..	..	..	..	46
40-44	67	..	..	..	..	..	..	26
45-49	37	..	..	..	..	..	..	26
50-54	27	..	..	..	..	..	..	24
55-59	16	..	..	..	..	..	..	9
60-64	11	..	..	..	..	..	..	36
65+	23	..	..	..	..	..	..	68
Females	791	..	..	..	..	..	..	982
0-4	40	..	..	..	..	..	..	83
5-9	113	..	..	..	..	..	..	222
10-14	196	..	..	..	..	..	..	198
15-19	150	..	..	..	..	..	..	157
20-24	96	..	..	..	..	..	..	79
25-29	47	..	..	..	..	..	..	47
30-34	33	..	..	..	..	..	..	40
35-39	21	..	..	..	..	..	..	35
40-44	28	..	..	..	..	..	..	18
45-49	15	..	..	..	..	..	..	23
50-54	19	..	..	..	..	..	..	21
55-59	9	..	..	..	..	..	..	5
60-64	8	..	..	..	..	..	..	11
65+	16	..	..	..	..	..	..	43

b/ Figures for this country show actual number of disabled persons, by age and sex and by selected intellectual, other psychological, language and aural impairments.

Note. Column headings in italics show the national terminology.

Table 2 *(continued)*

Age and sex	Mental	Intellec-tual	Other psycho-logical	Language	Severe communi-cation	Aural	Total or profound hearing	Speech and hearing
ICIDH	M1.1	1	2	3	30	4	40	M40.1

KUWAIT, population census 1980

Age and sex	Mental	*Mental retardation*	Other	Language	*Mute*	Aural	*Deaf*	*Deaf and mute*
Males	..	142.4	..	..	29.1	..	16.6	23.6
0-4	..	18.5	..	..	4.6	..	2.8	3.7
5-9	..	150.7	..	..	58.1	..	14.0	46.3
10-14	..	385.7	..	..	87.9	..	18.4	90.5
15-19	..	488.7	..	..	70.0	..	21.8	52.9
20-24	..	190.4	..	..	22.1	..	19.3	15.2
25-29	..	78.2	..	..	10.5	..	5.8	11.7
30-34	..	52.5	..	..	5.2	..	6.6	3.9
35-39	..	47.7	..	..	11.1	..	9.5	4.8
40-44	..	34.4	..	..	11.5	..	13.4	0.0
45-49	..	32.1	..	..	8.8	..	17.5	5.8
50-54	..	39.0	..	..	4.3	..	21.7	8.7
55-59	..	25.1	..	..	8.4	..	41.8	8.4
60-64	..	68.9	..	..	27.6	..	96.5	0.0
65-69	..	26.4	..	..	52.8	..	237.6	26.4
70-74	..	317.0	..	..	39.6	..	158.5	0.0
75-79	..	326.3	..	..	0.0	..	407.8	0.0
80-84	..	228.1	..	..	228.1	..	342.1	0.0
85+	..	369.0	..	..	184.5	..	738.0	0.0
Females	..	115.3	..	..	17.0	..	11.4	16.3
0-4	..	22.9	..	..	2.9	..	2.9	1.0
5-9	..	131.3	..	..	31.2	..	11.1	25.6
10-14	..	247.9	..	..	40.6	..	16.3	33.9
15-19	..	286.3	..	..	41.4	..	14.4	43.2
20-24	..	146.6	..	..	9.6	..	17.4	15.4
25-29	..	85.2	..	..	3.8	..	3.8	9.5
30-34	..	47.2	..	..	9.0	..	4.5	11.2
35-39	..	29.7	..	..	3.0	..	0.0	0.0
40-44	..	19.9	..	..	4.0	..	11.9	11.9
45-49	..	36.7	..	..	6.1	..	0.0	0.0
50-54	..	61.4	..	..	0.0	..	8.8	0.0
55-59	..	70.0	..	..	0.0	..	56.0	0.0
60-64	..	17.5	..	..	0.0	..	35.1	0.0
65-69	..	122.3	..	..	30.6	..	61.1	0.0
70-74	..	0.0	..	..	0.0	..	149.4	37.3
75-79	..	74.5	..	..	0.0	..	297.8	0.0
80-84	..	104.1	..	..	0.0	..	0.0	0.0
85+	..	678.0	..	..	0.0	..	0.0	0.0

Note. Column headings in italics show the national terminology.

Table 2 (continued)

Age and sex	Mental	Intellectual	Other psychological	Language	Severe communication	Aural	Total or profound hearing	Speech and hearing
ICIDH	M1.1	1	2	3	30	4	40	M40.1

LEBANON, national survey of handicapped 1981 b/

	Mentally disabled	Mongoloid			Mute		Deaf	Deaf and mute
Both sexes disabled	5 940	1 281	..	..	4 434	..	2 720	2 208

NEPAL, national survey 1980

		Mental retardation				Total auditory	Deaf or hearing handicapped	Deaf-mute
Both sexes	..	223.0	..	..	..	1 150.0	754.0	196.0
<5	..	14.0	..	..	..	115.0	72.0	43.0
5-14	..	244.0	..	..	..	1 548.0	867.0	731.0
15-24	..	348.0	..	..	..	1 201.0	707.0	494.0
25-39	..	267.0	..	..	..	929.0	592.0	377.0
40-59	..	219.0	..	..	..	1 206.0	973.0	233.0
60-74	..	143.0	..	..	..	1 903.0	1 665.0	238.0
75+	..	0.0	..	..	..	5 101.0	4 965.0	236.0

b/ Figures for this country show actual number of disabled persons, by age and sex and by selected intellectual, other psychological, language and aural impairments.

Note. Column headings in italics show the national terminology.

Table 2 *(continued)*

Age and sex	Mental	Intellec-tual	Other psycho-logical	Language	Severe communi-cation	Aural	Total or profound hearing	Speech and hearing
ICIDH	M1.1	1	2	3	30	4	40	M40.1

PAKISTAN, population census 1981

Age and sex		*Mentally retarded*	*Insane*					*Deaf and mute*
Males	..	47.4	30.5	..	..	..	..	43.3
0-4	..	5.8	5.1	..	..	..	..	21.4
5-9	..	33.5	16.9	..	..	..	..	82.8
10-14	..	56.8	28.9	..	..	..	..	68.7
15-19	..	52.1	36.1	..	..	..	..	40.8
20-24	..	63.1	29.8	..	..	..	..	32.4
25-29	..	61.4	35.5	..	..	..	..	14.8
30-34	..	59.6	43.3	..	..	..	..	15.6
35-39	..	55.2	31.7	..	..	..	..	20.3
40-44	..	64.2	56.3	..	..	..	..	20.1
45-49	..	53.8	41.0	..	..	..	..	11.9
50-54	..	60.0	51.5	..	..	..	..	19.7
55-59	..	45.7	39.7	..	..	..	..	39.7
60+	..	71.5	55.6	..	..	..	..	73.0
Females	..	45.2	27.3	..	..	..	..	75.9
0-4	..	4.7	4.9	..	..	..	..	17.7
5-9	..	19.0	8.0	..	..	..	..	57.7
10-14	..	40.7	24.7	..	..	..	..	70.9
15-19	..	56.7	36.4	..	..	..	..	77.7
20-24	..	45.8	24.4	..	..	..	..	67.0
25-29	..	54.0	31.1	..	..	..	..	102.3
30-34	..	57.9	43.9	..	..	..	..	100.2
35-39	..	73.2	31.0	..	..	..	..	78.9
40-44	..	69.1	39.2	..	..	..	..	98.9
45-49	..	55.7	51.0	..	..	..	..	93.4
50-54	..	60.3	65.2	..	..	..	..	112.3
55-59	..	52.8	39.0	..	..	..	..	95.3
60+	..	130.5	62.1	..	..	..	..	187.9

Note. Column headings in italics show the national terminology.

Table 2 *(continued)*

Age and sex	Mental	Intellec-tual	Other psycho-logical	Language	Severe communi-cation	Aural	Total or profound hearing	Speech and hearing
ICIDH	M1.1	1	2	3	30	4	40	M40.1

PHILIPPINES, national survey 1980

	Mental impairment							
Males	412.4	..	..	..	..	..	..	..
< 1	0.0	..	..	..	..	..	..	..
1–4	135.6	..	..	..	..	..	..	..
5–9	382.8	..	..	..	..	..	..	..
10–14	264.9	..	..	..	..	..	..	..
15–19	607.3	..	..	..	..	..	..	..
20–24	487.8	..	..	..	..	..	..	..
25–29	778.5	..	..	..	..	..	..	..
30–34	603.0	..	..	..	..	..	..	..
35–39	680.3	..	..	..	..	..	..	..
40–44	4 502.0	..	..	..	..	..	..	..
45–49	183.8	..	..	..	..	..	..	..
50–54	0.0	..	..	..	..	..	..	..
55–59	763.4	..	..	..	..	..	..	..
60–64	293.3	..	..	..	..	..	..	..
65–69	0.0	..	..	..	..	..	..	..
70–74	606.1	..	..	..	..	..	..	..
75+	584.8	..	..	..	..	..	..	..
Females	387.1	..	..	..	..	..	..	..
< 1	0.0	..	..	..	..	..	..	..
1–4	0.0	..	..	..	..	..	..	..
5–9	172.9	..	..	..	..	..	..	..
10–14	382.8	..	..	..	..	..	..	..
15–19	520.3	..	..	..	..	..	..	..
20–24	480.5	..	..	..	..	..	..	..
25–29	487.0	..	..	..	..	..	..	..
30–34	397.2	..	..	..	..	..	..	..
35–39	615.0	..	..	..	..	..	..	..
40–44	554.8	..	..	..	..	..	..	..
45–49	1 111.1	..	..	..	..	..	..	..
50–54	354.0	..	..	..	..	..	..	..
55–59	489.0	..	..	..	..	..	..	..
60–64	917.4	..	..	..	..	..	..	..
65–69	0.0	..	..	..	..	..	..	..
70–74	0.0	..	..	..	..	..	..	..
75+	0.0	..	..	..	..	..	..	..

Note. Column headings in italics show the national terminology.

Table 2 (continued)

Age and sex	Mental	Intellec-tual	Other psycho-logical	Language	Severe communi-cation	Aural	Total or profound hearing	Speech and hearing
ICIDH	M1.1	1	2	3	30	4	40	M40.1

PHILIPPINES, national survey 1980 (cont'd)

					Communi-cation	*Aural*		
Males	..	..	..	..	78.9	242.6	..	..
< 15	..	..	..	..	72.9	160.5	..	..
15–64	..	..	..	..	77.3	265.2	..	..
65+	..	..	..	..	171.8	859.1	..	..
Females	..	..	..	..	77.4	190.6	..	..
< 15	..	..	..	..	74.1	118.6	..	..
15–64	..	..	..	..	73.8	158.2	..	..
65+	..	..	..	..	177.6	1 598.6	..	..

				Aphasia	*Mutism*		*Total hearing loss*	
Males	..	..	..	54.6	206.2	..	121.3	..
< 15	..	..	..	43.8	291.8	..	131.3	..
15–64	..	..	..	22.1	132.6	..	99.4	..
65+	..	..	..	687.3	343.6	..	343.6	..
Females	..	..	..	59.6	154.8	..	137.0	..
< 15	..	..	..	44.5	133.4	..	89.0	..
15–64	..	..	..	52.7	179.3	..	137.1	..
65+	..	..	..	355.2	0.0	..	710.5	..

Note. Column headings in italics show the national terminology.

Table 2 *(continued)*

Age and sex	Mental	Intellectual	Other psychological	Language	Severe communication	Aural	Total or profound hearing	Speech and hearing
ICIDH	**M1.1**	**1**	**2**	**3**	**30**	**4**	**40**	**M40.1**

SINGAPORE, continuous registration system of disabled persons 1985 b/

		Intellectual	Psychiatric			Hearing		
Both sexes	..	3 472	286	..	..	2 875	..	..
0-4	..	36	0	..	..	32	..	..
5-13	..	802	0	..	..	322	..	..
14-19	..	834	0	..	..	384	..	..
20-29	..	1 403	40	..	..	869	..	..
30-39	..	346	95	..	..	460	..	..
40-49	..	38	91	..	..	209	..	..
50-59	..	9	59	..	..	181	..	..
60-69	..	3	0	..	..	166	..	..
70-79	..	0	1	..	..	179	..	..
80+	..	1	0	..	..	73	..	..

b/ Figures for this country show actual number of disabled persons by age and sex and by selected intellectual, other psychological, language and aural impairments.

Note. Column headings in italics show the national terminology.

Table 2 *(continued)*

Age and sex	Mental	Intellec-tual	Other psycho-logical	Language	Severe communi-cation	Aural	Total or profound hearing	Speech and hearing
ICIDH	**M1.1**	**1**	**2**	**3**	**30**	**4**	**40**	**M40.1**

SRI LANKA, *population census 1981*

Age and sex					*Mute*		*Deaf*	*Deaf and mute*
Males	..	..	..	..	89.2	..	24.7	69.1
< 1	..	..	..	..	2.4	..	0.5	1.0
1-4	..	..	..	..	53.0	..	3.4	36.7
5-9	..	..	..	..	111.3	..	10.7	70.8
10-14	..	..	..	..	125.5	..	20.3	92.9
15-19	..	..	..	..	132.0	..	21.1	104.4
20-24	..	..	..	..	100.4	..	15.8	69.8
25-29	..	..	..	..	85.0	..	15.7	66.2
30-34	..	..	..	..	66.4	..	12.6	65.8
35-39	..	..	..	..	79.7	..	20.8	67.6
40-44	..	..	..	..	58.5	..	23.8	57.6
45-49	..	..	..	..	56.9	..	21.7	56.0
50-54	..	..	..	..	60.9	..	36.6	53.5
55-59	..	..	..	..	57.8	..	51.0	52.8
60-64	..	..	..	..	54.9	..	72.3	54.4
65-69	..	..	..	..	68.0	..	85.9	45.6
70-74	..	..	..	..	54.3	..	110.7	50.2
75+	..	..	..	..	40.0	..	187.0	40.9
Females	..	..	..	..	70.0	..	21.8	56.5
< 1	..	..	..	..	1.5	..	0.0	1.0
1-4	..	..	..	..	45.5	..	4.1	29.0
5-9	..	..	..	..	89.8	..	10.1	57.1
10-14	..	..	..	..	98.4	..	17.3	77.4
15-19	..	..	..	..	104.1	..	15.4	82.8
20-24	..	..	..	..	73.0	..	11.2	57.8
25-29	..	..	..	..	68.9	..	14.0	54.3
30-34	..	..	..	..	51.5	..	15.0	49.5
35-39	..	..	..	..	59.4	..	15.6	53.6
40-44	..	..	..	..	47.7	..	28.4	45.9
45-49	..	..	..	..	46.2	..	38.2	51.2
50-54	..	..	..	..	46.8	..	37.5	52.2
55-59	..	..	..	..	45.8	..	47.3	49.8
60-64	..	..	..	..	36.1	..	58.9	31.7
65-69	..	..	..	..	32.0	..	64.9	38.6
70-74	..	..	..	..	31.3	..	103.6	31.3
75+	..	..	..	..	29.9	..	151.5	42.9

Note. Column headings in italics show the national terminology.

Table 2 *(continued)*

Age and sex	Mental	Intellec-tual	Other psycho-logical	Language	Severe communi-cation	Aural	Total or profound hearing	Speech and hearing
ICIDH	M1.1	1	2	3	30	4	40	M40.1

TURKEY, population census 1975

Age and sex	Mental	Intellec-tual	Other psycho-logical	Language	Severe communi-cation	Aural	*Deaf*	*Deaf and mute*
Males	..	..	..	..	..	..	139.6	125.5
0–4	..	..	..	..	..	..	193.5	65.2
5–9	..	..	..	..	..	..	39.8	107.9
10–14	..	..	..	..	..	..	134.0	145.4
15–19	..	..	..	..	..	..	53.5	106.5
20–24	..	..	..	..	..	..	89.4	125.5
25–29	..	..	..	..	..	..	60.0	97.9
30–34	..	..	..	..	..	..	472.1	187.0
35–39	..	..	..	..	..	..	81.9	132.3
40–44	..	..	..	..	..	..	95.5	133.3
45–49	..	..	..	..	..	..	115.1	112.8
50–54	..	..	..	..	..	..	144.1	142.6
55–59	..	..	..	..	..	..	184.1	172.4
60–64	..	..	..	..	..	..	239.0	192.7
65+	..	..	..	..	..	..	385.4	257.1
Unknown	..	..	..	..	..	..	28.7	82.3
Females	..	..	..	..	..	..	225.9	106.6
0–4	..	..	..	..	..	..	1 182.8	209.5
5–9	..	..	..	..	..	..	31.4	82.5
10–14	..	..	..	..	..	..	80.9	105.8
15–19	..	..	..	..	..	..	35.7	80.2
20–24	..	..	..	..	..	..	47.1	80.0
25–29	..	..	..	..	..	..	34.2	67.1
30–34	..	..	..	..	..	..	55.3	77.4
35–39	..	..	..	..	..	..	43.4	75.0
40–44	..	..	..	..	..	..	57.1	76.2
45–49	..	..	..	..	..	..	54.0	78.9
50–54	..	..	..	..	..	..	95.8	88.0
55–59	..	..	..	..	..	..	94.2	97.3
60–64	..	..	..	..	..	..	140.2	120.9
65+	..	..	..	..	..	..	264.3	165.7
Unknown	..	..	..	..	..	..	97.0	89.3

Note. Column headings in italics show the national terminology.

Table 2 *(continued)*

Age and sex	Mental	Intellec-tual	Other psycho-logical	Language	Severe communi-cation	Aural	Total or profound hearing	Speech and hearing
ICIDH	M1.1	1	2	3	30	4	40	M40.1

AUSTRIA, sample survey on physical disabilities 1976

Age and sex	Mental	Intellectual	Other psychological	*Speech disturbance*	*Mute*	*Hearing*	*Deaf in both ears*	
Both sexes	..	..	..	335.4	32.6	4 569.5	77.7	..
0–5	..	..	..	19.4	0.0	19.4	0.0	..
6–9	..	..	..	166.0	62.3	352.8	0.0	..
10–14	..	..	..	206.1	14.7	412.2	13.2	..
15–19	..	..	..	296.1	49.4	411.3	86.4	..
20–29	..	..	..	169.5	22.6	644.1	63.8	..
30–39	..	..	..	217.4	10.9	1 380.6	48.3	..
40–49	..	..	..	226.9	45.4	2 144.1	66.5	..
50–59	..	..	..	483.8	11.5	4 998.8	75.0	..
60–69	..	..	..	626.5	51.1	10 139.4	131.8	..
70–79	..	..	..	706.8	34.5	19 634.5	255.2	..
80+	..	..	..	1 168.5	184.5	34 132.8	204.8	..
Males	..	..	..	427.0	25.8	4 829.0	82.1	..
Females	..	..	..	249.1	3.8	4 269.7	68.3	..

DENMARK, living conditions survey 1976

Age and sex	Mental	Intellectual	Other psychological	Language	*Hearing problems*			
Males 20–69	..	..	..	..	..	13 000.0	..	..
20–29	..	..	..	..	..	4 000.0	..	..
30–44	..	..	..	..	..	8 000.0	..	..
45–59	..	..	..	..	..	18 000.0	..	..
60–69	..	..	..	..	..	28 000.0	..	..
Females 20–69	..	..	..	..	..	7 000.0	..	..
20–29	..	..	..	..	..	2 000.0	..	..
30–44	..	..	..	..	..	4 000.0	..	..
45–59	..	..	..	..	..	10 000.0	..	..
60–69	..	..	..	..	..	14 000.0	..	..
Both sexes 20–69	..	..	..	..	..	10 000.0	..	..

Note. Column headings in italics show the national terminology.

Table 2 *(continued)*

Age and sex	Mental	Intellec-tual	Other psycho-logical	Language	Severe communi-cation	Aural	Total or profound hearing	Speech and hearing
ICIDH	M1.1	1	2	3	30	4	40	M40.1

FINLAND, survey on living conditions 1978

Age and sex	Mental	Intellectual	Other psychological	Language	Severe communication	Diminished hearing ability	Total or profound hearing	Speech and hearing
Males 15+	..	..	..	..	..	9 000.0	..	..
15-24	..	..	..	..	..	2 000.0	..	..
25-44	..	..	..	..	..	4 000.0	..	..
45-64	..	..	..	..	..	14 000.0	..	..
65+	..	..	..	..	..	32 000.0	..	..
Females 15+	..	..	..	..	..	11 000.0	..	..
15-24	..	..	..	..	..	1 000.0	..	..
25-44	..	..	..	..	..	3 000.0	..	..
45-64	..	..	..	..	..	16 000.0	..	..
65+	..	..	..	..	..	37 000.0	..	..

FEDERAL REPUBLIC OF GERMANY, national sample survey 1983
(Compilation of state registration system of disabled persons) b/

Age and sex	Mental	Mental development disturbances	Brain-organic attacks, no neuro-logical symptoms	Speech	Severe communication	Hearing; also deafness	Hearing & balance	Speech and hearing
Both sexes	..	154 789	70 276	9 266	..	151 394	19 053	..
<4	..	2 352	378	47	..	314	106	..
4-5	..	2 433	383	110	..	416	118	..
6-14	..	20 314	3 485	1 004	..	3 391	1 091	..
15-17	..	12 530	2 502	292	..	1 673	486	..
18-24	..	34 290	7 857	667	..	4 091	1 277	..
25-34	..	29 576	9 059	665	..	5 203	1 766	..
35-44	..	18 663	9 767	778	..	9 938	2 130	..
45-54	..	15 307	11 906	1 404	..	21 161	2 334	..
55-59	..	5 687	7 131	1 047	..	21 861	1 672	..
60-61	..	2 128	2 902	439	..	10 531	776	..
62-64	..	2 306	3 099	577	..	11 587	917	..
65+	..	9 203	11 807	2 236	..	61 228	6 380	..

b/ Figures for this country show actual number of disabled persons by age and sex and by selected intellectual, other psycho-logical, language and aural impairments.

Note. Column headings in italics show the national terminology.

Table 2 *(continued)*

Age and sex	Mental	Intellec-tual	Other psycho-logical	Language	Severe communi-cation	Aural	Total or profound hearing	Speech and hearing
ICIDH	M1.1	1	2	3	30	4	40	M40.1

NORWAY, *level of living survey 1983*

			Nervous condition		*Reduced hearing*			
Males	..	..	3 000.0	..	..	4 000.0	..	..
16-24	..	..	1 000.0	..	..	2 000.0	..	..
25-44	..	..	1 000.0	..	..	2 000.0	..	..
45-66	..	..	5 000.0	..	..	6 000.0	..	..
67-79	..	..	6 000.0	..	..	15 000.0	..	..
Females	..	..	4 000.0	..	..	3 000.0	..	..
16-24	..	..	1 000.0	..	..	1 000.0	..	..
25-44	..	..	2 000.0	..	..	1 000.0	..	..
45-66	..	..	5 000.0	..	..	4 000.0	..	..
67-79	..	..	8 000.0	..	..	10 000.0	..	..

SWEDEN, *living conditions survey 1980/81*

					Hearing			
Males	..	..	..	..	..	9 000.0	..	..
16-44	..	..	..	..	..	2 900.0	..	..
45-64	..	..	..	..	..	12 500.0	..	..
65-74	..	..	..	..	..	19 000.0	..	..
75-84	..	..	..	..	..	27 400.0	..	..
Females	..	..	..	..	..	5 200.0	..	..
16-44	..	..	..	..	..	1 600.0	..	..
45-64	..	..	..	..	..	4 600.0	..	..
65-74	..	..	..	..	..	10 700.0	..	..
75-84	..	..	..	..	..	20 500.0	..	..

Note. Column headings in italics show the national terminology.

Table 2 *(continued)*

Age and sex	Mental	Intellec- tual	Other psycho- logical	Language	Severe communi- cation	Aural	Total or profound hearing	Speech and hearing
ICIDH	M1.1	1	2	3	30	4	40	M40.1

UNITED KINGDOM (NORTHERN IRELAND), household survey of handicapped persons 1978 d/

			Psychiatric disorders		*Disorders of communication*			
Both sexes	..	..	100.0	..	100.0	..	..	..
0-4	..	..	0.1	..	0.6	..	..	..
5-14	..	..	0.8	..	6.4	..	..	..
15-24	..	..	0.8	..	5.4	..	..	..
25-34	..	..	2.3	..	3.6	..	..	..
35-44	..	..	5.6	..	4.7	..	..	..
45-54	..	..	10.6	..	6.4	..	..	..
55-64	..	..	23.1	..	13.0	..	..	..
65-74	..	..	32.6	..	24.5	..	..	..
75+	..	..	24.3	..	35.6	..	..	..
Both sexes								
Prevalence per 100 000	..	..	8 400.0	..	13 300.0	..	..	..

d/ Percentage distribution of disabled persons by age and prevalence of disability for selected intellectual other psychological, language and aural impairments.

Note. Column headings in italics show the national terminology.

Table 2 *(continued)*

Age and sex	Mental	Intellec-tual	Other psycho-logical	Language	Severe communi-cation	Aural	Total or profound hearing	Speech and hearing
ICIDH	**M1.1**	**1**	**2**	**3**	**30**	**4**	**40**	**M40.1**

AUSTRALIA, national survey of handicapped persons 1981

Age and sex	*Total mental disorders*	*Mental retar- dation*	*Mental disorders*			*Hearing loss*		
Both sexes	2 748.2	758.3	2 088.8	..	..	3 629.3	..	..
0-4	575.7	389.7	*	..	..	620.0	..	..
5-14	1 841.2	1 385.8	545.0	..	..	1 378.0	..	..
15-24	1 594.0	995.2	701.8	..	..	939.7	..	..
25-34	1 969.6	562.1	1 500.4	..	..	1 559.6	..	..
35-44	2 613.5	404.2	2 286.8	..	..	2 530.5	..	..
45-54	3 439.2	304.2	3 227.5	..	..	4 047.6	..	..
55-64	5 018.7	336.6	4 779.4	..	..	7 741.2	..	..
65-74	4 628.8	545.9	4 192.1	..	..	11 091.7	..	..
75+	10 591.7	2 248.5	8 796.8	..	..	23 116.4	..	..

AUSTRALIA, national survey of handicapped persons 1981

Age and sex		*Mild mental retar- dation* e/	*Other psychoses* e/					
Both sexes								
< 15	..	389.4	*					
15-24	..	503.6	*	..	..	..	..	..
25-34	..	371.9	*	..	..	..	..	..
35-44	..	249.2	*	..	..	..	..	..
45-54	..	..	264.6	..	..	..	..	..
55-64	..	..	239.3	..	..	..	..	..
65-74	..	..	327.5	..	..	..	..	..
75+	..	..	*	..	..	..	..	..
Males	..	346.4	162.9	..	..	..	..	..
Females	..	305.7	99.2	..	..	..	..	..
Both sexes	..	326.0	130.9	..	..	..	..	..

e/ Numerator excludes mild cases that: (i) do not reduce ability to perform activities; (ii) do not require an aid.

* Estimate not published because its relative standard error was too large: its standard error was greater than 25 per cent of the estimate.

Note. Column headings in italics show the national terminology.

Table 3. Disabled persons per 100,000 population by age and sex and by selected ocular, visceral, and skeletal impairments

This table provides the number of disabled persons per 100,000 population according to age group and sex for: ocular; total visual impairment: both eyes; profound visual impairment: one eye; unspecified other paralysis of limb; unspecified other motor impairment of limb; transverse deficiency of upper arm; transverse deficiency of lower leg; and unspecified transverse deficiency of proximal limb parts. The rates presented were calculated by the Statistical Office based upon numbers or rates provided in the published reports.

Description of variables

The type of impairments reported are based upon codes 5-7 of the ICIDH impairment code. Reasonably comparable national data were placed in the same ICIDH column. Only selected impairments that countries reported are presented in table 3. A complete list of impairments reported by the 63 surveys of the 55 countries in DISTAT is provided below according to the number of national surveys utilizing the 5-7 codes. Codes for 8 (Disfiguring impairments) and 9 (Generalized impairments) that were used by the 55 countries are not shown in table 3 of the *Compendium*. Statistics for disfigurement and generalized impairments are, however, available in DISTAT and are also utilized as columns in tables 6 through 12 of the *Compendium*.

Impairment description	ICIDH code	Number of surveys coded into this category
CODE 5: OCULAR IMPAIRMENTS		
Ocular	5.0	20
Total visual loss, both eyes	51.0	29
Near-total visual loss: both eyes	51.3	5
Moderate visual loss: both eyes	53	1
Unspecified moderate visual loss: both eyes	53.9	1
Profound visual impairment: one eye	54.0	7
Near-total visual loss: one eye, other not stated	54.5	1
Other visual impairment	57	3
Other visual, colour vision	57.5	2
Other vision	57.8	4
CODE 6: VISCERAL		
Visceral	6	5
Cardio-respiratory function	61	7
Shortness of breath	61.0	3
Other breathing disturbances	61.1	2
Other respiratory disturbance	61.11*	1
Other respiratory disturbances	61.12*	1
Other cardio-respiratory function	61.8	5
Gastro-intestinal function	62	3
Unspecified gastro-intestinal function	62.9	1
Urinary function	63	1
Other urinary function	63.8	1
Reproductive function	64	1
Other reproductive function	64.9	1
Internal organ deficiency	65	1
Other internal organ deficiency	65.9	1
Other internal organ	66	2
Other internal organs	66.8	3
Mastication and swallowing	68	1
Olfaction and other special functions	69	2

Impairment description	ICIDH code	Number of surveys coded into this category
(continued)		
CODE 7: SKELETAL		
Skeletal	7	4
Skeletal and/or motor	7.1*	7
Mechanical and motor of face	70.2	1
Posture	70.5	8
Unspecified posture	70.59	2
Dwarfism	70.6	1
Mechanical of limb	71	1
Mixed and other upper limb: mechanical	71.8	6
Mixed and other mechanical of limb	71.9	7
Bilateral complete paralysis of lower limb: paraplegia	72.3	7
Unspecified spastic paralysis of more than one limb	72.9	3
Bilateral paralysis of upper limbs	73.0	2
Paralysis of dominant upper limb	73.1	2
Other paralysis of lower limb	73.4	2
Paralysis of upper and lower limbs on same side	73.5	3
Paralysis of all four limbs	73.7	2
Other flaccid paralysis of limb	73.85	2
Unspecified other paralysis of limb	73.9	12
Other motor of limb	74	3
Other bilateral motor of upper limbs	74.0	3
Other motor of dominant upper limb	74.1	1
Other bilateral motor of lower limbs	74.3	2
Other motor of lower limb	74.4	2
Other motor impairment of limb: other	74.8	5
Unspecified other motor of limb	74.9	20
Unspecified other motor of limb: tremor NOS	74.92	1
Unspecified other motor of limb: limping NOS	74.97	1

Impairment description	ICIDH code	Number of surveys coded into this category
CODE 7 (*continued*)		
Transverse deficiency of upper arm	75.1	9
Transverse deficiency of upper arms	75.11*	2
Transverse deficiency of carpus	75.3	3
Transverse deficiency of carpi	75.31	1
Transverse deficiency of thigh	75.5	1
Transverse deficiency of lower leg	75.6	10
Transverse deficiency of lower legs	75.61	4
Transverse deficiency of tarsus	75.7	1
Transverse deficiency of tarsi	75.71	1
Transverse deficiencies, more than one site-proximal limb parts	75.8	3
Transverse deficiency unspecified of proximal limb parts	75.9	7
Other transverse deficiency of phalanges of fingers	76.3	2
Transverse deficiency of phalanges of fingers-first ray, complete	76.31	1

NOS: Not otherwise specified

*Not an ICIDH code, but devised to accommodate items not readily coded with ICIDH categories

Statistical definitions

The definitions of each of the impairment codes in table 3 of the *Compendium* are taken from WHO/ICIDH. They are as shown below.

Ocular impairments (5). Ocular impairments relate not only to the eye, but also to its associated structures and functions, including the eyelids. The most important subclass of ocular impairment is made up of impairments relating to the function of vision (*WHO/ICIDH. Manual*, p.78).

Total visual: both eyes (51.0). This category is defined in the *WHO/ICIDH Manual* as an impairment of visual acuity. This indicates that there is a total impairment of both eyes.

Profound visual: one eye (54). Profound visual impairment of one eye.

Unspecified other: Paralysis of limb (73.9). Other paralysis of limb with the nature of the paralysis unspecified.

Unspecified other: Motor, of limb (74.9). Other motor impairment of limb, with the nature of the impairment unspecified.

Transverse deficiency (75). Transverse deficiencies present, essentially as an amputation-like stump; they may arise as a failure of formation of the parts, or as the result of surgical intervention. A deficiency is customarily identified by the level at which the limb terminates (the most proximal part that is missing), it being understood that all elements distal to the level named are absent. The International Society for Prosthetics and Orthotics (ISPO) has developed a preferred nomenclature and has recommended abbreviations for describing the appropriate levels, and these have been incorporated in the classification (*WHO/ICIDH Manual*, p. 100-101).

(75.1) indicates a transverse deficiency of upper arm (Ar) and includes shoulder disarticulation.

(75.6) indicates a transverse deficiency of lower leg.

(75.9) indicates an unspecified transverse deficiency of proximal limb parts and includes upper limb (UL) transverse deficiency, lower limb (LL) transverse deficiency, and deficiency of hand or foot not otherwise specified.

Codes **8** and **9** are not utilized in table 3. They are, however, shown below for information since these codes are used in tables 6-12.

Impairment description	ICIDH code	Number of surveys coded into this category
CODE 8: DISFIGURING		
Deficiency in head region	75.6	10
Cleft palate	75.61	4
Other dentofacial deficiency	80.5	1
Other disfigurement of trunk	83	2
Congenital deformity	84	2
Congenital deformity: disfigurement of metacarpus and hand	84.03	1
Congenital deformity: disfigurement of knee and leg	84.06	1
Congenital deformity: disfigurement of ankle, foot and toe	84.07	1
Other disfigurement	87	6
Other and unspecified disfigurement	87.9	10
CODE 9: GENERALIZED		
Generalized, sensory and other	9	3
Multiple, of all classes	90.0	10
Other sensory: pain	98.3	2
Other	99	26
Unspecified other	99.9	8
Impairment status not ascertained	0	5

3. Disabled persons per 100,000 population by age and sex and by selected ocular, visceral, and skeletal impairments

Age and sex	Ocular	Total visual both eyes	Profound visual one eye	Unspecified other Paralysis of limb	Motor: of limb	Transverse deficiency Upper arm	Lower leg	Unspecified transverse deficiency of proximal limb parts
ICIDH	5	51.0	54	73.9	74.9	75.1	75.6	75.9

COMOROS, population census 1980

		Blind			*Motor*			*Loss of limb*
Males	..	201.7	..	..	664.9	..	..	82.0
0–4	..	14.3	..	..	167.7	..	..	28.5
5–9	..	50.0	..	..	396.3	..	..	33.3
10–14	..	52.1	..	..	386.3	..	..	69.4
15–19	..	85.4	..	..	617.7	..	..	46.0
20–24	..	95.8	..	..	478.9	..	..	78.4
25–29	..	115.6	..	..	504.3	..	..	115.6
30–34	..	146.9	..	..	802.4	..	..	22.6
35–39	..	246.1	..	..	902.5	..	..	191.4
40–44	..	213.3	..	..	1 242.3	..	..	112.9
45–49	..	282.5	..	..	1 311.5	..	..	282.5
50–54	..	452.4	..	..	1 085.8	..	..	162.9
55–59	..	548.4	..	..	1 608.8	..	..	219.4
60–64	..	603.9	..	..	1 718.9	..	..	162.6
65–59	..	1 046.8	..	..	2 203.9	..	..	275.5
70–74	..	1 347.3	..	..	2 170.7	..	..	112.3
75–79	..	1 748.6	..	..	2 404.4	..	..	218.6
80–84	..	2 799.7	..	..	2 624.7	..	..	262.5
85+	..	4 645.5	..	..	2 445.0	..	..	244.5
Not stated	..	266.3	..	..	1 331.6	..	..	0.0
Females	..	185.6	..	..	384.4	..	..	50.6
0–4	..	14.5	..	..	119.7	..	..	10.9
5–9	..	34.5	..	..	179.4	..	..	44.9
10–14	..	48.8	..	..	195.3	..	..	43.9
15–19	..	30.7	..	..	226.9	..	..	42.9
20–24	..	58.7	..	..	264.3	..	..	14.7
25–29	..	17.0	..	..	348.4	..	..	68.0
30–34	..	142.6	..	..	387.1	..	..	50.9
35–39	..	177.5	..	..	646.7	..	..	63.4
40–44	..	220.1	..	..	712.2	..	..	129.5
45–49	..	210.0	..	..	700.0	..	..	70.0
50–54	..	357.5	..	..	1 144.1	..	..	107.3
55–59	..	470.9	..	..	1 198.6	..	..	42.8
60–64	..	864.6	..	..	1 008.6	..	..	120.1
65–59	..	800.5	..	..	1 200.8	..	..	133.4
70–74	..	1 306.7	..	..	1 306.7	..	..	115.3
75–79	..	2 356.0	..	..	1 701.6	..	..	0.0
80–84	..	2 698.5	..	..	1 233.6	..	..	231.3
85+	..	5 537.8	..	..	1 597.4	..	..	0.0
Not stated	..	230.4	..	..	691.2	..	..	0.0

Note. Column headings in italics show the national terminology.

Table 3 *(continued)*

Age and sex	Ocular	Total visual both eyes	Profound visual one eye	Unspecified other Paralysis of limb	Motor: of limb	Transverse deficiency Upper arm	Lower leg	Unspecified transverse deficiency of proximal limb parts
ICIDH	5	51.0	54	73.9	74.9	75.1	75.6	75.9

EGYPT, population census 1976

		Blind	*Sight loss in one eye*			*Loss of upper limbs*	*Loss of lower limbs*	
Males	..	105.9	77.6	..	..	33.3	27.2	..
0-4	..	2.6	0.6	..	..	0.5	0.6	..
5-9	..	79.5	8.6	..	..	2.8	3.5	..
10-14	..	104.5	20.6	..	..	7.5	10.8	..
15-19	..	69.7	47.8	..	..	12.0	23.0	..
20-24	..	60.2	81.5	..	..	28.1	34.7	..
25-29	..	50.1	93.7	..	..	49.0	44.1	..
30-34	..	67.7	121.7	..	..	63.2	46.7	..
35-39	..	83.2	149.8	..	..	70.6	40.1	..
40-44	..	114.0	163.1	..	..	78.7	46.4	..
45-49	..	123.0	172.9	..	..	83.1	50.3	..
50-54	..	174.6	195.8	..	..	81.3	59.4	..
55-59	..	236.9	213.7	..	..	86.3	60.6	..
60-64	..	344.6	198.4	..	..	89.2	60.2	..
65-69	..	478.8	187.5	..	..	72.2	58.4	..
70-74	..	680.8	165.5	..	..	60.8	59.8	..
75+	..	988.3	167.3	..	..	48.2	49.4	..
Not stated	..	387.9	232.7	..	..	116.4	77.6	..
Females	..	69.5	23.3	..	..	2.9	3.3	..
0-4	..	1.8	0.9	..	..	0.1	0.3	..
5-9	..	52.2	5.1	..	..	2.0	1.9	..
10-14	..	57.0	9.6	..	..	2.7	2.8	..
15-19	..	46.1	18.2	..	..	2.9	3.3	..
20-24	..	35.3	24.2	..	..	3.0	3.3	..
25-29	..	21.4	23.0	..	..	2.1	2.9	..
30-34	..	35.4	26.6	..	..	2.9	2.7	..
35-39	..	34.9	30.0	..	..	3.7	3.5	..
40-44	..	58.0	37.8	..	..	3.9	4.3	..
45-49	..	59.3	38.9	..	..	4.6	3.5	..
50-54	..	110.0	48.9	..	..	4.3	5.9	..
55-59	..	128.6	58.7	..	..	5.3	6.8	..
60-64	..	253.3	69.9	..	..	7.3	9.0	..
65-69	..	346.1	84.2	..	..	5.8	7.0	..
70-74	..	572.1	92.0	..	..	7.7	13.2	..
75+	..	893.9	91.4	..	..	6.7	14.4	..
Not stated	..	188.9	125.9	..	..	0.0	0.0	..

ETHIOPIA, survey of children 1981

		Visual (blind)	*Paralysis*			*Arm amputation*	*Leg amputation*	
Both sexes 0-14	..	27.3	..	68.7	..	3.4	2.2	

Note. Column headings in italics show the national terminology.

Table 3 *(continued)*

Age and sex	Ocular	Total visual both eyes	Profound visual one eye	Unspecified other Paralysis of limb	Motor: of limb	Transverse deficiency Upper arm	Lower leg	Unspecified transverse deficiency of proximal limb parts
ICIDH	**5**	**51.0**	**54**	**73.9**	**74.9**	**75.1**	**75.6**	**75.9**

MALI, population census 1976

Blindness

Males	..	760.8	..	..	..	..	..	..
0–4	..	45.0	..	..	..	..	..	..
5–9	..	119.9	..	..	..	..	..	..
10–14	..	127.2	..	..	..	..	..	..
15–19	..	176.0	..	..	..	..	..	..
20–24	..	267.9	..	..	..	..	..	..
25–29	..	424.8	..	..	..	..	..	..
30–34	..	666.6	..	..	..	..	..	..
35–39	..	852.6	..	..	..	..	..	..
40–44	..	1 185.6	..	..	..	..	..	..
45–49	..	1 539.6	..	..	..	..	..	..
50–54	..	2 043.6	..	..	..	..	..	..
55–59	..	2 473.6	..	..	..	..	..	..
60–64	..	3 621.8	..	..	..	..	..	..
65–69	..	4 374.5	..	..	..	..	..	..
70–74	..	6 302.9	..	..	..	..	..	..
75–79	..	7 796.4	..	..	..	..	..	..
80–84	..	8 104.5	..	..	..	..	..	..
85–89	..	9 659.5	..	..	..	..	..	..
90–94	..	9 847.4	..	..	..	..	..	..
95+	..	10 924.4	..	..	..	..	..	..
Not stated	..	503.8	..	..	..	..	..	..
Females	..	772.7	..	..	..	..	..	..
0–4	..	43.8	..	..	..	..	..	..
5–9	..	85.7	..	..	..	..	..	..
10–14	..	121.1	..	..	..	..	..	..
15–19	..	331.6	..	..	..	..	..	..
20–24	..	515.0	..	..	..	..	..	..
25–29	..	585.4	..	..	..	..	..	..
30–34	..	744.9	..	..	..	..	..	..
35–39	..	855.1	..	..	..	..	..	..
40–44	..	1 116.2	..	..	..	..	..	..
45–49	..	1 389.5	..	..	..	..	..	..
50–54	..	1 903.3	..	..	..	..	..	..
55–59	..	2 290.3	..	..	..	..	..	..
60–64	..	3 343.7	..	..	..	..	..	..
65–69	..	4 547.7	..	..	..	..	..	..
70–74	..	5 846.8	..	..	..	..	..	..
75–79	..	7 304.2	..	..	..	..	..	..
80–84	..	7 963.7	..	..	..	..	..	..
85–89	..	9 026.5	..	..	..	..	..	..
90–94	..	8 870.8	..	..	..	..	..	..
95+	..	9 934.4	..	..	..	..	..	..
Not stated	..	802.1	..	..	..	..	..	..

Note. Column headings in italics show the national terminology.

Table 3 *(continued)*

Age and sex	Ocular	Total visual both eyes	Profound visual one eye	Unspecified other Paralysis of limb	Motor: of limb	Transverse deficiency Upper arm	Lower leg	Unspecified transverse deficiency of proximal limb parts
ICIDH	5	51.0	54	73.9	74.9	75.1	75.6	75.9

ST. HELENA, national survey 1976

		Blind						
Males	..	198.9	..	..	..	..	..	..
Females	..	151.9	..	..	..	..	..	..

SWAZILAND, national survey 1983

		Blind		*Physically disabled*				
Both sexes	..	352.6	..	..	1 327.5	..	..	..

Note. Column headings in italics show the national terminology.

Table 3 *(continued)*

Age and sex	Ocular	Total visual both eyes	Profound visual one eye	Unspecified other Paralysis of limb	Motor: of limb	Transverse deficiency Upper arm	Lower leg	Unspecified transverse deficiency of proximal limb parts
ICIDH	5	51.0	54	73.9	74.9	75.1	75.6	75.9

TUNISIA, population census 1975

		Blind			*Motor impairment*			
Males	..	241.9	..	..	293.2	..	..	..
0-4	..	6.6	..	..	24.2	..	..	..
5-9	..	36.0	..	..	93.5	..	..	..
10-14	..	45.2	..	..	151.4	..	..	..
15-19	..	74.8	..	..	239.9	..	..	..
20-29	..	111.3	..	..	284.8	..	..	..
30-39	..	166.4	..	..	279.8	..	..	..
40-49	..	284.9	..	..	429.3	..	..	..
50-59	..	636.7	..	..	740.9	..	..	..
60+	..	1 961.8	..	..	1 243.4	..	..	..
Not stated	..	466.2	..	..	233.1	..	..	..
Females	..	202.2	..	..	148.0	..	..	..
0-4	..	6.9	..	..	22.9	..	..	..
5-9	..	17.6	..	..	77.8	..	..	..
10-14	..	36.5	..	..	103.9	..	..	..
15-19	..	32.5	..	..	146.4	..	..	..
20-29	..	77.5	..	..	113.9	..	..	..
30-39	..	124.8	..	..	128.2	..	..	..
40-49	..	221.0	..	..	148.7	..	..	..
50-59	..	494.6	..	..	208.3	..	..	..
60+	..	2 250.9	..	..	905.9	..	..	..
Not stated	..	266.0	..	..	266.0	..	..	..

TUNISIA, population census 1984

		Blind			*Motor impairment*			
Males	..	204.5	..	..	393.7	..	..	..
< 5	..	17.3	..	..	11.5	..	..	..
5-14	..	31.2	..	..	123.8	..	..	..
15-59	..	171.5	..	..	450.8	..	..	..
60+	..	1 437.6	..	..	1 703.9	..	..	..
Females	..	141.7	..	..	231.2	..	..	..
< 5	..	22.3	..	..	22.3	..	..	..
5-14	..	34.0	..	..	96.1	..	..	..
15-59	..	108.5	..	..	246.8	..	..	..
60+	..	1 153.4	..	..	1 129.6	..	..	..

Note. Column headings in italics show the national terminology.

Table 3 *(continued)*

Age and sex	Ocular	Total visual both eyes	Profound visual one eye	Unspecified other Paralysis of limb	Motor: of limb	Transverse deficiency Upper arm	Lower leg	Unspecified transverse deficiency of proximal limb parts
ICIDH	5	51	54	73.9	74.9	75.1	75.6	75.9

CANADA, health and disability survey 1983-84 a/

	Seeing				*Mobility*			
Males	1 432.1	..	..	..	6 903.9	..	..	..
15-34	415.1	..	..	..	1 775.8	..	..	..
35-54	891.3	..	..	..	4 936.6	..	..	..
55-64	1 841.6	..	..	..	16 114.2	..	..	..
65+	6 883.0	..	..	..	24 483.8	..	..	..
Females	2 014.5	..	..	..	9 745.4	..	..	..
15-34	461.5	..	..	..	2 584.2	..	..	..
35-54	924.0	..	..	..	7 084.2	..	..	..
55-64	2 282.3	..	..	..	18 596.8	..	..	..
65+	9 186.0	..	..	..	30 843.9	..	..	..
Both sexes	1 729.7	..	..	..	8 350.8	..	..	..
15-34	426.8	..	..	..	2 179.9	..	..	..
35-54	907.5	..	..	..	6 027.4	..	..	..
55-64	2 114.5	..	..	..	17 444.9	..	..	..
65+	8 191.9	..	..	..	28 098.5	..	..	..

JAMAICA, survey of handicapped children in schools 1978 b/

	Visual				*Physical*			
Males 4-11	48	..	..	..	8	..	..	..
Females 4-11	47	..	..	..	4	..	..	..

----

a/ Since these national labels were coded into DISTAT, it was concluded that the Canadian definitions were actually disabilities and not impairments. ICIDH disability codes for seeing(5), and mobility(4) should have been used, rather than the above mentioned impairment codes.

b/ Figures for this country show actual number of disabled persons by age and sex and by selected ocular, visceral and skeletal impairments.

Note. Column headings in italics show the national terminology.

Table 3 *(continued)*

Age and sex	Ocular	Total visual both eyes	Profound visual one eye	Unspecified other Paralysis of limb	Motor: of limb	Transverse deficiency Upper arm	Lower leg	Unspecified transverse deficiency of proximal limb parts
ICIDH	5	51.0	54	73.9	74.9	75.1	75.6	75.9

NETHERLANDS ANTILLES, general census of population and housing 1981.

		Blind			*Physical*			
Males	..	240.8	..	..	1 154.7	..	..	..
0-4	..	28.4	..	..	293.1	..	..	..
5-9	..	26.1	..	..	530.7	..	..	..
10-14	..	49.9	..	..	499.2	..	..	..
15-19	..	22.2	..	..	718.5	..	..	..
20-24	..	52.4	..	..	873.4	..	..	..
25-29	..	63.6	..	..	667.7	..	..	..
30-34	..	46.4	..	..	730.4	..	..	..
35-39	..	200.9	..	..	731.8	..	..	..
40-44	..	168.7	..	..	1 298.9	..	..	..
45-49	..	214.7	..	..	1 639.3	..	..	..
50-54	..	306.3	..	..	1 955.7	..	..	..
55-59	..	493.5	..	..	2 699.6	..	..	..
60-64	..	765.0	..	..	3 685.7	..	..	..
65-69	..	487.6	..	..	3 856.4	..	..	..
70-74	..	1 954.2	..	..	4 957.1	..	..	..
75-79	..	3 724.2	..	..	5 388.3	..	..	..
80-84	..	4 795.7	..	..	7 815.3	..	..	..
85+	..	9 187.3	..	..	8 127.2	..	..	..
Females	..	270.5	..	..	821.5	..	..	..
0-4	..	69.1	..	..	365.2	..	..	..
5-9	..	45.0	..	..	306.2	..	..	..
10-14	..	59.6	..	..	485.3	..	..	..
15-19	..	30.3	..	..	356.6	..	..	..
20-24	..	61.0	..	..	357.0	..	..	..
25-29	..	37.2	..	..	549.1	..	..	..
30-34	..	52.0	..	..	437.0	..	..	..
35-39	..	24.8	..	..	582.0	..	..	..
40-44	..	57.3	..	..	530.2	..	..	..
45-49	..	191.1	..	..	972.7	..	..	..
50-54	..	106.1	..	..	955.0	..	..	..
55-59	..	260.7	..	..	1 251.3	..	..	..
60-64	..	577.5	..	..	2 252.4	..	..	..
65-69	..	647.9	..	..	2 123.8	..	..	..
70-74	..	1 634.9	..	..	3 425.5	..	..	..
75-79	..	2 463.9	..	..	5 288.5	..	..	..
80-84	..	6 222.2	..	..	4 711.1	..	..	..
85+	..	7 497.0	..	..	8 222.5	..	..	..

Note. Column headings in italics show the national terminology.

Table 3 *(continued)*

Age and sex	Ocular	Total visual both eyes	Profound visual one eye	Unspecified other Paralysis of limb	Motor: of limb	Transverse deficiency Upper arm	Lower leg	Unspecified transverse deficiency of proximal limb parts
ICIDH	5	51.0	54	73.9	74.9	75.1	75.6	75.9

PANAMA, general census of population and housing 1980

Blind

Males 0-39	..	32.4	..	..	..	..	..	..
Females 0-39	..	24.4	..	..	..	..	..	..

TRINIDAD AND TOBAGO, survey of children 1982 b/ c/

	Visual				*Physical*			
Both sexes 3-16	317	..	..	..	43	..	..	..

UNITED STATES, national health interview survey, 1982
(Survey of civilian and non-institutionalized population)

	Visual			*Paralysis of extremities*				
Males								
< 45	3 240.0	..	..	290.0	..	..	..	..
45-64	7 120.0	..	..	*1 020.0	..	..	..	..
65-74	10 190.0	..	..	*2 590.0	..	..	..	..
75+	15 700.0	..	..	*1 970.0	..	..	..	..
Females								
< 45	1 560.0	..	..	*270.0	..	..	..	..
45-64	3 730.0	..	..	*610.0	..	..	..	..
65-74	6 440.0	..	..	*1 590.0	..	..	..	..
75+	12 210.0	..	..	*2 060.0	..	..	..	..

----

b/ Figures for this country show actual number of disabled persons by age and sex and by selected ocular, visceral and skeletal impairments.

c/ Non-response rates were significant (each about 50 per cent) at the two stages of screening and examination of the children in this survey.

* Refers to an estimate for which numerator has a relative standard error greater than 30 per cent.

Note. Column headings in italics show the national terminology.

Table 3 *(continued)*

Age and sex	Ocular	Total visual both eyes	Profound visual one eye	Unspecified other		Transverse deficiency		Unspecified transverse deficiency of proximal limb parts
				Paralysis of limb	Motor: of limb	Upper arm	Lower leg	
ICIDH	5	51.0	54	73.9	74.9	75.1	75.6	75.9

PERU, national census of population and housing 1981

Blind

Both sexes	..	19.2		..	..	..	..	..	..

Note. Column headings in italics show the national terminology.

Table 3 *(continued)*

Age and sex	Ocular	Total visual both eyes	Profound visual one eye	Unspecified other Paralysis of limb	Motor: of limb	Transverse deficiency Upper arm	Lower leg	Unspecified transverse deficiency of proximal limb parts
ICIDH	**5**	**51.0**	**54**	**73.9**	**74.9**	**75.1**	**75.6**	**75.9**

BAHRAIN, population census 1981

		Blind		*Paralysed*				*Amputee*
Males	..	343.8	..	159.7	..	..	..	115.7
0-4	..	9.0	..	72.2				
5-9	..	58.2	..	153.4	..	..	..	13.5
10-14	..	75.6	..	174.4	..	..	..	21.2
15-19	..	118.2	..	230.8	..	..	..	11.6
20-24	..	140.9	..	72.5	..	..	..	61.9
25-29	..	95.1	..	55.8	..	..	..	48.3
30-34	..	131.2	..	49.8	..	..	..	36.1
35-39	..	155.9	..	70.9	..	..	..	54.3
40-44	..	271.3	..	78.8	..	..	..	120.4
45-49	..	620.1	..	97.3	..	..	..	157.5
50-54	..	957.9	..	345.5	..	..	..	316.1
55-59	..	1 661.8	..	391.0	..	..	..	455.4
60-64	..	3 004.3	..	1 089.5	..	..	..	537.6
65-69	..	3 838.9	..	1 132.8	..	..	..	858.4
70+	..	7 229.4	..	1 979.0	..	..	..	1 321.6
					..	..	..	928.9
Females	..	333.6	..	166.4	..	..	..	49.3
0-4	..	23.2	..	32.4				
5-9	..	10.8	..	134.5	..	..	..	4.6
10-14	..	47.0	..	117.6	..	..	..	16.1
15-19	..	56.7	..	136.0	..	..	..	17.6
20-24	..	65.8	..	119.7	..	..	..	22.7
25-29	..	21.9	..	65.8	..	..	..	12.0
30-34	..	121.0	..	110.0	..	..	..	21.9
35-39	..	293.4	..	69.9	..	..	..	0.0
40-44	..	342.8	..	62.3	..	..	..	14.0
45-49	..	386.5	..	96.6	..	..	..	77.9
50-54	..	1 363.1	..	376.0	..	..	..	173.9
55-59	..	1 851.2	..	370.2	..	..	..	188.0
60-64	..	2 644.1	..	693.5	..	..	..	222.1
65-69	..	3 755.9	..	626.0	..	..	..	390.1
70+	..	6 484.9	..	2 643.5	..	..	..	391.2
					..	..	..	537.0

Note. Column headings in italics show the national terminology.

Table 3 *(continued)*

Age and sex	Ocular	Total visual both eyes	Profound visual one eye	Unspecified other		Transverse deficiency		Unspecified transverse deficiency of proximal limb parts
				Paralysis of limb	Motor: of limb	Upper arm	Lower leg	
ICIDH	5	51.0	54	73.9	74.9	75.1	75.6	75.9

CHINA, annual population survey 1983
(special children's question on disability)

Age and sex	Ocular	*Blind* Total visual both eyes	Profound visual one eye	Paralysis of limb	Motor: of limb	Upper arm	Lower leg	Unspecified...
Males	..	25.9	..	..	..	..	..	..
0	..	0.0	..	..	..	..	..	..
1	..	17.1	..	..	..	..	..	..
2	..	53.8	..	..	..	..	..	..
3	..	0.0	..	..	..	..	..	..
4	..	18.1	..	..	..	..	..	..
5	..	37.5	..	..	..	..	..	..
6	..	0.0	..	..	..	..	..	..
7	..	36.2	..	..	..	..	..	..
8	..	34.4	..	..	..	..	..	..
9	..	31.1	..	..	..	..	..	..
10	..	44.3	..	..	..	..	..	..
11	..	13.7	..	..	..	..	..	..
12	..	38.8	..	..	..	..	..	..
13	..	38.0	..	..	..	..	..	..
14	..	13.1	..	..	..	..	..	..
Females	..	13.9	..	..	..	..	..	..
0	..	0.0	..	..	..	..	..	..
1	..	18.7	..	..	..	..	..	..
2	..	19.5	..	..	..	..	..	..
3	..	0.0	..	..	..	..	..	..
4	..	0.0	..	..	..	..	..	..
5	..	0.0	..	..	..	..	..	..
6	..	41.4	..	..	..	..	..	..
7	..	19.2	..	..	..	..	..	..
8	..	0.0	..	..	..	..	..	..
9	..	50.0	..	..	..	..	..	..
10	..	15.4	..	..	..	..	..	..
11	..	15.0	..	..	..	..	..	..
12	..	0.0	..	..	..	..	..	..
13	..	13.4	..	..	..	..	..	..
14	..	14.0	..	..	..	..	..	..

Note. Column headings in italics show the national terminology.

Table 3 *(continued)*

Age and sex	Ocular	Total visual both eyes	Profound visual one eye	Unspecified other Paralysis of limb	Motor: of limb	Transverse deficiency Upper arm	Lower leg	Unspecified transverse deficiency of proximal limb parts
ICIDH	5	51.0	54	73.9	74.9	75.1	75.6	75.9

HONG, KONG population census 1981

		Blind			*Physically disabled*			
Both sexes	..	88.0	..	..	309.0	..	..	..
0–4	..	5.0	..	..	28.0	..	..	..
5–9	..	10.0	..	..	39.0	..	..	..
10–14	..	4.0	..	..	86.0	..	..	..
0–14	..	..	..	..	..	..	..	..
15–19	..	8.0	..	..	144.0	..	..	..
20–24	..	14.0	..	..	206.0	..	..	..
25–29	..	28.0	..	..	195.0	..	..	..
30–34	..	29.0	..	..	176.0	..	..	..
35–39	..	52.0	..	..	142.0	..	..	..
40–44	..	60.0	..	..	183.0	..	..	..
45–49	..	89.0	..	..	234.0	..	..	..
50+	..	..	..	..	..	..	..	..
50–54	..	113.0	..	..	303.0	..	..	..
55–59	..	134.0	..	..	465.0	..	..	..
60–64	..	216.0	..	..	914.0	..	..	..
65+	..	759.0	..	..	1 930.0	..	..	..

Note. Column headings in italics show the national terminology.

Table 3 *(continued)*

Age and sex	Ocular	Total visual both eyes	Profound visual one eye	Unspecified other Paralysis of limb	Motor: of limb	Transverse deficiency Upper arm	Lower leg	Unspecified transverse deficiency of proximal limb parts
ICIDH	5	51.0	54	73.9	74.9	75.1	75.6	75.9

INDIA, national survey of handicapped 1981

	Visual			*Locomotor*				
Urban								
Males	294.0	..	..	..	800.0	..	..	..
0-4	29.0	..	..	..	628.0	..	..	..
5-14	100.0	..	..	..	859.0	..	..	..
15-39	136.0	..	..	..	601.0	..	..	..
40-59	281.0	..	..	..	873.0	..	..	..
60+	3 291.0	..	..	..	2 444.0	..	..	..
Females	425.0	..	..	..	544.0	..	..	..
0-4	21.0	..	..	..	448.0	..	..	..
5-14	72.0	..	..	..	562.0	..	..	..
15-39	96.0	..	..	..	346.0	..	..	..
40-59	467.0	..	..	..	560.0	..	..	..
60+	4 968.0	..	..	..	2 060.0	..	..	..
Rural								
Males	444.0	..	..	..	1 047.0	..	..	..
0-4	41.0	..	..	..	522.0	..	..	..
5-14	71.0	..	..	..	817.0	..	..	..
15-39	125.0	..	..	..	876.0	..	..	..
40-59	462.0	..	..	..	1 458.0	..	..	..
60+	4 573.0	..	..	..	3 079.0	..	..	..
Females	670.0	..	..	..	597.0	..	..	..
0-4	37.0	..	..	..	342.0	..	..	..
5-14	60.0	..	..	..	515.0	..	..	..
15-39	106.0	..	..	..	402.0	..	..	..
40-59	715.0	..	..	..	744.0	..	..	..
60+	7 155.0	..	..	..	2 154.0	..	..	..

Note. Column headings in italics show the national terminology.

Table 3 *(continued)*

Age and sex	Ocular	Total visual both eyes	Profound visual one eye	Unspecified other Paralysis of limb	Motor: of limb	Transverse deficiency Upper arm	Lower leg	Unspecified transverse deficiency of proximal limb parts
ICIDH	5	51.0	54	73.9	74.9	75.1	75.6	75.9

INDONESIA, population census 1980

		Blind			*Physical handicap*			
Both sexes	..	126.4	..	..	182.4	..	..	..
0-14	..	68.6	..	..	160.1	..	..	..
15+	..	166.2	..	..	197.8	..	..	..

JAPAN, national survey of handicapped adults 1980 b/

	Visual			*Physical*				
Both sexes	336 000	..	..	..	1 127 000	..	..	..

JORDAN, national registration campaign 1979 b/

		Blind		*Partially paralysed*	*Amputation* Arm	Leg	
Total	..	2 088	..	4 857	78	352	..

----

b/ Figures for this country show actual number of disabled persons by age and sex and by selected ocular, visceral and skeletal impairments.

Note. Column headings in italics show the national terminology.

Table 3 *(continued)*

Age and sex	Ocular	Total visual both eyes	Profound visual one eye	Unspecified other Paralysis of limb	Motor: of limb	Transverse deficiency Upper arm	Lower leg	Unspecified transverse deficiency of proximal limb parts
ICIDH	5	51.0	54	73.9	74.9	75.1	75.6	75.9

JORDAN, agricultural census 1983 b/

	Visual				*Physical*			
Males	740	..	..	..	2490	..	..	..
0–4	22	..	..	..	181	..	..	..
5–9	37	..	..	..	332	..	..	..
10–14	41	..	..	..	377	..	..	..
15–19	40	..	..	..	301	..	..	..
20–24	32	..	..	..	179	..	..	..
25–29	35	..	..	..	96	..	..	..
30–34	26	..	..	..	77	..	..	..
35–39	41	..	..	..	86	..	..	..
40–44	32	..	..	..	99	..	..	..
45–49	35	..	..	..	81	..	..	..
50–54	53	..	..	..	105	..	..	..
55–59	37	..	..	..	85	..	..	..
60–64	60	..	..	..	114	..	..	..
65+	249	..	..	..	377	..	..	..
Females	496	..	..	..	1 338	..	..	..
0–4	16	..	..	..	120	..	..	..
5–9	27	..	..	..	211	..	..	..
10–14	34	..	..	..	222	..	..	..
15–19	36	..	..	..	180	..	..	..
20–24	19	..	..	..	96	..	..	..
25–29	12	..	..	..	69	..	..	..
30–34	14	..	..	..	21	..	..	..
35–39	29	..	..	..	31	..	..	..
40–44	20	..	..	..	39	..	..	..
45–49	23	..	..	..	33	..	..	..
50–54	34	..	..	..	41	..	..	..
55–59	23	..	..	..	26	..	..	..
60–64	33	..	..	..	51	..	..	..
65+	176	..	..	..	198	..	..	..

b/ Figures for this country show actual number of disabled persons by age and sex and by selected ocular, visceral and skeletal impairments.

Note. Column headings in italics show the national terminology.

Table 3 *(continued)*

Age and sex	Ocular	Total visual both eyes	Profound visual one eye	Unspecified other		Transverse deficiency		Unspecified transverse deficiency of proximal limb parts
				Paralysis of limb	Motor: of limb	Upper arm	Lower leg	
ICIDH	5	51.0	54	73.9	74.9	75.1	75.6	75.9

KUWAIT, population census 1980

		Blind	*Sight in one eye*	*Paralysis*		*Loss of arm*	*Loss of leg*	
Males	..	60.8	61.8	101.8	..	5.0	9.1	..
0-4	..	4.6	1.8	19.4	..	0.9	0.0	..
5-9	..	8.6	2.2	134.5	..	3.2	3.2	..
10-14	..	15.7	13.1	220.4	..	3.9	14.4	..
15-19	..	21.8	24.9	247.4	..	6.2	12.4	..
20-24	..	9.7	42.8	85.5	..	8.3	2.8	..
25-29	..	19.8	46.7	26.8	..	1.2	5.8	..
30-34	..	24.9	51.2	34.1	..	5.2	6.6	..
35-39	..	36.6	84.3	22.3	..	4.8	8.0	..
40-44	..	47.8	124.4	28.7	..	3.8	11.5	..
45-49	..	70.0	131.3	58.3	..	14.6	20.4	..
50-54	..	138.7	199.4	95.4	..	8.7	34.7	..
55-59	..	392.9	334.4	259.2	..	25.1	41.8	..
60-64	..	634.0	358.4	358.4	..	27.6	0.0	..
65-69	..	1 425.6	660.0	739.2	..	0.0	79.2	..
70-74	..	1 981.0	911.3	832.0	..	0.0	79.2	..
75-79	..	2 773.2	571.0	1 141.9	..	0.0	81.6	..
80-84	..	4 218.9	798.2	1 254.3	..	0.0	0.0	..
85+	..	3 321.0	553.5	922.5	..	0.0	0.0	..
Females	..	40.9	22.4	92.0	..	0.9	4.0	..
0-4	..	2.9	1.0	22.9	..	1.0	2.9	..
5-9	..	12.2	6.7	123.5	..	0.0	1.1	..
10-14	..	13.5	5.4	143.6	..	1.4	4.1	..
15-19	..	10.8	10.8	171.0	..	0.0	1.8	..
20-24	..	13.5	13.5	92.6	..	0.0	1.9	..
25-29	..	9.5	11.4	30.3	..	0.0	1.9	..
30-34	..	13.5	20.2	29.2	..	2.2	4.5	..
35-39	..	47.5	41.5	14.8	..	3.0	3.0	..
40-44	..	83.6	51.8	39.8	..	0.0	11.9	..
45-49	..	67.2	85.5	67.2	..	0.0	0.0	..
50-54	..	175.3	96.4	113.9	..	0.0	8.8	..
55-59	..	140.1	70.0	140.1	..	14.0	0.0	..
60-64	..	368.2	140.3	263.0	..	0.0	17.5	..
65-69	..	550.3	214.0	336.3	..	0.0	0.0	..
70-74	..	746.8	485.4	522.8	..	0.0	37.3	..
75-79	..	1 489.2	74.5	968.0	..	0.0	74.5	..
80-84	..	2 081.2	416.2	936.5	..	0.0	104.1	..
85+	..	2 203.4	169.5	1 864.4	..	0.0	339.0	..

Note. Column headings in italics show the national terminology.

Table 3 *(continued)*

Age and sex	Ocular	Total visual both eyes	Profound visual one eye	Unspecified other Paralysis of limb	Motor: of limb	Transverse deficiency Upper arm	Lower leg	Unspecified transverse deficiency of proximal limb parts
ICIDH	**5**	**51.0**	**54**	**73.9**	**74.9**	**75.1**	**75.6**	**75.9**

LEBANON, national survey of handicapped 1981 b/

		Blind only		*Paralysis only*	*Other physical only*			*Loss of limb only*
Both sexes								
Total disabled	..	1 266	..	4 962	542	..	..	979
Total disabilities	..	1 576	..	6 852	1 353	..	..	1 051

NEPAL, national survey 1980

	Total visual	*Bilateral sight loss/ blind*	*Loss of sight in one eye*					
Both sexes	886.0	485.0	401.0	..	..	..	..	..
<5	116.0	116.0	0.0	..	..	..	..	..
5-14	216.0	90.0	126.0	..	..	..	..	..
15-24	415.0	224.0	191.0	..	..	..	..	..
25-39	860.0	488.0	372.0	..	..	..	..	..
40-59	2 096.0	1 000.0	1 096.0	..	..	..	..	..
60-74	3 662.0	2 426.0	1 236.0	..	..	..	..	..
75+	6 856.0	3 783.0	3 073.0	..	..	..	..	..

b/ Figures for this country show actual number of disabled persons by age and sex and by selected ocular, visceral and skeletal impairments.

Note. Column headings in italics show the national terminology.

Table 3 *(continued)*

Age and sex	Ocular	Total visual both eyes	Profound visual one eye	Unspecified other Paralysis of limb	Motor: of limb	Transverse deficiency Upper arm	Lower leg	Unspecified transverse deficiency of proximal limb parts
ICIDH	5	51.0	54	73.9	74.9	75.1	75.6	75.9

PAKISTAN, population census 1981

Blind

Males	..	84.5	..	..	..	..	..	..
0-4	..	26.7	..	..	..	..	..	..
5-9	..	17.6	..	..	..	..	..	..
10-14	..	17.7	..	..	..	..	..	..
15-19	..	21.2	..	..	..	..	..	..
20-24	..	36.7	..	..	..	..	..	..
25-29	..	34.6	..	..	..	..	..	..
30-34	..	42.0	..	..	..	..	..	..
35-39	..	50.5	..	..	..	..	..	..
40-44	..	43.0	..	..	..	..	..	..
45-49	..	62.5	..	..	..	..	..	..
50-54	..	138.3	..	..	..	..	..	..
55-59	..	180.3	..	..	..	..	..	..
60+	..	655.2	..	..	..	..	..	..
Females	..	186.8	..	..	..	..	..	..
0-4	..	22.1	..	..	..	..	..	..
5-9	..	13.4	..	..	..	..	..	..
10-14	..	25.2	..	..	..	..	..	..
15-19	..	95.3	..	..	..	..	..	..
20-24	..	242.7	..	..	..	..	..	..
25-29	..	304.7	..	..	..	..	..	..
30-34	..	284.3	..	..	..	..	..	..
35-39	..	224.8	..	..	..	..	..	..
40-44	..	191.3	..	..	..	..	..	..
45-49	..	195.5	..	..	..	..	..	..
50-54	..	260.1	..	..	..	..	..	..
55-59	..	337.3	..	..	..	..	..	..
60+	..	1 127.6	..	..	..	..	..	..

Note. Column headings in italics show the national terminology.

Table 3 *(continued)*

Age and sex	Ocular	Total visual both eyes	Profound visual one eye	Unspecified other Paralysis of limb	Unspecified other Motor: of limb	Transverse deficiency Upper arm	Transverse deficiency Lower leg	Unspecified transverse deficiency of proximal limb parts
ICIDH	5	51.0	54	73.9	74.9	75.1	75.6	75.9

PHILIPPINES, national survey 1980

	Ocular
Males	479.2
< 15	218.8
15-64	563.5
65+	2 233.7
Females	428.8
< 15	266.9
15-64	442.9
65+	2 131.4

(Columns for Males and Females rows all show ".." for: Total visual both eyes, Profound visual one eye, Paralysis of limb, Motor of limb, Upper arm, Lower leg, proximal limb parts.)

		Blind both eyes	*Blind one eye*	*1-limb paralysis*	*Polio*	*Right and left upper*	*Right and left lower*	*More than one extremity*
Males	..	175.9	363.9	454.9	266.9	103.1	91.0	18.2
< 15	..	43.8	131.3	233.4	262.6	14.6	14.6	14.6
15-64	..	176.8	442.0	519.3	276.2	143.6	143.6	22.1
65+	..	1 718.2	1 890.0	2 061.9	171.8	515.5	171.8	0.0
Females	..	202.5	315.6	232.3	226.3	6.0	11.9	6.0
< 15	..	29.7	103.8	252.0	281.7	0.0	14.8	14.8
15-64	..	168.7	337.4	158.2	200.4	10.5	10.5	0.0
65+	..	2 841.9	2 486.7	1 243.3	0.0	0.0	0.0	0.0

Note. Column headings in italics show the national terminology.

Table 3 *(continued)*

Age and sex	Ocular	Total visual both eyes	Profound visual one eye	Unspecified other		Transverse deficiency		Unspecified transverse deficiency of proximal limb parts
				Paralysis of limb	Motor: of limb	Upper arm	Lower leg	
ICIDH	5	51.0	54	73.9	74.9	75.1	75.6	75.9

SINGAPORE, continuous registration system of disabld persons 1985 b/

	Visual				*Neuro-muscular*			
Both sexes	1 061	..	..	..	784	..	..	..
0-4	1	..	..	..	2	..	..	..
5-13	50	..	..	..	180	..	..	..
14-19	83	..	..	..	163	..	..	..
20-29	161	..	..	..	257	..	..	..
30-39	151	..	..	..	146	..	..	..
40-49	129	..	..	..	24	..	..	..
50-59	135	..	..	..	9	..	..	..
60-69	156	..	..	..	2	..	..	..
70-79	136	..	..	..	0	..	..	..
80+	59	..	..	..	1	..	..	..

b/ Figures for this country show actual number of disabled persons by age and sex and by selected ocular, visceral and skeletal impairments.

Note. Column headings in italics show the national terminology.

Table 3 (continued)

Age and sex	Ocular	Total visual both eyes	Profound visual one eye	Unspecified other Paralysis of limb	Motor: of limb	Transverse deficiency Upper arm	Lower leg	Unspecified transverse deficiency of proximal limb parts
ICIDH	5	51.0	54	73.9	74.9	75.1	75.6	75.9

SRI LANKA, population census 1981

		Blind					*Loss of one leg*	
Males	..	67.1	..	..	..	..	30.3	..
< 1	..	3.9	..	..	..	..	1.4	..
1-4	..	14.7	..	..	..	..	3.1	..
5-9	..	25.2	..	..	..	..	4.7	..
10-14	..	31.7	..	..	..	..	6.0	..
15-19	..	37.4	..	..	..	..	9.4	..
20-24	..	40.4	..	..	..	..	17.8	..
25-29	..	49.4	..	..	..	..	20.7	..
30-34	..	51.8	..	..	..	..	31.3	..
35-39	..	67.6	..	..	..	..	43.0	..
40-44	..	74.8	..	..	..	..	53.5	..
45-49	..	86.7	..	..	..	..	65.0	..
50-54	..	106.3	..	..	..	..	83.0	..
55-59	..	137.2	..	..	..	..	102.0	..
60-64	..	212.1	..	..	..	..	100.1	..
65-69	..	272.7	..	..	..	..	107.6	..
70-74	..	331.1	..	..	..	..	98.4	..
75+	..	511.8	..	..	..	..	100.5	..
Females	..	58.4	..	..	..	..	7.4	..
< 1	..	7.5	..	..	..	..	1.0	..
1-4	..	15.1	..	..	..	..	1.6	..
5-9	..	24.5	..	..	..	..	2.6	..
10-14	..	27.7	..	..	..	..	3.5	..
15-19	..	29.4	..	..	..	..	4.4	..
20-24	..	31.1	..	..	..	..	6.1	..
25-29	..	38.5	..	..	..	..	5.3	..
30-34	..	42.7	..	..	..	..	9.0	..
35-39	..	59.7	..	..	..	..	7.7	..
40-44	..	57.8	..	..	..	..	8.9	..
45-49	..	74.4	..	..	..	..	11.0	..
50-54	..	102.9	..	..	..	..	13.9	..
55-59	..	127.1	..	..	..	..	17.9	..
60-64	..	219.9	..	..	..	..	21.5	..
65-69	..	250.5	..	..	..	..	17.2	..
70-74	..	346.8	..	..	..	..	31.3	..
75+	..	494.5	..	..	..	..	37.9	..

Note. Column headings in italics show the national terminology.

Table 3 *(continued)*

Age and sex	Ocular	Total visual both eyes	Profound visual one eye	Unspecified other Paralysis of limb	Motor: of limb	Transverse deficiency Upper arm	Lower leg	Unspecified transverse deficiency of proximal limb parts
ICIDH	5	51.0	54	73.9	74.9	75.1	75.6	75.9

TURKEY, population census 1975

Age and sex		Blind	*Loss of sight in one eye*	*Paralysed*	*Lame*			
Males	..	139.6	250.0	52.0	493.3	..	..	..
0-4	..	75.6	47.1	18.9	106.1	..	..	..
5-9	..	43.3	70.8	41.5	272.6	..	..	..
10-14	..	69.2	169.1	38.6	303.1	..	..	..
15-19	..	56.0	118.8	43.8	333.3	..	..	..
20-24	..	78.3	181.1	40.6	366.9	..	..	..
25-29	..	93.1	197.4	40.6	419.9	..	..	..
30-34	..	154.4	313.7	36.8	550.6	..	..	..
35-39	..	152.7	321.9	38.7	670.5	..	..	..
40-44	..	170.6	358.0	45.4	784.0	..	..	..
45-49	..	190.3	407.1	55.9	879.2	..	..	..
50-54	..	244.1	474.7	76.6	1 013.3	..	..	..
55-59	..	332.5	667.9	105.0	1 261.1	..	..	..
60-64	..	432.3	822.5	163.4	1 377.5	..	..	..
65+	..	858.3	1 184.5	240.2	1 621.3	..	..	..
Unknown	..	89.9	118.6	19.1	181.8	..	..	..
Females	..	114.7	153.3	38.2	345.0	..	..	..
0-4	..	163.6	130.4	17.7	169.2	..	..	..
5-9	..	39.2	55.7	30.0	265.4	..	..	..
10-14	..	73.6	131.4	29.6	313.6	..	..	..
15-19	..	37.3	66.1	22.9	290.4	..	..	..
20-24	..	46.7	84.0	24.5	247.5	..	..	..
25-29	..	43.4	88.1	24.0	262.6	..	..	..
30-34	..	66.4	114.1	22.6	309.0	..	..	..
35-39	..	75.0	125.0	22.8	351.9	..	..	..
40-44	..	86.0	145.5	27.2	383.9	..	..	..
45-49	..	92.8	163.6	33.9	418.1	..	..	..
50-54	..	145.7	231.3	47.7	512.5	..	..	..
55-59	..	184.0	309.9	69.5	662.0	..	..	..
60-64	..	289.4	412.7	105.2	760.5	..	..	..
65+	..	642.0	724.6	205.6	973.9	..	..	..
Unknown	..	248.4	194.1	34.9	388.1	..	..	..

Note. Column headings in italics show the national terminology.

174

Table 3 *(continued)*

Age and sex	Ocular	Total visual both eyes	Profound visual one eye	Unspecified other Paralysis of limb	Motor: of limb	Transverse deficiency Upper arm	Lower leg	Unspecified transverse deficiency of proximal limb parts
ICIDH	**5**	**51.0**	**54**	**73.9**	**74.9**	**75.1**	**75.6**	**75.9**

AUSTRIA, sample survey on physical disabilities 1976

	Visual impair-ments	Blind in both eyes	Blind in one eye	Feet paralysed	Foot other	Arm missing	Lower leg missing	
Both sexes								
	8 392.2	67.1	520.3	..	..	..	..	..
0-5	639.8	5.8	37.7	..	..	..	..	..
6-9	1 868.0	0.0	100.9	..	..	..	..	..
10-14	2 473.5	0.0	56.9	..	..	..	..	..
15-19	2 335.9	0.0	121.5	..	..	..	..	..
20-29	3 141.6	37.7	267.0	..	..	..	..	..
30-39	4 011.3	0.0	268.8	..	..	..	..	..
40-49	5 139.0	15.4	231.3	..	..	..	..	..
50-59	12 819.6	153.8	564.1	..	..	..	..	..
60-69	17 568.1	17.6	1 018.9	..	..	..	..	..
70-79	26 650.6	186.6	1 998.8	..	..	..	..	..
80+	37 761.4	1 095.1	3 247.5	..	..	..	..	..
Males	7 136.1	71.4	620.8	43.0	891.3	154.8	100.3	..
Females	9 378.1	65.6	422.0	35.6	655.7	50.8	22.9	..

DENMARK, living conditions survey 1976

	Vision problems							
Males 20+	8 000.0	..	..	..	..	..	..	..
20-29	5 000.0	..	..	..	..	..	..	..
30-44	6 000.0	..	..	..	..	..	..	..
45-59	11 000.0	..	..	..	..	..	..	..
60-69	12 000.0	..	..	..	..	..	..	..
Females 20+	11 000.0	..	..	..	..	..	..	..
20-29	8 000.0	..	..	..	..	..	..	..
30-44	7 000.0	..	..	..	..	..	..	..
45-59	15 000.0	..	..	..	..	..	..	..
60-69	18 000.0	..	..	..	..	..	..	..
Both sexes 20+	9 000.0	..	..	..	..	..	..	..

Note. Column headings in italics show the national terminology.

Table 3 *(continued)*

| Age and sex | Ocular | Total visual both eyes | Profound visual one eye | Unspecified other | | Transverse deficiency | | Unspecified transverse deficiency of proximal limb parts |
				Paralysis of limb	Motor: of limb	Upper arm	Lower leg	
ICIDH	5	51.0	54	73.9	74.9	75.1	75.6	75.9

FINLAND, survey on living conditions 1978

Age and sex	*Diminished ability to see*							
Males 15+	3 000.0	..	..	..	..	..	..	..
15-24	0.0	..	..	..	..	..	..	..
25-44	1 000.0	..	..	..	..	..	..	..
45-64	8 000.0	..	..	..	..	..	..	..
65+	7 000.0	..	..	..	..	..	..	..
Females 15+	6 000.0	..	..	..	..	..	..	..
15-24	1 000.0	..	..	..	..	..	..	..
25-44	2 000.0	..	..	..	..	..	..	..
45-64	8 000.0	..	..	..	..	..	..	..
65+	19 000.0	..	..	..	..	..	..	..

FEDERAL REPUBLIC OF GERMANY, national sample survey 1983 b/ d/

Age and sex	*Blindness/ eye loss/ difficulty seeing*	*Blindness*			*One upper and one lower limb function reduced*	*Amputee one upper limb*	*Amputee one lower limb*	*Amputee of three or four limbs*
Both sexes	271 134	52 783	..	..	67 352	37 532	87 830	1 728
< 4	556	240	..	..	134	82	25	12
4-5	478	203	..	..	153	65	27	7
6-14	4 288	1 151	..	..	1 135	375	243	19
15-17	2 666	550	..	..	632	272	260	14
18-24	8 759	1 488	..	..	2 222	864	1 338	91
25-34	13 346	2 361	..	..	3 367	1 454	2 312	112
35-44	19 579	3 361	..	..	5 067	2 382	4 193	135
45-54	31 981	4 838	..	..	9 358	4 510	8 660	246
55-59	26 515	4 006	..	..	9 327	6 974	16 307	275
60-61	13 096	2 026	..	..	4 866	3 720	8 661	157
62-64	15 678	2 589	..	..	5 917	4 319	10 222	170
65+	134 192	29 970	..	..	25 174	12 515	35 582	490

b/ Figures for this country show actual numbers of disabled persons by age and sex and by selected ocular, visceral and skeletal impairments.

d/ These numbers exclude Bavaria, which did not specify these disability groups. The denominator is therefore smaller than that of the previous pages.

Note. Column headings in italics show the national terminology.

Table 3 *(continued)*

Age and sex	Ocular	Total visual both eyes	Profound visual one eye	Unspecified other Paralysis of limb	Motor: of limb	Transverse deficiency Upper arm	Lower leg	Unspecified transverse deficiency of proximal limb parts
ICIDH	**5**	**51.0**	**54**	**73.9**	**74.9**	**75.1**	**75.6**	**75.9**

FEDERAL REPUBLIC OF GERMANY, national sample survey 1983 b/ d/

					Reduction in all combina- tions limb function			*All combinations limb loss/ partial loss*
Both sexes	..	..	..	..	946 323	..	..	143 868
< 4	..	..	..	..	1 520	..	..	141
4–5	..	..	..	..	1 467	..	..	115
6–14	..	..	..	..	10 708	..	..	752
15–17	..	..	..	..	6 658	..	..	628
18–24	..	..	..	..	26 879	..	..	2 750
25–34	..	..	..	..	4 457	..	..	4 422
35–44	..	..	..	..	76 286	..	..	7 704
45–54	..	..	..	..	144 616	..	..	15 350
55–59	..	..	..	..	136 170	..	..	26 439
60–61	..	..	..	..	68 402	..	..	14 112
62–64	..	..	..	..	82 002	..	..	16 556
65+	..	..	..	..	346 858	..	..	54 899

NORWAY, level of living survey 1983

	Reduced eye sight							
Males	2 000.0	..	..	..	..	..	..	..
16–24	1 000.0	..	..	..	..	..	..	..
25–44	1 000.0	..	..	..	..	..	..	..
45–66	2 000.0	..	..	..	..	..	..	..
67–79	5 000.0	..	..	..	..	..	..	..
Females	2 000.0	..	..	..	..	..	..	..
16–24	1 000.0	..	..	..	..	..	..	..
25–44	1 000.0	..	..	..	..	..	..	..
45–66	2 000.0	..	..	..	..	..	..	..
67–79	8 000.0	..	..	..	..	..	..	..

---

b/ Figures for this country show actual numbers of disabled persons by age and sex and by selected ocular, visceral and skeletal impairments.

d/ These numbers exclude Bavaria, which did not specify these disability groups. The denominator is therefore smaller than that of the previous pages.

Note. Column headings in italics show the national terminology.

Table 3 *(continued)*

Age and sex	Ocular	Total visual both eyes	Profound visual one eye	Unspecified other Paralysis of limb	Unspecified other Motor: of limb	Transverse deficiency Upper arm	Transverse deficiency Lower leg	Unspecified transverse deficiency of proximal limb parts
ICIDH	**5**	**51.0**	**54**	**73.9**	**74.9**	**75.1**	**75.6**	**75.9**

SWEDEN, living conditions survey 1980/81

	Reduced eye sight							
Males	1 100.0	..	..	..	..	..	..	..
16-44	200.0	..	..	..	..	..	..	..
45-64	1 000.0	..	..	..	..	..	..	..
65-74	1 500.0	..	..	..	..	..	..	..
75-84	9 200.0	..	..	..	..	..	..	..
Females	1 900.0	..	..	..	..	..	..	..
16-44	200.0	..	..	..	..	..	..	..
45-64	1 100.0	..	..	..	..	..	..	..
65-74	3 200.0	..	..	..	..	..	..	..
75-84	12 600.0	..	..	..	..	..	..	..

UNITED KINGDOM (NORTHERN IRELAND), household survey of handicapped persons 1978 e/

	Disorders of vision			*Polio, polyneuritis, muscular dystrophy*				
Both sexes	100.0	..	..	100.0	..	..	..	..
0-4	0.5	..	..	0.9	..	..	..	..
5-14	3.9	..	..	3.8	..	..	..	..
15-24	3.7	..	..	6.5	..	..	..	..
25-34	3.9	..	..	16.1	..	..	..	..
35-44	4.2	..	..	13.7	..	..	..	..
45-54	7.4	..	..	14.9	..	..	..	..
55-64	14.2	..	..	20.6	..	..	..	..
65-74	28.2	..	..	19.8	..	..	..	..
75+	34.1	..	..	3.6	..	..	..	..
Both sexes								
Total prevalence	12 200.0	..	..	1 800.0	..	..	..	..

----

e/ Percentage distribution of disabled persons by age, and prevalence of disability, according to selected ocular, visceral and skeletal impairments.

Note. Column headings in italics show the national terminology.

Table 3 *(continued)*

Age and sex	Ocular	Total visual both eyes	Profound visual one eye	Unspecified other Paralysis of limb	Motor: of limb	Transverse deficiency Upper arm	Lower leg	Unspecified transverse deficiency of proximal limb parts
ICIDH	5	51.0	54	73.9	74.9	75.1	75.6	75.9

AUSTRALIA, national survey of handicapped persons 1981

	Sight loss				*Other physical condition*			
Both sexes	1 331.8	..	..	..	2 954.2	..	..	..
0-4	*	..	..	..	1 240.0	..	..	..
5-14	471.0	..	..	..	1 253.4	..	..	..
15-24	467.9	..	..	..	1 145.9	..	..	..
25-34	494.5	..	..	..	1 580.7	..	..	..
35-44	636.8	..	..	..	2 037.7	..	..	..
45-54	1 005.3	..	..	..	3 928.6	..	..	..
55-64	1 787.6	..	..	..	5 961.1	..	..	..
65-74	3 559.0	..	..	..	7 838.4	..	..	..
75+	14 497.0	..	..	..	14 378.7	..	..	..

AUSTRALIA, national survey of handicapped persons 1981

Paralysis f̲/

Both sexes								
< 15	..	..	..	132.5	..	..	..	..
15-24	..	..	..	134.8	..	..	..	..
25-34	..	..	..	181.7	..	..	..	..
35-44	..	..	..	*	..	..	..	..
45-54	..	..	..	238.1	..	..	..	..
55-64	..	..	..	448.8	..	..	..	..
65-74	..	..	..	884.3	..	..	..	..
75+	..	..	..	1 380.7	..	..	..	..
Males	..	..	..	299.9	..	..	..	..
Females	..	..	..	244.5	..	..	..	..
Both sexes	..	..	..	272.1	..	..	..	..

----

f̲/ Numerator excludes mild cases that: (i) do not reduce ability to perform activities;
(ii) do not require an aid.

* Denotes an estimate not published because its relative standard error was too large: its standard error was greater than 25 per cent of the estimate.

Note. Column headings in italics show the national terminology.

**Table 4. Disabled persons per 100,000 population by age and sex
and selected disabilities**

This table provides the number of disabled persons per 100,000 population by age group and sex, according to type of disability. The rates presented were calculated by the Statistical Office, based upon numbers or rates provided in the published reports.

Description of variables

The type of disabilities reported are based upon codes 1-9 of the ICIDH disability codes. Reasonably comparable national data were placed in the same ICIDH column. All types of disabilities reported by countries are presented. A complete list of disabilities reported by the 63 surveys of the 55 countries in DISTAT is provided below according to the number of national surveys utilizing the disability codes. Note that single-digit numbers for disability codes are broader categories than the double-digit codes; double-digit codes are subheadings of the single digit codes. For example, all disability codes starting with the digit 1, i.e., 1, 10, 18, are behavioural disabilities. Codes beginning with the digit 2, i.e., 25, 28 etc., are specific communication disabilities.

In some cases, it was difficult to distinguish between impairment and disability codes. For example, it was not always clear in the national reports whether a country was referring to an "ocular" impairment (impairment code 5) or a "seeing" disability (disability codes 25-27), especially when a general reference to vision problem was stated. In similar cases, the coders for DISTAT decided, through judgement, whether it was an impairment or a disability code. This decision was usually based upon what other groups of categories of disablement were used in the survey and upon the intention stated in the census or survey reports.

Disability description	ICIDH code	Number of surveys coded into this category
CODE 1: BEHAVIOUR		
Occupational role	18	3
CODE 2: COMMUNICATION		
Listening to speech	23	1
Detailed visual tasks	26	1
CODE 3: PERSONAL CARE		
Clothing	35	1
Making food ready	37.3	1
Other feeding: chewing	38.2	1
CODE 4: LOCOMOTOR (MOBILITY)		
Locomotor	4	3
Walking	40	2
Climbing stairs	42	2
Standing transfer	46.2	1
Other transfer	46.8	1
Lifting	48	2
Other locomotor	49	1
CODE 5: BODY DISPOSITION		
Retrieval	52	1
CODE 6: DEXTERITY		
CODE 7: SITUATIONAL		
Other situational	78	2
CODE 8: PARTICULAR SKILLS		
CODE 9: OTHER ACTIVITY RESTRICTIONS		
Other activity restrictions	9	3
Other activity restrictions: certified disabled	9.1*	
Other activity restrictions: partial	9.2*	1
Other activity restrictions: self-reported	9.9*	1

*Not an ICIDH code, but devised to accommodate items not readily coded with ICIDH categories

Statistical definitions

The definitions of each of the disability codes in table 4 of the *Compendium* are taken from WHO/ICIDH. They are as shown below:

Behaviour (1). In the ICIDH definition, the reference is to an individual's awareness and ability to conduct self, in everyday activities and towards others, including the ability to learn (self-awareness, appearance, location in time and space, identification of objects and persons, avoidance of self-injury, potentially dangerous conduct, wandering).

Occupational role (18). Disturbance in the ability to organize and participate in routine activities connected with the occupation of time: not merely confined to a person's performance of work, but involves motivation, co-operation, conformity to work routine, organization of activities in temporal sequence, decision-making ability, response to emergencies, quick decisions and action.

Communication (2). Refers to an individual's ability to generate and emit messages, and to receive and understand messages (speaking, listening, seeing, other communication disabilities such as writing, nonverbal expression, and the like).

Listening to speech (23). Loss or reduction of the ability to receive verbal messages.

Detailed visual tasks (26). Loss or reduction of the ability to execute tasks requiring adequate visual acuity, such as reading, recognition of faces, writing, and visual manipulation.

Personal care (3). Refers to an individual's ability to look after self in regard to basic physiological activities, such as excretion and feeding (preparing food, serving food, eating, drinking, chewing, swallowing), hygiene (bathing of body, dental care, hands and fingernails), dressing, sleeping (difficulty getting up, unable to decide to go to bed, changing into pajamas).

Clothing (35). Includes underclothes, skirts and trousers, jackets and shirts, coats, doing buttons, hooks, zippers, and the like.

Making food ready (37.3). Includes all aspects of cutting meat, buttering bread and the like.

Other feeding: chewing (38.2). Includes mastication.

Locomotor (mobility) (4). Refers to an individual's ability to execute distinctive activities associated with moving self, and objects, from place to place (walking, climbing, running, getting in and out of transport vehicles, lifting and carrying).

Walking (40). Includes ambulation on flat terrain.

Climbing stairs (42). Includes negotiation of flight of stairs and similar man-made obstacles such as ladders.

Standing transfer (46.2). Difficulty in standing transfer to or from bed associated with manipulative problems.

Other transfer (46.8).

Lifting (48). Includes carrying of items.

Other locomotor (49). All locomotor disabilities not included in the other sub-headings of code 4.

Body disposition (5). Refers to an individual's ability to execute distinctive activities associated with the disposition of body parts, e.g., reaching, kneeling, crouching, maintaining posture.

Retrieval (52). Picking up objects from floor and bending.

Dexterity (6). Refers to adroitness and skill in bodily movements, including manipulative skills and the ability to regulate control mechanisms, e.g., fingering, gripping, holding, foot movements.

Situational (7). An attempted description of disturbances of activity performances that are situation-specific, i.e., dependence upon life-sustaining equipment and special procedures or care, such as special diet; environmentally induced such as tolerance to heat or cold, sunlight, barometric pressure, noise, illumination, dust, other allergens, chemical agents.

Other situational (78). All situational disabilities not included in the other sub-headings of code 7.

Other activity restrictions (9). As yet, not specified in ICIDH beyond a general statement that this code provides a way of meeting needs not satisfied in other parts of the classification.

4. Disabled persons per 100,000 population by age, sex and selected type of disabilities

Age and sex	Disabilities	
	Walking disability	Climbing stairs disability
ICIDH	40	42

DENMARK, living conditions survey, 1976

	Difficulty in walking 15 minutes	*Difficulty in climbing stairs*
Males 20-69	10 000.0	8 000.0
20-29	3 000.0	4 000.0
30-44	5 000.0	5 000.0
45-59	13 000.0	10 000.0
60-69	27 000.0	18 000.0
Females 20-69	11 000.0	9 000.0
20-29	3 000.0	3 000.0
30-44	5 000.0	4 000.0
45-59	15 000.0	13 000.0
60-69	28 000.0	23 000.0
Both sexes 20-69	10 000.0	9 000.0

Age and sex	Locomotor disability
ICIDH	4

FINLAND, survey on living conditions, 1978

	Diminished moving ability
Males, 15+	21 000.0
15-24	1 000.0
25-44	5 000.0
45-64	40 000.0
65+	75 000.0
Females, 15+	29 000.0
15-24	2 000.0
25-44	10 000.0
45-64	47 000.0
65+	83 000.0

Note. Column headings in italics show the national terminology.

Table 4 (continued)

Age and sex	Disabilities per 100,000 population					
	Disability in listening to speech	Disability in detailed visual tasks	Clothing disability	Making food	Other feeding disability: chewing	Walking disability
ICIDH	23	26	35	37.3	38.2	40

NEW ZEALAND, social indicators survey, 1980

	Hearing conversa- tions	Reading news- paper print	Dressing and undressing	Cutting own food	Biting and chewing hard foods	Walking 400 metres
Both sexes, 15+	3 000	1 000	1 000	1 000	4 000	4 000
15–54	1 000	..	..	..	2 000	1 000
55–64	4 000	2 000	1 000	1 000	6 000	6 000
65+	10 000	6 000	4 000	2 000	11 000	19 000

	Climbing stairs disability	Standing transfer disability	Other transfer disability	Lifting disability	Retrieval disability	Other situational disability
	42	46.2	6.8	48	52	78

	Walking up/down stairs	Getting in/out of bed	Moving between rooms	Carrying a 5-kg object 10 metres	Bending down to pick up shoe	One or more functional disabilities
Both sexes, 15+	6 000	1 000	1 000	4 000	2 000	13 000
15–54	2 000	..	..	1 000	1 000	6 000
55–64	10 000	1 000	1 000	6 000	3 000	21 000
65+	25 000	4 000	3 000	18 000	11 000	44 000

Note. Column headings in italics show the national terminology.

Table 5. Population, disabled persons and disabilities by type of impairment or disability, and prevalence rate by age, sex and urban/rural residence

Table 5 presents for each available source the number of disabled persons, disabilities, and total persons and type of impairment or disability, age group and sex for urban and rural residence. The prevalence of disability per 100,000 population, by age-group and sex for urban and rural areas, has also been calculated by the Statistical Office and presented in the table. All references to ICIDH codes prefaced with an M (for example, M1.1), indicate that the codes are not ICIDH codes, but are devised to accommodate items not readily coded within ICIDH categories.

Description of variables

Not all rural and urban populations in table 5 are similar in concept and description. The classifications of residence used by the countries in their national publications were maintained. Footnotes are added to the country data of table 5, as needed, in order to clarify their national classification of residence.

Limitations

Table 5 has all the limitations in the estimated prevalence rates that were described in detail in the notes for table 1. Table 5 has the additional problem of differential variation in countries in their descriptions and classifications of urban and rural residence.

5. Population, disabled persons and disabilities by type of impairment or disability, and prevalence rate by age, sex and urban/rural residence

Residence, age and sex	Population surveyed	Disabilities	Impairment status not ascertained	Prevalence rate per 100,000 population	
ICIDH			0		

CENTRAL AFRICAN REPUBLIC, population census 1975

Residence, age and sex	Population surveyed	*Infirm population*	*Undetermined*	*Infirm population*	*Undetermined*
Urban					
Males 10+	202 310	1 923	7 397	950.5	3 656.3
Females 10+	215 541	1 455	1 790	675.0	830.5
Bangui					
Males 10+	388 835	5 986	48 786	1 539.5	12 546.7
Females 10+	434 071	5 446	6 852	1 254.6	1 578.5
Rural					
Males 10+	83 865	423	2 291	504.4	2 731.8
Females 10+	85 005	240	690	282.3	811.7

	Disabled persons	Disabilities

EGYPT, national survey 1979-1981 a/

	Disabled persons	Disabilities
Urban		
Both sexes	456	694
Under 15	79	137
15-24	78	141
25-34	44	66
35-44	46	54
45-54	56	75
55-64	72	104
65+	81	117
Rural		
Both sexes	652	905
Under 15	..	175
15-24	..	87
25-34	..	90
35-44	..	95
45-54	..	107
55-64	..	120
65+	..	231

a/ Number of disabled persons and disabilities reported by age, sex and urban/rural residence.
Note. Column headings in italics show the national terminology.

Table 5 *(continued)*

Residence, age and sex	Mental	Severe communication:	Aural	Ocular	Other cardio-respiratory function	Posture	Mechanical: Mixed and other upper limb	Mixed and other limb
ICIDH	**M1.1**	**30**	**4**	**5**	**61.8**	**70.5**	**71.8**	**71.9**

EGYPT, national survey 1979-1981 (cont'd)

	Mental	*Mutism*	*Hearing*	*Vision*	*Debility*	*Spine*	*Upper limb*	*Lower limb*
Urban								
Both sexes	64	59	51	158	17	13	101	231
Under 15	17	18	7	8	3	1	16	67
15-24	23	20	14	11	5	3	24	41
25-34	9	7	3	14	1	1	11	20
35-44	4	5	6	19	0	1	6	13
45-54	2	3	4	29	2	1	12	22
55-64	3	2	6	34	2	2	17	38
65+	6	4	11	43	4	4	15	30
Rural								
Both sexes	46	76	108	289	22	15	120	229
Under 15	15	30	20	16	2	3	22	67
15-24	6	14	10	19	4	3	13	18
25-34	7	12	12	25	0	1	13	20
35-44	9	8	11	42	3	0	12	10
45-54	3	5	14	37	1	1	18	28
55-64	2	1	15	50	1	3	19	29
65+	4	6	26	100	11	4	23	57

Note. Column headings in italics show the national terminology.

Table 5 *(continued)*

			Prevalence per 100,000 population		
Residence, age and sex	Population surveyed	Disabled persons	Disabled persons	Other psychological impairments	Total visual impairment of both eyes
ICIDH				2	51.0

MALI, population census 1976

				Insanity	*Blindness*
Urban					
Males	529 215	10 356	1 956.9	210.7	558.0
0-4	100 416	129	128.5	0.0	45.8
5-9	80 816	704	871.1	143.5	136.1
10-14	60 647	527	869.0	75.8	95.6
15-19	58 662	491	837.0	88.6	78.4
20-24	46 239	573	1 239.2	233.6	183.8
25-29	36 390	663	1 821.9	302.3	409.5
30-34	30 895	761	2 463.2	417.5	605.3
35-39	27 926	942	3 373.2	530.0	895.2
40-44	22 479	944	4 199.5	551.6	1 116.6
45-49	17 864	822	4 601.4	492.6	1 332.3
50-54	14 692	838	5 703.8	442.4	1 865.0
55-59	10 659	726	6 811.1	431.6	2 242.2
60-64	8 630	765	8 864.4	486.7	3 719.6
65-69	5 043	454	9 002.6	238.0	3 390.8
70-74	3 460	412	11 907.5	549.1	5 606.9
75-79	2 084	268	12 859.9	191.9	6 525.9
80-84	1 086	160	14 733.0	368.3	8 195.2
85-89	423	62	14 657.2	0.0	8 747.0
90-94	274	41	14 963.5	729.9	9 489.1
95+	405	70	17 284.0	0.0	11 358.0
Not stated	125	4	3 200.0	0.0	0.0
Females	547 614	8 315	1 518.4	136.8	437.0
0-4	99 453	105	105.6	0.0	45.2
5-9	82 665	324	391.9	16.9	89.5
10-14	65 075	444	682.3	49.2	66.1
15-19	60 765	541	890.3	67.5	241.9
20-24	47 487	582	1 225.6	92.7	433.8
25-29	43 143	739	1 712.9	143.7	498.3
30-34	35 504	716	2 016.7	214.1	538.0
35-39	28 505	689	2 417.1	259.6	652.5
40-44	22 007	677	3 076.3	404.4	727.0
45-49	15 445	531	3 438.0	414.4	912.9
50-54	13 238	539	4 071.6	483.5	944.3
55-59	8 928	451	5 051.5	604.8	1 332.9
60-64	9 337	584	6 254.7	524.8	1 852.8
65-69	5 032	351	6 975.4	635.9	2 504.0
70-74	4 610	380	8 243.0	520.6	3 080.3
75-79	2 650	265	10 000.0	377.4	4 452.8
80-84	1 789	168	9 390.7	559.0	4 192.3
85-89	679	76	11 192.9	589.1	4 418.3
90-94	548	60	10 948.9	547.4	6 386.9
95+	661	90	13 615.7	453.9	6 202.7
Not stated	93	3	3 225.8	0.0	1 075.3

Note. Column headings in italics show the national terminology.

Table 5 *(continued)*

Residence, age and sex	Population surveyed	Disabled persons	Prevalence per 100,000 population		
			Disabled persons	Other psychological impairments	Total visual impairment of both eyes
ICIDH				2	51.0

MALI, population census 1976 (cont'd)

				Insanity	*Blindness*
Rural					
Males	2 594 518	85 962	3 313.2	213.3	802.2
0-4	486 599	1 052	216.2	6.4	44.8
5-9	411 456	4 841	1 176.6	58.3	116.7
10-14	282 160	4 007	1 420.1	93.6	134.0
15-19	249 945	4 001	1 600.8	124.0	198.8
20-24	172 152	4 211	2 446.1	496.7	290.4
25-29	163 705	4 420	2 700.0	304.2	428.2
30-34	154 834	5 779	3 732.4	421.7	678.8
35-39	133 457	6 015	4 507.1	429.4	843.7
40-44	116 947	6 584	5 629.9	460.0	1 198.8
45-49	93 466	6 329	6 771.4	379.8	1 579.2
50-54	89 927	7 135	7 934.2	448.1	2 072.8
55-59	66 919	6 224	9 300.8	298.9	2 510.5
60-64	67 990	7 688	11 307.5	344.2	3 609.4
65-69	35 236	4 816	13 667.8	363.3	4 515.3
70-74	28 430	4 653	16 366.5	386.9	6 387.6
75-79	15 065	2 926	19 422.5	278.8	7 972.1
80-84	13 005	2 455	18 877.4	330.6	8 096.9
85-89	4 070	879	21 597.1	172.0	9 754.3
90-94	4 052	857	21 150.0	666.3	9 871.7
95+	4 831	1 079	22 334.9	331.2	10 888.0
Not stated	272	11	4 044.1	2 205.9	735.3
Females	2 723 571	88 574	3 252.1	174.6	840.1
0-4	489 941	1 005	205.1	4.5	43.5
5-9	400 186	2 991	747.4	36.5	85.0
10-14	256 884	3 142	1 223.1	76.3	135.1
15-19	272 743	4 601	1 686.9	104.5	351.6
20-24	218 355	5 160	2 363.1	150.7	532.6
25-29	223 875	6 416	2 865.9	169.7	602.1
30-34	190 446	7 290	3 827.9	249.4	783.4
35-39	137 444	6 240	4 540.0	288.8	897.1
40-44	125 822	7 235	5 750.2	410.1	1 184.2
45-49	83 008	5 788	6 972.8	456.6	1 478.2
50-54	90 369	7 635	8 448.7	512.3	2 043.8
55-59	53 989	5 266	9 753.8	526.0	2 448.6
60-64	72 129	8 379	11 616.7	526.8	3 536.7
65-69	31 800	4 402	13 842.8	512.6	4 871.1
70-74	33 137	5 107	15 411.8	546.2	6 231.7
75-79	14 080	2 460	17 471.6	348.0	7 840.9
80-84	16 042	2 871	17 896.8	380.3	8 384.2
85-89	3 697	752	20 340.8	297.5	9 872.9
90-94	4 367	792	18 136.0	274.8	9 182.5
95+	4 976	1 029	20 679.3	482.3	10 430.1
Not stated	281	13	4 626.3	711.7	711.7

Note. Column headings in italics show the national terminology.

Table 5 *(continued)*

Residence, age and sex	Prevalence per 100,000 population				
	Other impairment of vision	Impairment of cardio-respiratory function	Other impairments of internal organs	Other dis-figurement	Other impairment
ICIDH	57.8	61	66.8	87	99

MALI, population census 1976 (cont'd)

	Oncho-cerciasis	Tuber-culosis	Sleeping sickness	Leprosy	Other
Urban					
Males	111.3	65.6	14.9	245.5	750.9
0-4	2.0	4.0	0.0	1.0	75.7
5-9	22.3	121.3	13.6	79.2	355.1
10-14	24.7	9.9	3.3	47.8	611.7
15-19	20.5	0.0	5.1	68.2	576.2
20-24	62.7	41.1	6.5	95.2	616.4
25-29	96.2	35.7	11.0	241.8	725.5
30-34	129.5	74.4	6.5	346.3	883.6
35-39	182.6	75.2	21.5	594.4	1 074.3
40-44	289.2	93.4	8.9	836.3	1 303.4
45-49	352.7	167.9	78.4	811.7	1 365.9
50-54	442.4	231.4	54.5	959.7	1 708.4
55-59	525.4	234.5	112.6	956.9	2 307.9
60-64	602.5	266.5	81.1	1 019.7	2 688.3
65-69	713.9	238.0	79.3	813.0	3 529.6
70-74	520.2	231.2	0.0	896.0	4 104.0
75-79	1 151.6	191.9	48.0	527.8	4 222.6
80-84	184.2	92.1	0.0	1 012.9	4 880.3
85-89	236.4	236.4	0.0	236.4	5 200.9
90-94	1 094.9	1 094.9	0.0	365.0	2 189.8
95+	493.8	246.9	0.0	0.0	5 185.2
Not stated	0.0	0.0	0.0	0.0	3 200.0
Females	113.9	22.6	10.4	181.7	615.9
0-4	2.0	3.0	0.0	3.0	52.3
5-9	14.5	8.5	4.8	31.5	226.2
10-14	13.8	9.2	7.7	29.2	507.1
15-19	18.1	6.6	4.9	49.4	501.9
20-24	59.0	16.8	4.2	115.8	503.3
25-29	71.9	34.8	11.6	299.0	653.6
30-34	104.2	31.0	25.3	385.9	718.2
35-39	161.4	38.6	28.1	463.1	813.9
40-44	254.5	45.4	18.2	554.4	1 072.4
45-49	330.2	64.7	45.3	518.0	1 152.5
50-54	415.5	52.9	22.7	551.4	1 601.5
55-59	593.6	78.4	22.4	683.2	1 736.1
60-64	942.5	139.2	10.7	664.0	2 120.6
65-69	874.4	79.5	19.9	417.3	2 444.4
70-74	802.6	65.1	43.4	477.2	3 253.8
75-79	1 132.1	0.0	37.7	339.6	3 660.4
80-84	838.5	223.6	0.0	335.4	3 242.0
85-89	1 325.5	147.3	0.0	441.8	4 271.0
90-94	912.4	0.0	0.0	365.0	2 737.2
95+	756.4	0.0	0.0	453.9	5 748.9
Not stated	0.0	0.0	0.0	0.0	2 150.5

Note. Column headings in italics show the national terminology.

Table 5 (continued)

Residence, age and sex	Prevalence per 100,000 population				
	Other impairment of vision	Impairment of cardio-respiratory function	Other impairments of internal organs	Other dis-figurement	Other impairment
ICIDH	57.8	61	66.8	87	99

MALI, population census 1976 (cont'd)

	Oncho-cerciasis	Tuber-culosis	Sleeping sickness	Leprosy	Other
Rural					
Males	339.1	116.9	11.4	287.4	1 543.0
0-4	5.5	3.1	0.4	2.1	153.9
5-9	25.5	246.0	4.9	34.8	690.5
10-14	59.5	22.3	3.2	60.6	1 046.9
15-19	90.0	26.0	6.4	106.0	1 049.4
20-24	129.0	79.6	8.7	176.0	1 265.7
25-29	250.5	70.2	10.4	268.2	1 368.3
30-34	403.7	82.0	15.5	409.5	1 721.2
35-39	571.7	112.4	22.5	592.0	1 935.5
40-44	799.5	136.0	23.1	761.9	2 250.6
45-49	1 012.1	193.7	34.2	833.5	2 739.0
50-54	1 103.1	223.5	32.2	869.6	3 184.8
55-59	1 285.1	263.0	35.9	1 029.6	3 877.8
60-64	1 289.9	301.5	25.0	923.7	4 813.9
65-69	1 600.6	380.3	34.1	919.5	5 854.8
70-74	1 466.8	457.3	49.2	865.3	6 753.4
75-79	1 705.9	404.9	33.2	962.5	8 065.1
80-84	1 522.5	415.2	15.4	907.3	7 589.4
85-89	1 572.5	319.4	24.6	737.1	9 017.2
90-94	1 604.1	444.2	0.0	937.8	7 625.9
95+	1 593.9	372.6	0.0	641.7	8 507.6
Not stated	0.0	0.0	0.0	0.0	1 102.9
Females	306.3	62.8	10.1	315.1	1 543.1
0-4	4.3	4.5	1.0	4.1	143.3
5-9	22.0	36.7	2.5	26.7	538.0
10-14	41.7	24.5	2.7	74.4	868.5
15-19	71.9	29.0	4.4	125.4	1 000.2
20-24	118.6	33.0	6.0	235.9	1 286.4
25-29	200.1	41.5	11.6	372.5	1 468.2
30-34	346.0	70.4	16.8	539.3	1 822.6
35-39	456.9	74.2	23.3	667.9	2 131.8
40-44	714.5	126.4	22.3	814.6	2 478.1
45-49	850.5	157.8	24.1	921.6	3 084.0
50-54	1 029.1	200.3	31.0	940.6	3 691.5
55-59	1 296.6	190.8	35.2	963.2	4 293.5
60-64	1 418.3	219.1	16.6	899.8	4 999.4
65-69	1 594.3	264.2	31.4	874.2	5 695.0
70-74	1 542.1	274.6	30.2	799.7	5 987.3
75-79	1 647.7	248.6	7.1	894.9	6 484.4
80-84	1 583.3	180.8	43.6	473.8	6 850.8
85-89	1 622.9	135.2	0.0	622.1	7 790.1
90-94	1 305.2	229.0	22.9	480.9	6 640.7
95+	1 145.5	261.3	20.1	562.7	7 777.3
Not stated	355.9	0.0	0.0	355.9	2 491.1

Note. Column headings in italics show the national terminology.

Table 5 (continued)

Residence, age and sex	Population surveyed	Disabled persons	Prevalence per 100,000 population					
			Disabled persons	Mental handicap	Speech and hearing	Total visual: both eyes	Unspecified other motor: limb	Other
ICIDH				M1.1	M40.1	51.0	74.9	99

TUNISIA, population census 1975

	Population surveyed	Disabled persons	Disabled population	Mental handicap	Deaf and mute	Blind	Motor impairment	Other
Urban								
Males	1 401 510	14 310	1 021.0	190.5	112.7	239.0	338.2	140.6
0-4	199 540	170	85.2	0.0	10.0	10.0	35.1	30.1
5-9	200 670	770	383.7	64.8	129.6	24.9	114.6	49.8
10-14	196 900	1 450	736.4	177.8	162.5	66.0	213.3	116.8
15-19	163 910	1 350	823.6	256.2	140.3	54.9	268.4	103.7
20-29	202 220	1 910	944.5	316.5	108.8	84.1	311.5	123.6
30-39	137 730	1 250	907.6	225.1	123.4	145.2	297.7	116.2
40-49	127 540	1 680	1 317.2	305.8	78.4	345.0	431.2	156.8
50-59	85 930	1 780	2 071.5	290.9	81.5	535.3	872.8	314.2
60+	84 780	3 920	4 623.7	224.1	224.1	2 099.6	1 450.8	625.1
Not stated	2 280	30	1 315.8	438.6	0.0	438.6	438.6	0.0
Females	1 377 670	8 650	627.9	104.5	87.1	186.5	152.4	97.3
0-4	189 510	250	131.9	5.3	10.6	10.6	15.8	89.7
5-9	191 730	510	266.0	41.7	73.0	15.6	78.2	57.4
10-14	190 000	830	436.8	94.7	147.4	36.8	105.3	52.6
15-19	162 270	820	505.3	129.4	104.8	18.5	166.4	86.3
20-29	216 190	1 070	494.9	148.0	92.5	87.9	120.3	46.3
30-39	149 990	740	493.4	126.7	33.3	106.7	140.0	86.7
40-49	124 440	750	602.7	144.6	56.3	176.8	160.7	64.3
50-59	77 090	770	998.8	155.7	51.9	402.1	207.5	181.6
60+	74 580	2 910	3 901.9	201.1	308.4	2 064.9	831.3	496.1
Not stated	1 870	0	0.0	0.0	0.0	0.0	0.0	0.0

Note. Column headings in italics show the national terminology.

Table 5 *(continued)*

Residence, age and sex	Population surveyed	Disabled persons	Prevalence per 100,000 population					
			Disabled persons	Mental handicap	Speech and hearing	Total visual: both eyes	Unspecified other motor: limb	Other
ICIDH				M1.1	M40.1	51.0	74.9	99

TUNISIA, population census 1975 (cont'd)

			Disabled population	*Mental handicap*	*Deaf and mute*	*Blind*	*Motor impairment*	*Other*
Rural								
Males	1 426 030	12 490	875.9	124.8	92.6	244.7	248.9	164.8
0-4	255 710	130	50.8	0.0	11.7	3.9	15.6	19.6
5-9	216 330	640	295.8	32.4	87.8	46.2	74.0	55.5
10-14	179 480	740	412.3	66.9	117.0	22.3	83.6	122.6
15-19	157 050	1 040	662.2	178.3	82.8	95.5	210.1	95.5
20-29	184 060	1 510	820.4	168.4	108.7	141.3	255.4	146.7
30-39	126 700	1 110	876.1	205.2	47.4	189.4	260.5	173.6
40-49	121 680	1 540	1 265.6	271.2	98.6	221.9	427.4	246.5
50-59	86 840	1 770	2 038.2	230.3	115.2	737.0	610.3	345.5
60+	96 170	4 000	4 159.3	218.4	291.2	1 840.5	1 060.6	748.7
Not stated	2 010	10	497.5	0.0	0.0	497.5	0.0	0.0
Females	1 372 040	8 250	601.3	80.9	60.5	217.9	143.6	98.4
0-4	246 860	150	60.8	0.0	0.0	4.1	28.4	28.4
5-9	206 860	380	183.7	4.8	53.2	19.3	77.3	29.0
10-14	166 210	570	342.9	54.1	84.2	36.1	102.3	66.2
15-19	145 130	480	330.7	55.1	48.2	48.2	124.0	55.1
20-29	196 620	860	437.4	152.6	30.5	66.1	106.8	81.4
30-39	138 570	650	469.1	144.3	36.1	144.3	115.5	28.9
40-49	124 420	860	691.2	104.5	72.3	265.2	136.6	112.5
50-59	76 560	940	1 227.8	169.8	78.4	587.8	209.0	182.9
60+	68 920	3 320	4 817.2	246.7	348.2	2 452.1	986.7	783.5
Not stated	1 890	40	2 116.4	0.0	529.1	529.1	529.1	529.1

Note. Column headings in italics show the national terminology.

Table 5 *(continued)*

Residence, age and sex	Population surveyed	Disabled persons	Prevalence per 100,000 population				
			Mental handicap	Speech and hearing	Total visual: both eyes	Unspecified other motor: limb	Other
ICIDH			M1.1	M40.1	51.0	74.9	99

TUNISIA, population census 1984 b/

			Mental handicap	*Deaf and mute*	*Blind*	*Motor impairment*	*Other*
Urban							
Males	1 869 010	1 016.0	276.1	122.0	199.6	351.0	67.4
Females	1 816 460	657.3	165.2	112.9	129.9	209.2	40.2
Rural							
Males	1 677 030	1 124.6	236.1	156.2	209.9	441.3	81.1
Females	1 612 950	667.7	120.9	104.2	155.0	256.1	31.6

b/ Figures for population surveyed taken from *Demographic Yearbook 1986.*

Note. Column headings in italics show the national terminology.

Table 5 (continued)

| Residence, age and sex | Numbers of impairments | | | |
	Disabled school population	Mental handicap	Other psycho-logical impairments	Unspecified impairment of behaviour pattern
ICIDH		M1.1	2	29.9

JAMAICA, survey of handicapped children in schools 1978 c/

		Mental	Emotional	Learning
Urban				
Both sexes 4-11	144	11	29	32
Rural				
Both sexes 4-11	523	104	65	190
Deep rural *				
Both sexes 4-11	53	10	2	32

| Numbers of impairments | | | |
Language impairments	Aural impairments	Ocular impairments	Unspecified other motor impairment of limb
3	4	5	74.9

	Speech	Auditory	Visual	Physical
Urban				
Both sexes 4-11	17	46	7	2
Rural				
Both sexes 4-11	23	54	79	8
Deep rural *				
Both sexes 4-11	1	2	4	2

c/ Number of disabled school children and disabilities reported, by age, sex and type of impairment.

* "Deep rural" was not defined in the published report.

Note. Column headings in italics show the national terminology.

Table 5 *(continued)*

			Prevalence per 100,000 population	
Residence, age and sex	Population surveyed	Disabled persons	Disabled persons	Other situational disability
ICIDH				78

UNITED STATES, census of population 1980

		Work disabled population	*Work disabled population*	*Prevented from work disabled population*
Urban				
Males (Ages 16-64)	52 367 038	4 443 601	8 485.5	3 633.2
Inside urbanized areas:	44 069 230	3 646 194	8 273.8	3 514.2
Central cities	20 845 439	1 925 017	9 234.7	4 217.8
Urban fringe	23 223 791	1 721 177	7 411.3	2 882.5
Outside urbanized areas:				
10,000 or more population	4 115 069	376 944	9 160.1	3 872.1
2,500-10,000 population	4 182 739	420 463	10 052.3	4 652.5
Females (Ages 16-64)	55 638 552	4 362 228	7 840.3	4 548.1
Inside urbanized areas:	46 795 506	3 585 718	7 662.5	4 423.5
Central cities	22 551 079	1 980 195	8 780.9	5 276.8
Urban fringe	24 244 427	1 605 523	6 622.2	3 629.8
Outside urbanized areas:				
10,000 or more population	4 373 948	368 648	8 428.3	4 864.1
2,500-10,000 population	4 469 098	407 862	9 126.3	5 543.1
Rural				
Males (Ages 16-64)	18 313 205	1 936 002	10 571.6	4 918.4
1,000-1,500 population	2 020 690	216 786	10 728.3	5 043.5
Females (Ages 16-64)	18 347 837	1 577 720	8 598.9	5 312.0
1,000-1,500 population	2 146 044	197 213	9 189.6	5 660.6
		Public transport disabled population		
Urban				
Both sexes (Age 65+)	17 906 942	2 697 643	15 064.8	..
Inside urbanized areas:	14 376 445	2 216 629	15 418.5	..
Central cities	7 584 064	1 243 598	16 397.5	..
Urban fringe	6 792 381	973 031	14 325.3	..
Outside urbanized areas:				
10,000 or more population	1 595 563	215 074	13 479.5	..
2,500-10,000 population	1 934 934	265 940	13 744.1	..
Rural				
Both sexes (Age 65+)	6 251 202	890 893	14 251.5	..
1,000-1,500 population	1 005 490	137 970	13 721.7	..

Note. Column headings in italics show the national terminology.

Table 5 *(continued)*

Residence, age and sex	Disabilities	Inter-mittent impairment of conscious-ness	Language	Aural	Tinnitus	Ocular	Other visual
ICIDH		21	3	4	47.2	5	57

UNITED STATES, national health interview survey, 1982 a/
(survey of civilian and non-institutionalized population)

		Epilepsy	Speech impairment	Hearing impair-ment	Tinnitus	Visual impair-ment	Cataracts
Urban							
Both sexes	49 372 000	757 000	1 624 000	12 689 000	3 292 000	5 770 000	3 424 000
SMSA: *							
Central city	19 613 000	370 000	637 000	5 064 000	1 213 000	2 342 000	1 625 000
Not central city	29 759 000	387 000	987 000	7 625 000	2 079 000	3 428 000	1 799 000
Rural							
Both sexes	74 925 000	1 186 000	2 362 000	19 775 000	5 130 000	8 700 000	5 124 000
Not SMSA	25 553 000	429 000	738 000	7 086 000	1 838 000	2 930 000	1 700 000

Other visual impair-ment, colour vision	Other impair-ment of vision	Impair-ment of posture	Mixed & other upper limb mechanical impairment	Mixed & other mechanical impairment of limb	Un-specified other paralysis of limb	Other transverse deficiency of phalanges of fingers
57.5	57.8	70.5	71.8	71.9	73.9	76.3

	Color blindness	Glaucoma	Back	Upper extremities	Lower extremities	Paralysis of extremities	Absence of extremities
Urban							
Both sexes	1 930 000	1 163 000	8 900 000	2 150 000	5 695 000	895 000	1 083 000
SMSA: *							
Central city	577 000	468 000	3 453 000	752 000	2 335 000	373 000	404 000
Not central city	1 353 000	695 000	5 447 000	1 398 000	3 360 000	522 000	679 000
Rural							
Both sexes	2 774 000	1 712 000	13 284 000	3 096 000	8 531 000	1 312 000	1 939 000
Not SMSA	844 000	549 000	4 384 000	946 000	2 836 000	417 000	856 000

a/ Number of disabled persons and impairments reported by sex and residence.
* Standard metropolitan statistical areas.
Note. Column headings in italics show the national terminology.

Table 5 *(continued)*

Residence, age and sex	Population surveyed	Disabled persons	Prevalence per 100,000 population
	VENEZUELA, census of population and housing 1981		
	(not economically active population)		
Urban			
Males	1 182 876	90 551	7 655.2
12-14	383 333	2 329	607.6
15-19	363 448	5 706	1 570.0
20-24	124 549	4 943	3 968.7
25-29	48 486	4 091	8 437.5
30-34	24 543	3 229	13 156.5
35-39	16 278	2 680	16 463.9
40-44	15 582	2 965	19 028.4
45-49	16 891	3 539	20 952.0
50-54	22 178	5 274	23 780.3
55-59	26 671	6 672	25 015.9
60-64	32 103	8 951	27 882.1
65+	108 814	40 172	36 918.0
Females	2 885 639	55 202	1 913.0
12-14	404 759	1 521	375.8
15-19	540 853	3 121	577.1
20-24	377 454	2 753	729.4
25-29	304 473	2 027	665.7
30-34	237 780	1 641	690.1
35-39	175 494	1 424	811.4
40-44	149 931	1 492	995.1
45-49	141 271	1 672	1 183.5
50-54	133 524	2 284	1 710.6
55-59	113 159	2 421	2 139.5
60-64	93 713	3 595	3 836.2
65+	213 228	31 251	14 656.1

Table 5 *(continued)*

Residence, age and sex	Population surveyed	Disabled persons	Prevalence per 100,000 population

VENEZUELA, census of population and housing 1981 (cont'd)
(not economically active population)

Intermediate*

Males	65 441	7 407	11 318.6
12-14	22 596	210	929.4
15-19	18 554	472	2 543.9
20-24	4 736	404	8 530.4
25-29	2 084	249	11 948.2
30-34	1 414	236	16 690.2
35-39	1 141	244	21 384.8
40-44	1 216	259	21 299.3
45-49	1 225	265	21 632.7
50-54	1 435	401	27 944.3
55-59	1 626	406	24 969.2
60-64	2 013	615	30 551.4
65+	7 401	3 646	49 263.6
Females	151 750	3 801	2 504.8
12-14	23 006	117	508.6
15-19	28 443	236	829.7
20-24	18 926	168	887.7
25-29	14 706	84	571.2
30-34	11 659	101	866.3
35-39	9 172	73	795.9
40-44	8 141	98	1 203.8
45-49	7 641	108	1 413.4
50-54	7 181	154	2 144.5
55-59	5 802	143	2 464.7
60-64	5 089	253	4 971.5
65+	11 984	2 266	18 908.5

* Semi-urban

Table 5 (continued)

Residence, age and sex	Population surveyed	Disabled persons	Prevalence per 100,000 population

VENEZUELA, census of population and housing 1981 (cont'd)
(not economically active population)

Residence, age and sex	Population surveyed	Disabled persons	Prevalence per 100,000 population
Rural			
Males	216 808	25 703	11 855.2
12-14	80 354	889	1 106.4
15-19	55 524	1 696	3 054.5
20-24	13 458	1 246	9 258.4
25-29	6 869	862	12 549.1
30-34	5 150	764	14 835.0
35-39	4 418	647	14 644.6
40-44	4 573	802	17 537.7
45-49	4 545	827	18 195.8
50-54	5 268	1 359	25 797.3
55-59	5 553	1 479	26 634.3
60-64	6 499	2 342	36 036.3
65+	24 597	12 790	51 998.2
Females	579 993	12 396	2 137.3
12-14	83 560	465	556.5
15-19	100 758	792	786.0
20-24	71 709	588	820.0
25-29	56 919	345	606.1
30-34	46 630	291	624.1
35-39	38 946	249	639.3
40-44	35 297	305	864.1
45-49	32 638	297	910.0
50-54	29 473	409	1 387.7
55-59	22 908	488	2 130.3
60-64	20 052	938	4 677.8
65+	41 103	7 229	17 587.5

Table 5 *(continued)*

Residence, age and sex	Population surveyed	Disabled persons	Prevalence per 100,000 population
	BURMA*, population census 1983		
	(not economically active population)		
Urban			
Males	1 271 784	5 062	398.0
10–14	527 702	476	90.2
15–19	336 688	608	180.6
20–24	122 839	515	419.2
25–29	43 236	398	920.5
30–34	22 070	325	1 472.6
35–39	17 116	356	2 079.9
40–44	17 805	319	1 791.6
45–49	20 111	311	1 546.4
50–54	22 514	282	1 252.6
55–59	22 599	237	1 048.7
60–64	37 744	263	696.8
65+	81 360	972	1 194.7
Females	2 316 630	3 810	164.5
10–14	496 935	446	89.8
15–19	393 930	452	114.7
20–24	302 512	320	105.8
25–29	222 028	266	119.8
30–34	165 718	178	107.4
35–39	123 554	159	128.7
40–44	109 531	162	147.9
45–49	102 909	181	175.9
50–54	95 069	237	249.3
55–59	77 706	201	258.7
60–64	73 322	277	377.8
65+	153 416	931	606.8

* Now Myanmar

Table 5 *(continued)*

Residence, age and sex	Population surveyed	Disabled persons	Prevalence per 100,000 population

BURMA, population census 1983 (cont'd)
(not economically active population)

Residence, age and sex	Population surveyed	Disabled persons	Prevalence per 100,000 population
Rural			
Males	3 378 973	21 632	640.2
10-14	1 427 985	1 868	130.8
15-19	616 465	2 143	347.6
20-24	280 187	1 904	679.5
25-29	186 137	1 361	731.2
30-34	132 117	1 381	1 045.3
35-39	104 392	1 178	1 128.4
40-44	90 455	1 192	1 317.8
45-49	92 942	1 420	1 527.8
50-54	92 415	1 386	1 499.8
55-59	75 762	1 370	1 808.3
60-64	78 888	1 578	2 000.3
65+	201 228	4 851	2 410.7
Females	6 066 567	19 496	321.4
10-14	1 353 137	1 321	97.6
15-19	820 387	1 207	147.1
20-24	701 882	1 088	155.0
25-29	608 968	909	149.3
30-34	475 945	885	185.9
35-39	362 874	808	222.7
40-44	331 231	991	299.2
45-49	311 036	926	297.7
50-54	289 907	1 445	498.4
55-59	221 636	1 369	617.7
60-64	199 968	2 158	1 079.2
65+	389 596	6 389	1 639.9

Table 5 *(continued)*

Residence, age and sex	Population surveyed	Disabled persons	Prevalence per 100,000 population

CHINA, annual population survey 1983
(special children's question on disability)

Urban

Both sexes

0-14	32 905	445	1 352.4
0	2 075	12	578.3
1	2 384	27	1 132.6
2	2 064	10	484.5
3	1 613	25	1 549.9
4	1 881	27	1 435.4
5	1 763	24	1 361.3
6	1 787	35	1 958.6
7	1 833	28	1 527.6
8	1 998	34	1 701.7
9	1 979	27	1 364.3
10	2 342	43	1 836.0
11	2 542	33	1 298.2
12	2 740	37	1 350.4
13	2 953	44	1 490.0
14	2 951	39	1 321.6

Rural

Both sexes

0-14	146 118	2 131	1 458.4
0	8 019	56	698.3
1	8 806	105	1 192.4
2	8 644	112	1 295.7
3	7 764	117	1 507.0
4	8 836	142	1 607.1
5	8 440	108	1 279.6
6	8 307	122	1 468.6
7	8 908	129	1 448.1
8	9 266	134	1 446.1
9	10 447	170	1 627.3
10	10 901	164	1 504.4
11	11 413	172	1 507.1
12	12 125	183	1 509.3
13	12 417	218	1 755.7
14	11 825	199	1 682.9

Table 5 *(continued)*

Residence, age and sex	Prevalence per 100,000 population					
	Disabled persons	Speech and hearing	Total visual impairment of both eyes	Congenital deformity	Other	Unspecified other
ICIDH		M40.1	51.0	84.0	99	99.9

CHINA, annual population survey 1983 (cont'd)
(special children's question on disability)

		Deaf and mute	*Blind*	*Congenitally abnormal*	*Other*	*Disabled after birth*
Urban						
Both sexes						
0-14	1 352.4	76.0	6.1	413.3	580.5	276.6
0	578.3	0.0	0.0	144.6	433.7	0.0
1	1 132.6	41.9	0.0	419.5	629.2	41.9
2	484.5	0.0	0.0	193.8	242.2	48.4
3	1 549.9	62.0	0.0	744.0	620.0	124.0
4	1 435.4	53.2	0.0	478.5	744.3	159.5
5	1 361.3	0.0	0.0	453.8	737.4	170.2
6	1 958.6	56.0	0.0	615.6	895.4	391.7
7	1 527.6	109.1	54.6	545.6	491.0	327.3
8	1 701.7	350.4	0.0	500.5	650.7	200.2
9	1 364.3	50.5	50.5	202.1	555.8	505.3
10	1 836.0	42.7	0.0	555.1	811.3	427.0
11	1 298.2	157.4	0.0	314.7	550.7	275.4
12	1 350.4	109.5	0.0	401.5	474.5	365.0
13	1 490.0	67.7	0.0	508.0	643.4	270.9
14	1 321.6	33.9	0.0	271.1	372.8	643.8
Rural						
Both sexes						
0-14	1 458.4	160.1	23.3	389.4	485.9	399.7
0	698.3	12.5	0.0	361.6	286.8	37.4
1	1 192.4	34.1	22.7	420.2	590.5	124.9
2	1 295.7	81.0	46.3	474.3	485.9	208.2
3	1 507.0	115.9	0.0	463.7	566.7	360.6
4	1 607.1	124.5	11.3	475.3	577.2	418.7
5	1 279.6	130.3	23.7	379.1	414.7	331.8
6	1 468.6	144.5	24.1	373.2	553.7	373.2
7	1 448.1	179.6	22.5	370.5	471.5	404.1
8	1 446.1	151.1	21.6	399.3	485.6	388.5
9	1 627.3	191.4	38.3	335.0	526.5	536.0
10	1 504.4	238.5	36.7	486.2	403.6	339.4
11	1 507.1	236.6	17.5	394.3	543.2	315.4
12	1 509.3	173.2	24.7	313.4	395.9	602.1
13	1 755.7	257.7	32.2	346.3	515.4	604.0
14	1 682.9	203.0	16.9	312.9	482.0	668.1

Note. Column headings in italics show the national terminology.

Table 5 *(continued)*

Residence, age and sex	Prevalence per 100,000 population			
	Language	Aural	Ocular	Unspecified other motor impairment of limb
ICIDH	3	4	5	74.9

INDIA, national survey of the handicapped 1981

	Speech	*Hearing*	*Visual*	*Locomotor*
Urban				
Males	342	386	294	800
0–4			29	628
5–14	506	266	100	859
15–39	304	216	136	601
40–59	203	386	281	873
60+	360	2 432	3 291	2 444
Females	207	395	425	544
0–4			21	448
5–14	345	220	72	562
15–39	159	198	96	346
40–59	122	468	467	560
60+	209	2 305	4 968	2 060
Rural				
Males	379	595	444	1 047
0–4			41	522
5–14	486	343	71	817
15–39	359	386	125	876
40–59	262	647	462	1 458
60+	345	2 660	4 573	3 079
Females	228	510	670	597
0–4			37	342
5–14	324	283	60	515
15–39	189	250	106	402
40–59	175	579	715	744
60+	225	2 597	7 155	2 154

Note. Column headings in italics show the national terminology.

Table 5 *(continued)*

Residence, age and sex	Population surveyed	Disabled persons	Disabilities
NEPAL, national survey 1980 <u>d</u>/			
Hills			
Males		471	534
<5			17
5-14			98
15-24			89
25-39			94
40-59			139
60-74			60
75+			37
Females		296	323
<5			14
5-14			57
15-24			49
25-39			58
40-59			77
60-74			44
75+			24
Both sexes	23 077	767	857
Terai region			
Males		382	448
<5			5
5-14			115
15-24			78
25-39			89
40-59			114
60-74			36
75+			11
Females		213	259
<5			5
5-14			78
15-24			46
25-39			52
40-59			46
60-74			28
75+			4
Both sexes	22 271	595	707

<u>d</u>/ Number of population, disabled persons and disabilities, by age, sex, urban/rural residence and type of impairment or disability.

Table 5 *(continued)*

Residence, age and sex	Intellectual impairments	Total or profound impairment of hearing	Speech and hearing	Total visual impairment of both eyes
ICIDH	1	40	M40.1	51.0

NEPAL, national survey 1980 (cont'd)

	Mental retardation	*Deaf/hearing handicapped*	*Deaf-mute*	*Bilateral sight loss/blind*
Hills				
Males	37	116	62	48
<5	0	2	0	4.
5-14	7	17	26	4
15-24	10	14	17	5
25-39	11	16	13	6
40-59	8	36	5	12
60-74	1	20	0	9
75+	0	11	1	8
Females	24	84	29	44
<5	1	1	2	1
5-14	3	16	12	3
15-24	7	16	8	2
25-39	7	15	5	7
40-59	4	19	2	13
60-74	2	9	0	14
75+	0	8	0	4
Terai region				
Males	20	94	48	81
<5	0	1	1	2
5-14	7	40	21	3
15-24	7	23	8	8
25-39	4	13	7	19
40-59	2	12	7	33
60-74	0	4	4	13
75+	0	1	0	3
Females	20	48	41	47
<5	0	1	0	1
5-14	10	23	22	0
15-24	7	10	11	5
25-39	1	7	4	10
40-59	2	4	3	15
60-74	0	2	1	15
75+	0	1	0	1
Both sexes	40	142	89	128

Note. Column headings in italics show the national terminology.

Table 5 *(continued)*

Residence, age and sex	Profound visual impairment of one eye	Skeletal impairments	Mixed & other upper limb mechanical impairment	Mixed & other mechanical impairment of limb
ICIDH	**54**	**7**	**71.8**	**71.9**

NEPAL, national survey 1980 (cont'd)

	Loss of sight in one eye	*Head, neck and spine*	*Upper limb*	*Lower limb*
Hills				
Males	57	27	77	110
<5	0	2	4	5
5–14	5	3	12	24
15–24	7	4	13	19
25–39	7	4	18	19
40–59	22	9	21	26
60–74	8	1	8	13
75+	8	4	1	4
Females	40	14	40	48
<5	0	0	3	6
5–14	4	3	8	8
15–24	2	1	5	8
25–39	4	1	8	11
40–59	18	4	8	9
60–74	8	3	4	4
75+	4	2	4	2
Both sexes	97	41	117	158
Terai region				
Males	58	18	47	82
<5	0	0	0	1
5–14	3	0	15	26
15–24	7	2	9	14
25–39	15	4	10	17
40–59	27	9	9	15
60–74	5	3	2	5
75+	1	0	2	4
Females	27	8	23	45
<5	0	1	1	1
5–14	2	2	5	14
15–24	1	1	5	6
25–39	6	2	8	14
40–59	13	2	3	4
60–74	5	0	1	4
75+	0	0	0	2
Both sexes	85	26	70	127

Note. Column headings in italics show the national terminology.

Table 5 *(continued)*

Residence, age and sex	Population surveyed	Disabled persons	Prevalence per 100,000 population
PAKISTAN, population census 1981			
Urban			
Males	12 767 061	38 130	298.7
0-4	1 813 400	1 427	78.7
5-9	1 838 576	3 564	193.8
10-14	1 652 953	4 122	249.4
15-19	1 364 875	3 308	242.4
20-24	1 158 623	2 419	208.8
25-29	943 733	1 794	190.1
30-34	756 849	1 452	191.8
35-39	668 089	1 462	218.8
40-44	605 619	1 785	294.7
45-49	489 784	1 340	273.6
50-54	459 260	2 217	482.7
55-59	241 930	1 396	577.0
60+	773 370	11 844	1 531.5
Females	11 074 410	39 545	357.1
0-4	1 765 789	1 215	68.8
5-9	1 712 959	2 266	132.3
10-14	1 466 505	3 533	240.9
15-19	1 175 344	3 363	286.1
20-24	949 670	3 715	391.2
25-29	775 592	3 685	475.1
30-34	634 286	3 113	490.8
35-39	607 538	2 432	400.3
40-44	526 031	2 357	448.1
45-49	391 915	1 705	435.0
50-54	336 609	2 021	600.4
55-59	182 411	1 213	665.0
60+	549 761	8 927	1 623.8

Table 5 *(continued)*

Residence, age and sex	Population surveyed	Disabled persons	Prevalence per 100,000 population

PAKISTAN, population census 1981 (cont'd)

Rural

Males

	30 322 750	127 277	419.7
0-4	4 387 034	5 555	126.6
5-9	4 972 911	15 775	317.2
10-14	4 203 791	12 705	302.2
15-19	2 827 638	7 419	262.4
20-24	2 111 153	6 104	289.1
25-29	1 947 694	5 110	262.4
30-34	1 631 275	5 037	308.8
35-39	1 452 491	4 257	293.1
40-44	1 331 637	4 270	320.7
45-49	1 120 519	3 520	314.1
50-54	1 178 632	5 311	450.6
55-59	617 558	4 240	686.6
60+	2 540 417	47 974	1 888.4

Females

	27 890 876	166 468	596.9
0-4	4 607 681	4 366	94.8
5-9	4 617 891	9 050	196.0
10-14	3 479 799	9 840	282.8
15-19	2 395 230	10 444	436.0
20-24	2 008 310	10 932	544.3
25-29	1 812 139	12 737	702.9
30-34	1 594 918	11 597	727.1
35-39	1 469 119	9 221	627.7
40-44	1 401 737	8 004	571.0
45-49	1 073 864	6 520	607.2
50-54	991 116	8 321	839.6
55-59	568 958	5 430	954.4
60+	1 870 114	60 006	3 208.7

Table 5 *(continued)*

Residence, age and sex	Intellectual	Psychological	Speech and hearing	Of both eyes	Unspecified disfigurement	Other
ICIDH	1	2	M40.1	51.0	87.9	99

PAKISTAN, population census 1981 (cont'd)

	Mentally retarded	Insane	Deaf and mute	Blind	Crippled	Other disabled
Urban						
Males	55.9	26.7	30.7	56.9	59.2	69.3
0-4	4.4	1.4	14.2	21.0	30.4	7.2
5-9	29.0	11.7	50.6	17.8	59.9	24.7
10-14	65.1	20.0	47.9	23.6	58.9	34.0
15-19	64.2	24.1	37.9	19.9	62.6	33.8
20-24	57.0	28.5	23.4	24.3	48.0	27.6
25-29	68.0	35.8	14.2	24.7	24.2	23.2
30-34	76.2	26.4	9.6	28.8	31.8	18.9
35-39	74.8	34.3	12.6	27.1	51.9	18.1
40-44	85.4	49.4	12.4	44.7	38.5	64.4
45-49	74.1	46.8	12.7	52.5	51.5	36.1
50-54	81.2	78.4	18.5	105.0	66.6	133.0
55-59	65.3	33.1	23.6	190.6	90.9	173.6
60+	100.3	57.9	74.5	453.9	219.7	625.2
Females	42.6	21.4	55.8	124.8	55.7	56.8
0-4	4.5	2.8	6.7	24.6	22.0	8.2
5-9	17.8	8.0	38.5	10.0	46.4	11.6
10-14	52.7	25.6	61.6	17.0	51.9	32.1
15-19	62.8	22.7	64.7	57.9	53.7	24.4
20-24	48.3	17.8	58.5	200.8	36.6	29.1
25-29	52.2	19.0	66.0	236.9	68.3	32.7
30-34	40.5	26.2	79.3	226.4	71.6	46.8
35-39	45.9	27.3	54.0	187.6	51.5	33.9
40-44	62.4	36.3	82.1	159.9	49.8	57.6
45-49	62.5	43.4	72.5	130.1	54.6	72.0
50-54	47.5	60.6	73.4	198.2	84.4	136.4
55-59	82.2	44.4	91.0	218.2	77.3	151.9
60+	97.5	45.7	129.3	645.7	190.4	515.1

Note. Column headings in italics show the national terminology.

Table 5 *(continued)*

Residence, age and sex	Intellectual	Psychological	Speech and hearing	Total visual: both eyes	Unspecified disfigurement	Other
ICIDH	**1**	**2**	**M40.1**	**51.0**	**87.9**	**99**

PAKISTAN, population census 1981 (cont'd)

	Mentally retarded	*Insane*	*Deaf and mute*	*Blind*	*Crippled*	*Other disabled*
Rural						
Males	43.9	32.1	48.6	96.2	85.7	113.2
0–4	6.4	6.6	24.4	29.1	32.5	27.6
5–9	35.2	18.9	94.7	17.5	84.0	67.0
10–14	53.5	32.4	76.8	15.4	76.3	47.8
15–19	46.2	41.9	42.3	21.8	69.7	40.4
20–24	66.5	30.6	37.3	43.5	69.2	42.1
25–29	58.2	35.3	15.1	39.4	83.0	31.3
30–34	51.9	51.1	18.4	48.1	73.2	66.1
35–39	46.2	30.5	23.9	61.3	82.9	48.3
40–44	54.6	59.4	23.6	42.2	85.4	55.5
45–49	45.0	38.5	11.6	66.9	80.1	72.0
50–54	51.8	41.1	20.2	151.3	81.1	105.2
55–59	38.1	42.3	46.0	176.3	169.2	214.7
60+	62.7	54.8	72.5	716.5	224.7	757.1
Females	46.2	29.7	84.0	211.5	92.0	133.5
0–4	4.7	5.7	21.9	21.1	24.5	16.8
5–9	19.5	8.0	64.9	14.6	58.1	30.9
10–14	35.6	24.3	74.9	28.7	79.3	40.0
15–19	53.7	43.1	84.1	113.6	91.3	50.1
20–24	44.7	27.5	71.0	262.5	81.1	57.6
25–29	54.8	36.3	117.8	333.8	100.5	59.7
30–34	64.8	50.9	108.5	307.4	121.4	74.0
35–39	84.5	32.5	89.2	240.1	100.8	80.5
40–44	71.6	40.2	105.2	203.1	89.6	61.3
45–49	53.3	53.8	101.0	219.4	87.0	92.7
50–54	64.7	66.8	125.5	281.1	131.7	169.8
55–59	43.4	37.3	96.7	375.4	161.2	240.4
60+	140.3	66.9	205.1	1 269.3	301.1	1 226.0

Note. Column headings in italics show the national terminology.

Table 5 *(continued)*

Residence, age and sex	Population surveyed	Disabled persons	Prevalence per 100 000 population
PHILIPPINES, census 1980			
Urban			
Males 15+	1 365 135	35 630	2 610.0
Females 15+	3 893 183	27 118	696.6
Rural			
Males 15+	1 391 487	64 619	4 643.9
Females 15+	6 911 249	57 003	824.8

Table 5 *(continued)*

Residence, age and sex	Population surveyed	Severe communi-cation	Total/ profound hearing loss	Speech and hearing	Total visual: both eyes	Bilateral paralysis	
						Lower limbs: paraplegia	Upper limbs
ICIDH		30	40	M40.1	51.0	72.3	73.0

SRI LANKA, population census 1981

		Mute	*Deaf*	*Deaf and mute*	*Blind*	*Paralysis of both legs*	*Paralysis of both hands*
Urban							
Males	1 665 539	69.5	11.9	52.7	50.1	63.3	23.9
<1	35 506	8.4	0.0	0.0	2.8	2.8	2.8
1–4	129 741	33.9	1.5	17.7	4.6	42.4	10.0
5–9	163 229	90.1	4.3	71.1	21.4	72.3	25.1
10–14	179 901	105.1	5.0	111.2	36.1	76.2	36.7
15–19	190 670	91.8	11.5	76.6	36.7	52.4	24.1
20–24	188 268	69.1	6.9	31.9	31.3	65.3	22.3
25–29	157 344	61.6	5.7	41.9	35.6	53.4	21.6
30–34	138 540	56.3	3.6	50.5	36.1	52.0	18.0
35–39	101 872	56.9	12.8	41.2	39.3	40.2	5.9
40–44	85 000	55.3	10.6	24.7	65.9	42.4	9.4
45–49	71 160	42.2	11.2	28.1	63.2	50.6	14.1
50–54	65 599	41.2	12.2	44.2	67.1	35.1	16.8
55–59	49 624	48.4	16.1	34.3	70.5	48.4	16.1
60–64	40 110	49.9	32.4	29.9	142.1	104.7	39.9
65–69	28 051	57.0	60.6	28.5	171.1	128.3	60.6
70–74	20 158	49.6	64.5	39.7	262.9	119.1	34.7
75+	20 770	48.1	120.4	28.9	380.4	313.0	139.6
Females	1 528 937	52.4	16.5	52.6	43.6	53.6	18.0
<1	34 320	0.0	0.0	0.0	0.0	0.0	0.0
1–4	125 135	18.4	4.8	16.8	4.8	32.8	10.4
5–9	159 746	72.0	11.3	61.3	24.4	58.2	25.0
10–14	172 157	76.1	17.4	94.7	26.7	45.9	21.5
15–19	175 161	67.4	10.3	91.3	35.4	38.8	14.8
20–24	165 288	57.5	7.9	52.0	26.6	53.8	17.5
25–29	138 538	46.9	7.9	37.5	28.9	40.4	13.0
30–34	121 241	44.5	8.2	34.6	32.2	49.5	15.7
35–39	90 461	48.6	8.8	34.3	42.0	32.1	12.2
40–44	72 620	34.4	13.8	38.6	31.7	45.4	11.0
45–49	63 275	42.7	26.9	33.2	37.9	30.0	7.9
50–54	57 502	38.3	19.1	20.9	76.5	41.7	10.4
55–59	45 106	35.5	17.7	46.6	66.5	64.3	6.7
60–64	36 135	24.9	41.5	33.2	88.6	83.0	33.2
65–69	28 678	24.4	45.3	27.9	167.4	132.5	27.9
70–74	19 543	10.2	81.9	35.8	276.3	184.2	56.3
75+	24 039	41.6	120.6	33.3	328.6	303.7	70.7

Note. Column headings in italics show the national terminology.

Table 5 *(continued)*

Residence, age and sex	Population surveyed	Prevalence per 100,000 population					
		Severe communi-cation	Total/ profound hearing loss	Speech and hearing	Total visual: both eyes	Bilateral paralysis	
						Lower limbs: paraplegia	Upper limbs
ICIDH		**30**	**40**	**M40.1**	**51.0**	**72.3**	**73.0**

SRI LANKA, population census 1981 (cont'd)

		Mute	Deaf	Deaf and mute	Blind	Paralysis of both legs	Paralysis of both hands
Rural							
Males	5 902 553	90.9	26.5	70.6	67.9	86.5	32.0
<1	171 817	1.2	0.6	1.2	4.1	4.1	2.3
1-4	612 066	54.4	2.9	37.9	16.3	70.6	24.2
5-9	694 678	112.6	11.8	67.5	24.0	84.9	30.1
10-14	684 010	124.9	23.1	85.2	28.8	78.1	34.9
15-19	624 529	139.1	22.9	107.8	35.1	78.5	37.1
20-24	565 070	106.0	17.5	79.1	40.7	73.8	29.2
25-29	480 203	89.3	17.5	71.4	51.2	79.5	27.1
30-34	430 983	66.8	13.7	67.5	52.4	82.6	26.9
35-39	321 131	84.1	21.5	70.7	72.6	78.2	21.2
40-44	275 922	56.9	24.6	63.4	73.2	76.1	22.5
45-49	237 999	58.0	21.4	63.4	87.4	76.5	26.9
50-54	218 568	63.1	41.2	54.4	112.6	86.0	24.7
55-59	171 904	59.3	56.4	55.8	150.1	109.9	45.4
60-64	143 793	52.9	79.3	59.8	215.6	112.0	43.8
65-69	105 772	67.1	86.0	49.2	286.5	144.7	65.2
70-74	77 406	55.6	118.9	53.0	328.1	188.6	62.0
75+	86 703	38.1	199.5	41.5	525.9	267.6	87.7
Females	5 751 332	71.2	22.3	55.3	57.4	62.5	23.3
<1	164 407	1.8	0.0	1.2	8.5	3.6	2.4
1-4	584 272	49.3	3.8	30.8	16.1	56.7	19.0
5-9	671 803	91.4	9.2	53.9	20.8	73.8	28.0
10-14	654 187	97.7	17.1	70.3	25.7	56.7	24.2
15-19	617 175	109.0	16.2	76.6	25.9	54.4	20.7
20-24	591 173	72.6	11.0	56.8	30.3	51.3	21.1
25-29	497 292	71.4	15.1	56.5	38.6	49.7	17.3
30-34	432 093	51.4	16.9	50.9	42.1	62.3	22.0
35-39	325 261	59.3	16.6	57.2	60.0	48.9	18.4
40-44	264 957	49.8	31.3	46.4	58.9	47.9	18.1
45-49	237 716	46.3	38.3	53.8	77.0	51.7	18.5
50-54	200 888	46.3	39.3	59.2	104.0	64.7	18.9
55-59	155 576	46.3	52.1	48.2	133.1	56.6	17.4
60-64	121 687	38.6	60.8	30.4	227.6	84.6	34.5
65-69	93 081	33.3	68.8	41.9	250.3	106.4	34.4
70-74	63 504	37.8	110.2	29.9	335.4	159.0	70.9
75+	76 262	26.2	160.0	44.6	527.1	236.0	91.8

Note. Column headings in italics show the national terminology.

Table 5 *(continued)*

Residence, age and sex	Population surveyed	Prevalence per 100,000 population					
		Paralysis of:		Transverse deficiency of:			
		Upper limb	Lower limb	Carpus	Carpi	Lower leg	Lower legs
ICIDH		73.1	73.4	75.3	75.31	75.6	75.61

SRI LANKA, population census 1981 (cont'd)

		Paralysis of one hand	*Paralysis of one leg*	*Loss of one hand*	*Loss of both hands*	*Loss of one leg*	*Loss of both legs*
Urban							
Males	1 665 539	48.9	67.5	12.7	1.6	25.0	7.0
<1	35 506	0.0	2.8	0.0	0.0	0.0	0.0
1-4	129 741	6.9	17.7	4.6	0.0	2.3	2.3
5-9	163 229	15.9	27.6	1.8	0.6	3.7	1.8
10-14	179 901	24.5	42.8	3.3	1.1	6.1	4.4
15-19	190 670	34.6	55.1	6.3	1.0	6.8	5.2
20-24	188 268	36.6	62.1	8.5	1.6	10.6	3.7
25-29	157 344	28.0	59.7	14.6	1.3	14.6	3.2
30-34	138 540	41.1	58.5	17.3	2.2	22.4	8.7
35-39	101 872	33.4	42.2	17.7	2.9	29.4	7.9
40-44	85 000	43.5	55.3	17.6	2.4	34.1	11.8
45-49	71 160	59.0	59.0	16.9	0.0	46.4	11.2
50-54	65 599	79.3	91.5	24.4	1.5	65.5	21.3
55-59	49 624	114.9	114.9	26.2	4.0	92.7	14.1
60-64	40 110	167.0	192.0	22.4	2.5	82.3	7.5
65-69	28 051	171.1	192.5	39.2	7.1	99.8	10.7
70-74	20 158	297.6	347.3	19.8	5.0	114.1	14.9
75+	20 770	288.9	351.5	38.5	4.8	120.4	24.1
Females	1 528 937	25.9	45.1	4.1	1.2	8.8	2.4
<1	34 320	2.9	0.0	0.0	0.0	0.0	0.0
1-4	125 135	6.4	8.8	0.8	0.0	1.6	1.6
5-9	159 746	13.8	26.9	2.5	1.9	2.5	2.5
10-14	172 157	16.3	41.2	2.3	0.0	2.3	2.9
15-19	175 161	16.0	33.7	2.3	1.1	5.7	0.6
20-24	165 288	25.4	44.2	0.6	1.8	5.4	3.0
25-29	138 538	14.4	35.4	5.1	0.0	5.1	2.9
30-34	121 241	16.5	42.9	2.5	0.0	9.1	1.6
35-39	90 461	15.5	31.0	3.3	1.1	9.9	1.1
40-44	72 620	20.7	45.4	4.1	1.4	4.1	1.4
45-49	63 275	23.7	28.4	6.3	1.6	7.9	1.6
50-54	57 502	33.0	59.1	5.2	0.0	15.7	0.0
55-59	45 106	57.6	73.2	8.9	0.0	20.0	0.0
60-64	36 135	77.5	85.8	11.1	2.8	33.2	0.0
65-69	28 678	122.0	132.5	10.5	7.0	17.4	3.5
70-74	19 543	87.0	143.3	20.5	5.1	56.3	10.2
75+	24 039	166.4	249.6	29.1	12.5	70.7	16.6

Note. Column headings in italics show the national terminology.

Table 5 *(continued)*

Residence, age and sex	Population surveyed	Prevalence per 100,000 population					
		Paralysis of:		Transverse deficiency of:			
		Upper limb	Lower limb	Carpus	Carpi	Lower leg	Lower legs
ICIDH		73.1	73.4	75.3	75.31	75.6	75.61

SRI LANKA, population census 1981 (cont'd)

		Paralysis of one hand	*Paralysis of one leg*	*Loss of one hand*	*Loss of both hands*	*Loss of one leg*	*Loss of both legs*
Rural							
Males	5 902 553	66.2	93.6	18.1	1.8	30.2	5.9
<1	171 817	0.6	3.5	0.6	0.0	1.2	0.0
1-4	612 066	10.6	16.8	3.4	0.8	3.1	2.6
5-9	694 678	27.2	34.7	3.2	0.7	4.8	3.6
10-14	684 010	43.7	53.1	6.4	1.8	5.1	3.9
15-19	624 529	49.8	67.4	9.6	1.8	9.6	3.2
20-24	565 070	54.0	86.0	15.4	1.4	18.6	3.7
25-29	480 203	55.2	88.9	16.5	1.2	22.3	5.0
30-34	430 983	53.8	100.7	22.0	1.6	32.5	6.0
35-39	321 131	53.9	96.2	28.0	3.1	43.0	6.5
40-44	275 922	75.4	111.6	28.3	1.8	57.3	8.7
45-49	237 999	97.5	141.2	37.0	3.4	64.7	12.6
50-54	218 568	112.1	180.7	46.7	1.4	83.3	13.7
55-59	171 904	151.2	188.5	43.6	1.7	101.2	8.7
60-64	143 793	207.9	240.6	36.2	7.6	100.8	18.1
65-69	105 772	221.2	253.4	45.4	4.7	104.0	12.3
70-74	77 406	253.2	310.1	58.1	2.6	93.0	7.8
75+	86 703	289.5	348.3	45.0	2.3	92.3	11.5
Females	5 751 332	37.3	56.1	4.7	0.7	6.6	2.1
<1	164 407	0.6	3.6	0.0	0.6	1.2	0.6
1-4	584 272	10.1	13.0	1.4	0.5	1.4	1.7
5-9	671 803	20.4	25.8	3.3	0.6	2.7	1.5
10-14	654 187	29.0	41.9	4.0	0.6	3.5	2.0
15-19	617 175	33.2	46.7	2.8	1.0	3.7	1.9
20-24	591 173	31.5	53.5	3.7	1.0	6.1	2.0
25-29	497 292	33.4	62.7	4.8	0.4	4.6	1.8
30-34	432 093	31.9	75.0	4.4	0.9	8.6	2.5
35-39	325 261	33.2	60.6	5.2	0.0	7.1	2.8
40-44	264 957	32.1	55.9	4.9	0.8	9.4	0.8
45-49	237 716	44.2	55.9	4.2	0.8	10.9	2.1
50-54	200 888	52.8	69.2	10.0	0.5	13.4	1.5
55-59	155 576	56.6	79.7	9.6	0.0	14.8	3.9
60-64	121 687	109.3	119.2	12.3	1.6	17.3	0.8
65-69	93 081	113.9	132.1	9.7	1.1	17.2	5.4
70-74	63 504	149.6	165.3	20.5	0.0	23.6	4.7
75+	76 262	195.4	279.3	11.8	0.0	26.2	7.9

Note. Column headings in italics show the national terminology.

Table 5 *(continued)*

Residence, age and sex	Population surveyed	Disabled persons	Prevalence per 100,000 population

THAILAND, national survey 1981

Urban

Males	4 210 860	35 530	843.8
0-6	738 100	3 040	411.9
7-10	468 650	2 150	458.8
11-14	369 220	2 750	744.8
15-19	451 410	3 320	735.5
20-24	429 940	4 030	937.3
25-29	424 020	2 650	625.0
30-34	371 840	4 280	1 151.0
35-39	246 260	1 590	645.7
40-49	319 690	4 650	1 454.5
50-59	211 160	2 240	1 060.8
60+	180 560	4 830	2 675.0
Females	4 254 260	22 430	527.2
0-6	719 060	1 740	242.0
7-10	439 190	2 190	498.6
11-14	357 850	2 810	785.2
15-19	454 290	2 210	486.5
20-24	436 710	1 470	336.6
25-29	428 360	1 950	455.2
30-34	366 080	2 010	549.1
35-39	248 360	1 460	587.9
40-49	343 220	880	256.4
50-59	233 310	2 300	985.8
60+	227 820	3 400	1 492.4

Rural

Males	19 723 800	176 000	892.3
0-6	3 488 830	12 600	361.2
7-10	2 502 800	17 290	690.8
11-14	2 195 640	18 370	836.7
15-19	2 307 310	20 760	899.7
20-24	1 885 200	19 970	1 059.3
25-29	1 562 520	10 380	664.3
30-34	1 309 630	9 170	700.2
35-39	1 008 410	11 320	1 122.6
40-49	1 486 540	18 060	1 214.9
50-59	1 079 820	17 270	1 599.3
60+	897 100	20 830	2 321.9
Females	19 432 510	133 560	687.3
0-6	3 452 850	19 500	564.8
7-10	2 303 610	9 810	425.9
11-14	2 109 970	12 620	598.1
15-19	2 232 710	19 690	881.9
20-24	1 810 620	13 230	730.7
25-29	1 506 430	2 900	192.5
30-34	1 256 220	6 990	556.4
35-39	985 430	4 660	472.9
40-49	1 558 940	6 890	442.0
50-59	1 156 900	12 080	1 044.2
60+	1 058 820	25 230	2 382.8

Table 5 *(continued)*

Residence, age and sex	Population surveyed	Disabled persons	Prevalence per 100,000 population

THAILAND, national survey of children and young adults (not in school) 1983

	Not in school population	*Not in school disabled population*	
Urban			
Males	507 800	14 620	2 879.1
6-11	27 650	2 120	7 667.3
12-14	23 950	1 270	5 302.7
15-19	153 020	3 980	2 601.0
20-24	303 170	7 230	2 384.8
Females	623 280	20 980	3 366.1
6-11	34 610	2 510	7 252.2
12-14	38 740	960	2 478.1
15-19	198 510	4 360	2 196.4
20-24	351 410	13 130	3 736.4
Rural			
Males	4 846 390	105 900	2 185.1
6-11	442 310	20 690	4 677.7
12-14	458 200	12 340	2 693.1
15-19	1 991 630	40 590	2 038.0
20-24	1 954 230	32 270	1 651.3
Females	4 901 310	97 820	1 995.8
6-11	414 830	14 470	3 488.2
12-14	556 620	16 500	2 964.3
15-19	2 044 230	26 460	1 294.4
20-24	1 885 620	40 370	2 140.9

Note. Column headings in italics show the national terminology.

Table 5 *(continued)*

Residence, age and sex	Population surveyed	Prevalence per 100,000 population			
		Impairments			Disabilities
		Aural	Ocular	Mastication & swallowing	Locomotor
ICIDH		4	5	68	4

FINLAND, survey on living conditions 1978

		Diminished hearing ability	*Diminished vision ability*	*Diminished ability to masticate*	*Diminished moving ability*
Urban					
Both sexes (Age 15+)					
Large cities/surroundings	950 000	7 000	4 000	12 000	19 000
Other densely populated areas	1 802 000	9 000	4 000	15 000	24 000
Rural					
Both sexes (Age 15+)					
Sparsely populated areas	975 000	14 000	7 000	27 000	33 000

Note. Column headings in italics show the national terminology.

Table 5 *(continued)*

Residence, age and sex	Population surveyed	Prevalence per 100,000 population

NORWAY, level of living survey 1983

		Disabled persons
Both sexes (Ages 16-79)	3 898	..
>100,000 inhabitants	725	18 000
20,000-99,000 inhabitants	445	18 000
<20,000 inhabitants	1 586	17 000
Sparsely populated	1 142	19 000

	Prevalence per 100,000 population					
Other psychological	**Aural**	**Ocular**	**Disabilities**			
			Occupational role	**Locomotor**	**Lifting**	
2	4	5	18	4	48	

	Nervous condition	*Reduced hearing*	*Reduced eye sight*	*Strongly reduced working capacity*	*Reduced mobility*	*Reduced capacity to carry*
Both sexes (Ages 16-79)	..	..	..	..	..	..
>100,000 inhabitants	4 000	4 000	3 000	9 000	12 000	6 000
20,000-99,000 inhabitants	2 000	3 000	1 000	12 000	9 000	5 000
<20,000 inhabitants	3 000	3 000	2 000	10 000	10 000	5 000
Sparsely populated	3 000	4 000	2 000	12 000	11 000	7 000

Note. Column headings in italics show the national terminology.

Table 5 *(continued)*

Residence, age and sex	Population surveyed	Disabled persons	Prevalence per 100,000 population
FIJI, employment/unemployment survey 1982 *(not economically active population)*			
Urban			
Males	61 100	1 000	1 636.7
0-14	48 700	200	410.7
15-24	8 200	300	3 658.5
25-44	600	200	33 333.3
45-64	1 900	200	10 526.3
65+	1 700	100	5 882.4
Females	101 400	500	493.1
0-14	44 100	100	226.8
15-24	19 100	100	523.6
25-44	26 000	100	384.6
45-64	10 300	100	970.9
65+	2 000	100	5 000.0
Rural			
Males	92 400	1 600	1 731.6
0-14	78 300	200	255.4
15-24	7 800	400	5 128.2
25-44	700	200	28 571.4
45-64	2 200	500	22 727.3
65+	3 500	200	5 714.3
Females	167 000	900	538.9
0-14	73 000	200	274.0
15-24	31 000	100	322.6
25-44	40 400	200	495.0
45-64	18 100	300	1 657.5
65+	4 400	100	2 272.7

Table 6. Educational characteristics of disabled persons, by age, sex and type of impairment or disability

Table 6 provides the number of disabled persons, by age, sex and type of impairment or disability, according to their educational characteristics. No rates were produced for this table by the Statistical Office: numbers are presented whenever possible. Where rates are given in the table, it is because the national publication did not present numbers, but rates instead. These rates are explained for each country, as needed. No adjustments to the national presentations were done by the Statistical Office, beyond standardizing the types of impairments and disabilities through use of the ICIDH classification scheme, as needed. All references to ICIDH codes prefaced with an M (for example, M1.1), indicate that the codes are not ICIDH codes, but are devised to accommodate items not readily coded within ICIDH categories.

Classifications used, tabulations produced, and types of impairments or disabilities presented are according to national description and specification. It was decided to do it this way so that researchers and interested government officials may review national work and consider the needs for standardization. It also allows each country description to be presented independently, so that ideas may be exchanged about ways to assess educational characteristics of disabled persons in the future. Country-specific footnotes are included when explanation is needed to understand findings in table 6.

Topics covered under educational characteristics vary greatly from country to country, and are probably partly influenced by educational systems available in the country and also by national educational policy. For example, some countries distinguish between educational attainment of disabled persons according to whether they attended regular or ordinary school systems; whether they attended special classes in these school systems; or whether they attended special schools (Australia, 1981; Ethiopia, 1981). Some questions concerned current school attendance (Philippines, 1980) or reason for not attending school (Kenya, 1981).

224

6. Educational characteristics of disabled persons by age, sex and type of impairment or disability

Educational characteristics, age and sex	Intellectual impairments	Other psycho-logical impairments	Aural impairments	Ocular impairments
ICIDH	1	2	4	5

AUSTRALIA, national survey of handicapped persons 1981

	Disabled population	*Mental retardation*	*Mental disorders*	*Hearing loss*	*Sight loss*
Educational attainment					
Both sexes ages 15-64					
Living in a household	651 700	29 500	116 200	114 300	38 100
Never attended school	9 100	3 300	*	*	*
Still attending school	10 700	4 900	*	*	*
Left school under 15 yrs.	211 900	8 400	46 200	37 000	13 100
Left school 15 yrs. and over	236 300	11 300	42 700	37 100	13 700
Post-school qualifications	183 800	*	25 300	37 300	9 500
Don't know	4 800	*	*	*	*
Both sexes ages 15-64					
Living in institution	25 600	14 500	11 200	2 300	2 700
Never attended school	5 300	5 100	1 600	500	600
Still attending school	1 300	1 200	*	*	*
Left school under 15 yrs.	4 600	1 800	2 500	600	500
Left school 15 yrs. and over	5 300	2 700	2 000	600	600
Post-school qualifications	1 900	*	800	*	*
Don't know	7 200	3 500	4 100	*	800
School attendance					
Both sexes ages 5-20					
Type of school/class	102 600	33 100	8 700	22 400	8 000
Ordinary school-ordinary class	60 900	10 000	5 200	14 700	4 900
Ordinary school-special class	23 600	12 600	*	4 200	*
Special school	18 100	10 500	*	3 500	*

----

* Subject to sampling variability too high for practical purposes.

Note. Column headings in italics show the national terminology.

Table 6 *(continued)*

Educational characteristics, age and sex	Shortness of breath	Other impairment of internal organs	Other impairments of internal organs	Other motor impairment of limb: other	Unspecified other motor impairment of limb
ICIDH	61.0	66	66.8	74.8	74.9

AUSTRALIA, national survey of handicapped persons, 1981 (cont'd)

	Respira-tory disease	Circula-tory disease	Nervous system disease	Musculo-skeletal disease	Other physical condition
Educational attainment					
Both sexes ages 15-64					
Living in a household	61 500	130 900	67 100	278 200	156 900
Never attended school	*	*	*	*	*
Still attending school	*	*	*	*	*
Left school under 15 yrs.	22 400	55 700	19 600	92 100	51 700
Left school 15 yrs. and over	20 900	40 600	26 300	98 200	54 000
Post-school qualifications	16 800	33 400	17 500	84 800	46 600
Don't know	*	*	*	*	*
Both sexes ages 15-64					
Living in institution	700	2 400	9 600	4 500	6 000
Never attended school	*	*	2 400	1 100	1 100
Still attending school	*	*	500	*	*
Left school under 15 yrs.	*	500	1 500	1 000	1 100
Left school 15 yrs. and over	*	600	1 800	900	1 200
Post-school qualifications	*	*	800	*	600
Don't know	*	800	2 500	1 000	1 800
School attendance					
Both sexes ages 5-20					
Type of school/class	15 100	*	14 100	8 600	21 700
Ordinary school-ordinary class	12 500	*	7 500	7 000	11 400
Ordinary school-special class	*	*	*	*	6 300
Special school	*	*	4 100	*	4 100

* Subject to sampling variability too high for practical purposes.
Note. Column headings in italics show the national terminology.

Table 6 *(continued)*

Educational characteristics, age and sex			Mental handicap	Total or profound impairment of hearing	Speech and hearing
ICIDH			M1.1	40	M40.1

BAHRAIN, population census 1981

	Total population	*Disabled population*	*Mentally handicapped*	*Deaf*	*Deaf and mute*
Educational attainment					
Males, ages 10+	163 720	2 044	355	134	116
Illiterate	34 867	1 462	259	86	76
Read and write	46 073	329	47	31	20
Primary	26 270	127	23	9	13
Intermediate	18 414	55	14	4	5
Secondary	23 103	45	10	2	2
Diploma	7 400	16	2	2	..
B.A. or B.Sc.	6 466	7	..	..	..
Master's degree	908	1	..	..	..
Ph.D. or equivalent	189	..	..	..	..
Not stated	30	2	..	..	..
Females, ages 10+	105 829	1 179	179	80	64
Illiterate	38 450	1 025	153	71	54
Read and write	24 681	91	19	4	5
Primary	13 461	28	2	2	2
Intermediate	8 947	18	3	2	3
Secondary	12 839	11	..	..	..
Diploma	4 215	4	2	1	..
B.A. or B.Sc.	2 898	2	..	..	..
Master's degree	247	..	..	..	..
Ph.D. or equivalent	39	..	..	..	..
Not stated	52	..	..	..	..

Note. Column headings in italics show the national terminology.

Table 6 *(continued)*

Educational characteristics, age and sex	Total visual impairment of both eyes	Unspecified other paralysis of limb	Transverse deficiency unspecified of proximal limb parts	Other impairment	Unspecified other impairment
ICIDH	51.0	73.9	75.9	99	99.9

BAHRAIN, population census 1981 (continued)

Educational attainment	*Blind*	*Paralysed*	*Amputee*	*Other*	*Not stated*
Males, ages 10+	691	282	230	236	..
Illiterate	562	178	155	146	..
Read and write	81	59	42	49	..
Primary	31	24	9	18	..
Intermediate	6	10	9	7	..
Secondary	4	9	8	10	..
Diploma	3	1	5	3	..
B.A. or B.Sc.	2	1	2	2	..
Master's degree	1	..	..	..	..
Ph.D. or equivalent	..	..	..	..	..
Not stated	1	..	..	1	..
Females, ages 10+	480	211	68	97	..
Illiterate	445	170	58	74	..
Read and write	22	22	3	16	..
Primary	11	5	2	4	..
Intermediate	1	7	1	1	..
Secondary	1	5	3	2	..
Diploma	..	1	..	..	..
B.A. or B.Sc.	..	1	1	..	..
Master's degree	..	..	..	..	..
Ph.D. or equivalent	..	..	..	..	..
Not stated	..	..	..	..	..

Note. Column headings in italics show the national terminology.

Table 6 *(continued)*

Educational characteristics, age and sex	Population surveyed	Disabled persons
CANADA, health and disability survey 1983-84		
Educational attainment		
Both sexes, aged 15-24	4 335 000	165 000
0-8 years	281 000	28 000
High school	2 863 000	110 000
Some post-secondary education	644 000	16 000
Post-secondary certificate/diploma	395 000	9 000
University degree	153 000	..
Both sexes, aged 25-34	4 335 000	230 000
0-8 years	280 000	41 000
High school	2 200 000	122 000
Some post-secondary education	442 000	19 000
Post-secondary certificate/diploma	727 000	30 000
University degree	687 000	18 000
Both sexes, aged 35-54	5 840 000	581 000
0-8 years	1 283 000	202 000
High school	2 702 000	262 000
Some post-secondary education	358 000	30 000
Post-secondary certificate/diploma	735 000	53 000
University degree	762 000	33 000
Both sexes, aged 55-64	2 270 000	561 000
0-8 years	889 000	274 000
High school	968 000	221 000
Some post-secondary education	102 000	19 000
Post-secondary certificate/diploma	165 000	29 000
University degree	145 000	18 000
Both sexes, aged 65+	2 356 000	910 000
0-8 years	1 200 000	521 000
High school	828 000	291 000
Some post-secondary education	77 000	27 000
Post-secondary certificate/diploma	141 000	47 000
University degree	111 000	25 000
Both sexes, 15+	19 136 000	2 448 000
0-8 years	3 934 000	1 066 000
High school	9 559 000	1 007 000
Some post-secondary education	1 622 000	111 000
Post-secondary certificate/diploma	2 162 000	168 000
University degree	1 858 000	95 000

Table 6 *(continued)*

Educational characteristics, age and sex	Disabled persons	Mental handicap	Severe impairment of communi-cation	Total or profound impairment of hearing	Speech and hearing
ICIDH		M1.1	30	40	M40.1

EGYPT, population census 1976

Educational attainment		*Mentally disabled*	*Mute*	*Deaf*	*Deaf and mute*
Males, aged 10+	77 683	5 271	2 158	3 581	7 631
Illiterate	40 348	4 214	1 542	2 021	3 683
Read and write	16 519	257	296	920	1 575
Primary certificate	5 217	76	96	230	765
Certificate < intermediate	3 074	40	89	74	322
Intermediate	4 490	67	63	185	596
Diploma < university	176	4	5	4	31
University	2 827	11	36	112	545
Postgraduate diploma	64	0	0	1	8
Master's	44	0	0	0	9
Doctorate	47	0	0	4	12
Not available	4 869	602	31	30	85
Females, aged 10+	25 530	1 585	731	1 147	3 069
Illiterate	18 388	1 415	546	802	1 741
Read and write	2 326	40	56	185	450
Primary certificate	1 380	11	27	61	386
Certificate < intermediate	991	10	30	26	157
Intermediate	1 396	7	43	49	204
Diploma < university	91	1	6	1	13
University	404	2	15	17	78
Postgraduate diploma	3	0	0	0	2
Master's	5	0	1	0	1
Doctorate	2	0	0	0	0
Not available	544	99	7	6	37

Note. Column headings in italics show the national terminology.

Table 6 (continued)

Educational characteristics, age and sex	Total visual impairment of both eyes	Profound visual impairment of one eye	Transverse deficiency of upper arm	Transverse deficiency of lower leg	Other impairment
ICIDH	51.0	54	75.1	75.6	99

EGYPT, population census 1976 (cont'd)

	Blind	*Loss of sight in one eye*	*Loss of upper limbs*	*Loss of lower limbs*	*Other infirmities*
Educational attainment					
Males, aged 10+	17 751	14 240	6 127	4 980	15 944
Illiterate	7 800	7 416	2 854	2 403	8 423
Read and write	2 523	3 816	1 679	1 519	3 932
Primary certificate	1 534	792	414	372	938
Certificate < intermediate	870	586	176	267	650
Intermediate	790	989	477	281	1 050
Diploma < university	22	34	14	15	44
University	379	490	483	87	684
Postgraduate diploma	26	11	1	4	13
Master's	10	12	1	1	11
Doctorate	13	4	8	0	6
Not available	3 784	90	20	31	193
Females, aged 10+	11 270	4 047	468	543	2 672
Illiterate	8 610	2 968	271	439	1 598
Read and write	977	230	53	38	297
Primary certificate	566	140	37	29	123
Certificate < intermediate	407	191	28	14	128
Intermediate	473	343	39	14	224
Diploma < university	23	25	6	0	16
University	46	116	30	3	97
Postgraduate diploma	0	0	0	0	1
Master's	0	1	0	0	2
Doctorate	0	1	1	0	0
Not available	168	32	3	6	186

Note. Column headings in italics show the national terminology.

Table 6 (continued)

Educational characteristics, age and sex	Mental handicap	Severe impairment of communication	Aural impairments	Ocular impairments	Other impairment of cardio-respiratory function
ICIDH	M1.1	30	4	5	61.8

EGYPT, national survey 1979-1981

Educational attainment	*Mental*	*Mutism*	*Hearing*	*Vision*	*Debility*
Both sexes	64	59	51	158	17
Illiterate	44	37	32	118	16
Read and write	11	12	10	21	1
Primary	2	3	3	2	0
Secondary	1	4	3	8	0
University	0	0	2	5	0
Not ascertained	2	3	1	4	0

	Impairment of posture	Mixed and other upper limb mechanical impairment	Mixed and other mechanical impairment of limb
	70.5	71.8	71.9

Educational attainment	*Spine*	*Upper limb*	*Lower limb*
Both sexes	13	101	231
Illiterate	11	60	120
Read and write	1	18	38
Primary	0	9	20
Secondary	1	3	18
University	0	5	6
Not ascertained	0	6	29

Note. Column headings in italics show the national terminology.

Table 6 *(continued)*

Educational characteristics, age and sex	Disabled persons
ETHIOPIA, survey of children 1981	
School attendance	
Both sexes, aged 0-14	29 631
Attend formal education	2 375
Attend special education	536
Attend religious education	196
Do not go to school	19 032
No response	7 483

Table 6 *(continued)*

Educational characteristics, age and sex	Population surveyed	Disabled persons
HONG KONG, population census 1981 *		
Educational attainment (%)		
Both sexes		
Aged 15-24	100.0	100.0
No school/kindergarten	1.6	25.2
Primary	21.7	40.5
Secondary	64.6	30.5
Matriculated or higher	12.1	3.9
Aged 25-34	100.0	100.0
No school/kindergarten	4.1	26.3
Primary	36.9	43.1
Secondary	45.6	25.0
Matriculated or higher	13.3	5.6
Aged 35-44	100.0	100.0
No school/kindergarten	11.9	24.9
Primary	41.4	48.5
Secondary	33.2	22.2
Matriculated or higher	13.5	4.4
Aged 45-54	100.0	100.0
No school/kindergarten	29.4	37.6
Primary	46.8	48.7
Secondary	17.4	10.6
Matriculated or higher	6.5	3.1
Aged 55+	100.0	100.0
No school/kindergarten	47.4	56.4
Primary	37.1	31.6
Secondary	11.3	8.9
Matriculated or higher	4.2	3.1

----

* Percentage distribution of total and disabled population according to educational characteristics for selected age groups.

Table 6 *(continued)*

Educational characteristics, age and sex	Intellectual impairments	Other psycho-logical impairments	Total or profound impairment of hearing	Visual impairment of both eyes	Impairment of posture
ICIDH	1	2	40	51.0	70.5

HONG KONG, population census 1981 * (cont'd)

	Mentally retarded	Mentally ill	Severely deaf	Blind	Abnormal spine curvature
Educational attainment (%)					
Both sexes					
Total	100.0	100.0	100.0	100.0	100.0
No school/kindergarten	45.2	29.0	39.8	56.6	52.2
Primary	42.7	44.9	42.5	31.4	24.9
Secondary	11.3	22.6	15.3	9.9	17.5
Matriculated or higher	0.8	3.6	2.4	2.1	5.5

Complete paralysis of lower limbs paraplegia	Spastic paralysis of more than one limb	Of upper and lower limbs on same side	Deficiency unspecified of proximal limb parts
72.3	72.9	73.5	75.9

	Polio/ lower body paralysed	Spastic	One side of body paralysed	Loss of limb
Both sexes				
Total	100.0	100.0	100.0	100.0
No school/kindergarten	32.8	42.7	45.4	38.7
Primary	36.2	39.7	37.6	39.8
Secondary	23.8	14.1	12.0	17.6
Matriculated or higher	7.2	3.5	5.1	3.8

----

* Percentage distribution of disabled population according to educational characteristics for selected impairments.

Note. Column headings in italics show the national terminology.

Table 6 *(continued)*

Educational characteristics, age and sex	Mental handicap	Other psycho-logical impairment	Unspecified impairment of behaviour pattern
ICIDH	M1.1	2	29.9

JAMAICA, survey of handicapped children in schools 1978

School setting	School disabled population	Mental	Emotional	Learning
Both sexes, aged 4–11	654	241	87	115
Regular class, no special instruction	135	14	13	3
Regular class, special instruction	125	34	18	5
Resource room	172	119	18	19
Unit class	207	71	34	82
Special school, non-residential	13	3	2	6
Special school, residential	2	0	2	0

	Language impairments	Aural impairments	Ocular impairments	Unspecified other motor impairment of limb
	3	4	5	74.9

School setting	Speech	Auditory	Visual	Physical
Both sexes, aged 4–11	32	88	81	10
Regular class, no special instruction	9	34	55	7
Regular class, special instruction	18	41	8	1
Resource room	2	1	12	1
Unit class	2	11	6	1
Special school, non-residential	1	1	0	1
Special school, residential	0	0	0	0

Note. Column headings in italics show the national terminology.

Table 6 *(continued)*

	Disabled persons

KENYA, national survey of persons 1981

Persons who were eligible and did not seek to enrol at regular schools or training institutions, by reason for not enrolling

Total , both sexes, aged 15+	981
Parents unwilling	200
Educational costs	186
Disability	141
Lack of information	123
Other	150
Missing information	181

Persons eligible and who did not seek to enrol in special education

Total , both sexes, aged 15+	1 106
Lack of information	264
Educational/training costs	180
Parents/guardians unwilling	165
Due to disability	81
Other	184
Missing information	232

Persons who tried to enrol in regular school

Total , both sexes, aged 15+	702
Admitted and still enrolled	119
Admitted and completed	180
Left due to educational costs	150
Left due to disability/illness	150
Not admitted due to disability	91
Missing information	12

Persons who tried to enrol in special education

Total , both sexes, aged 15+	474
Admitted and completed	216
Admitted and still enrolled	93
Sent away for various reasons	99
Missing information	66

Table 6 *(continued)*

Educational characteristics, age and sex	Disabled persons	Intellectual	Severe: commun- ication	Total or profound: hearing	Speech and hearing	Total visual: both eyes
ICIDH			1	30	40	M40.1	51.0

KUWAIT, population census 1980

			Mental retardation	*Mute*	*Deaf*	*Deaf and mute*	*Blind*
Educational attainment							
Males, aged 10+	3 400		946	167	113	136	459
Illiterate	1 930		648	101	62	34	362
Read and write	587		132	35	20	29	35
Elementary	506		126	22	21	50	16
Intermediate	237		36	8	4	16	14
Secondary	93		4	1	5	7	16
Post-secondary college attended	18		..	..	1	..	8
University and above	29		..	..	0	..	8
Females, aged 10+	1 632		528	68	53	71	224
Illiterate	1 153		428	43	33	28	202
Read and write	160		45	9	5	14	8
Elementary	200		42	11	8	22	4
Intermediate	77		10	4	3	3	2
Secondary	36		3	1	2	4	7
Post-secondary college attended	3		..	..	2	..	..
University and above	3		..	..	0	..	1
School attendance							
Males, aged 4+	865		224	60	36	113	21
Kindergarten	10		3	..	1	3	..
Elementary	364		100	34	15	49	5
Intermediate	352		98	20	17	49	9
Secondary	126		22	5	3	11	5
Between secondary & university	3		1	1	..	..	0
University	9		..	..	..	..	2
Postgraduate	..		..	..	..	..	..
Other	1		..	..	..	1	..
Females, aged 4+	446		104	28	19	54	8
Kindergarten	10		6	..	..	..	..
Elementary	208		52	18	8	29	4
Intermediate	158		36	8	8	21	2
Secondary	61		8	2	3	3	2
Between secondary & university	4		1	..	..	1	..
University	5		1	..	..	..	..
Postgraduate	..		..	..	..	..	..
Other	..		..	..	..	..	..

Note. Column headings in italics show the national terminology.

Table 6 *(continued)*

Educational characteristics, age and sex	Profound Visual: one eye	Unspecified other paralysis of limb	Transverse deficiency				Other
			Upper arm	Upper arms	Lower leg	Lower legs	
ICIDH	54	73.9	75.1	M75.11	75.6	75.61	99

KUWAIT, population census 1980 (cont'd)

	Sight in one eye	Paralysis	Loss of arm	Loss of arms	Loss of leg	Loss of legs	Other
Educational attainment							
Males, aged 10+	476	645	35	1	68	10	344
Illiterate	246	310	9	1	24	6	127
Read and write	123	106	5	..	20	1	81
Elementary	50	131	9	..	14	2	65
Intermediate	31	81	7	..	6	1	33
Secondary	18	13	2	..	3	..	24
Post-secondary college attended	2	2	..	..	..	..	5
University and above	6	2	3	..	1	..	9
Females, aged 10+	123	400	4	..	19	7	135
Illiterate	97	230	2	..	11	5	74
Read and write	4	56	..	..	2	..	17
Elementary	13	71	2	..	5	..	22
Intermediate	2	38	..	..	..	1	14
Secondary	6	5	..	..	1	1	6
Post-secondary college attended	..	..	..	..	..	..	1
University and above	1	..	..	..	..	..	1
School attendance							
Males, aged 4+	22	286	7	..	16	1	79
Kindergarten	..	1	..	..	..	..	2
Elementary	4	111	1	..	5	..	40
Intermediate	12	110	3	..	9	..	25
Secondary	5	61	3	..	2	1	8
Between secondary & university	..	..	..	..	..	..	1
University	1	3	..	..	..	..	3
Postgraduate	..	..	..	..	..	..	..
Other	..	..	..	..	..	..	..
Females, aged 4+	14	180	1	..	3	2	33
Kindergarten	1	2	..	..	..	..	1
Elementary	4	83	..	..	2	..	8
Intermediate	7	59	1	..	1	..	15
Secondary	1	33	..	..	..	1	8
Between secondary & university	..	1	..	..	..	..	1
University	1	2	..	..	..	1	..
Postgraduate	..	..	..	..	..	..	..
Other	..	..	..	..	..	..	..

Note. Column headings in italics show the national terminology.

Table 6 *(continued)*

Educational characteristics, age and sex	Occupational role disability	Locomotor disability
ICIDH	18	4

NORWAY, level of living survey 1983

	Strongly reduced working capacity	*Reduced mobility*
Educational attainment		
Both sexes, aged 16–79	405	406
Above primary school level (%)	27	25
University level (%)	2	4
In vocational training in 1982 (%)	10	12
Total number, economically active in 1982	115	115

Note. Column headings in italics show the national terminology.

Table 6 *(continued)*

Educational characteristics, age and sex	Disabled persons	Severe impairment of communication	Total or profound impairment of hearing	Speech and hearing
ICIDH		30	40	M40.1

PERU, national census of population and housing 1981

		Mute	*Deaf*	*Deaf and mute*
Educational attainment				
Total	26 560	3 909	4 886	1 346
No education	9 310	1 989	1 936	643
Initial or pre-school	604	93	104	26
Primary, completed	3 819	362	689	146
Primary, not completed	6 928	905	1 292	252
Primary, not specified	515	63	80	22
Secondary, completed	1 400	96	197	59
Secondary, not completed	1 968	138	273	69
Secondary, not specified	184	12	32	10
Superior, not university, completed	195	11	35	9
Superior, not university, not completed	141	9	24	6
Superior, university, completed	350	14	56	15
Superior, university, not completed	233	12	36	10
Not specified	604	142	103	51
Less than 5 years old	309	63	29	28

	Total visual impairment of both eyes	Multiple impairment of all classes	Other impairment
	51.0	90.0	99

	Blind	*Other multiple*	*Other impairments*
Educational attainment			
Total	3 258	611	12 550
No education	1 181	285	3 276
Initial or pre-school	61	10	310
Primary, completed	486	72	2 064
Primary, not completed	823	133	3 523
Primary, not specified	75	15	260
Secondary, completed	158	22	868
Secondary, not completed	230	38	1 220
Secondary, not specified	24	–	106
Superior, not university, completed	26	4	110
Superior, not university, not completed	20	1	81
Superior, university, completed	49	5	211
Superior, university, not completed	30	4	141
Not specified	75	11	222
Less than 5 years old	20	11	158

Note. Column headings in italics show the national terminology.

Table 6 *(continued)*

Educational characteristics, age and sex	Population surveyed	Mental handicap	Multiple impairments of all classes
ICIDH		**M1.1**	**90.0**

PHILIPPINES, national survey 1980

		Mental impairment	*Mixed impairments*
Educational attainment			
Both sexes, total	19 678	102	27
None	1 106	30	14
Some years in primary	2 108	20	3
Finished primary	1 352	4	2
Some years in elementary	2 039	6	1
Finished elementary	3 987	10	2
Some years in secondary	3 454	13	4
Finished secondary	2 267	10	0
Some years in college	1 757	7	1
College graduate	1 501	2	0
Unknown	107	0	0

Note. Column headings in italics show the national terminology.

Table 6 *(continued)*

Educational characteristics, age and sex	Mental handicap	Severe: communi- cation	Aural	Ocular	Visceral
ICIDH	**M1.1**	**30**	**4**	**5**	**6**

PHILIPPINES, national survey 1980 (cont'd)

	Mental impairment	*Communi- cation*	*Aural*	*Ocular*	*Visceral*
School attendance					
Males, aged 0-14	18	5	11	15	24
Attend school independently	0	0	4	8	4
Attend school with assistance	2	1	0	0	1
Attend special class	0	2	0	0	0
Stopped school due to disability	3	0	1	1	0
Not applicable	13	2	6	6	19
Females, aged 0-14	13	5	8	18	12
Attend school independently	2	0	4	9	5
Attend school with assistance	2	1	0	3	0
Attend special class	1	0	0	1	0
Stopped school due to disability	2	0	2	0	1
Not applicable	6	4	2	5	6
Males, aged 15-64	45	7	24	51	82
Attend school independently	1	0	4	6	4
Attend school with assistance	0	0	1	3	0
Attend special class	0	0	0	2	0
Stopped school due to disability	18	2	6	3	4
Not applicable	26	5	13	37	74
Females, aged 15-64	55	7	15	42	66
Attend school independently	4	0	3	3	3
Attend school with assistance	1	0	0	1	0
Attend special class	1	0	0	0	0
Stopped school due to disability	19	0	2	8	0
Not applicable	30	7	10	30	63
Males, aged 65+	2	1	5	13	19
Attend school independently	0	0	0	0	0
Attend school with assistance	0	0	0	0	0
Attend special class	0	0	0	0	0
Stopped school due to disability	0	0	0	0	0
Not applicable	2	1	5	13	19
Females, aged 65+	0	1	9	12	11
Attend school independently	0	0	0	0	0
Attend school with assistance	0	0	0	0	0
Attend special class	0	0	0	0	0
Stopped school due to disability	0	0	0	0	0
Not applicable	0	1	9	12	11

Note. Column headings in italics show the national terminology.

6. Educational characteristics of disabled persons by age, sex and type of impairment or disability

Educational characteristics, age and sex	Skeletal	Other and unspecified disfigure- ment	Generalized, sensory and other
ICIDH	7	87.9	9

PHILIPPINES, national survey 1980 (cont'd)

	Skeletal	*Disfiguring*	*Two- category combinations*
School attendance			
Males, aged 0-14	41	10	57
Attend school independently	14	4	12
Attend school with assistance	2	1	2
Attend special class	0	0	2
Stopped school due to disability	4	0	12
Not applicable	21	5	29
Females, aged 0-14	43	10	34
Attend school independently	17	5	8
Attend school with assistance	4	0	4
Attend special class	0	0	3
Stopped school due to disability	3	1	0
Not applicable	19	4	19
Males, aged 15-64	146	14	152
Attend school independently	17	1	10
Attend school with assistance	1	0	4
Attend special class	2	0	2
Stopped school due to disability	15	3	18
Not applicable	111	10	118
Females, aged 15-64	67	8	118
Attend school independently	4	0	5
Attend school with assistance	2	0	2
Attend special class	1	0	0
Stopped school due to disability	7	3	12
Not applicable	53	5	99
Males, aged 65+	26	1	69
Attend school independently	0	0	0
Attend school with assistance	0	0	0
Attend special class	0	0	0
Stopped school due to disability	0	0	0
Not applicable	26	1	69
Females, aged 65+	23	0	55
Attend school independently	0	0	0
Attend school with assistance	0	0	0
Attend special class	0	0	0
Stopped school due to disability	0	0	0
Not applicable	23	0	55

Note. Column headings in italics show the national terminology.

Table 6 (continued)

Educational characteristics, age and sex	Population surveyed	Impairments		Disabilities		
		Aural	Ocular	Occupational role	Locomotor	Other Locomotor
ICIDH		4	5	18	4	49

SWEDEN, living conditions survey 1980/81 *

		Reduced hearing	Reduced eye sight	Reduced work capacity	Mobility	Serious mobility disability
Educational attainment						
Both sexes, aged 16-84						
Pre-secondary education	2 812 000	7.8	1.2	13.8	9.3	3.7
Secondary education	2 195 000	5.1	0.5	8.0	4.1	1.7
Post-secondary education	994 000	2.4	0.1	3.1	2.0	0.8

----

* Percentage of total population that is disabled at each level of educational attainment according to type of impairment or disability.

Note. Column headings in italics show the national terminology.

Table 6 (continued)

Educational characteristics, age and sex	Mental handicap	Speech and hearing	Total visual impairment of both eyes	Unspecified other motor impairment of limb	Other impairment
ICIDH	M1.1	M40.1	51.0	74.9	99

TUNISIA, population census 1975

	Disabled population	Mental handicap	Deaf and mute	Blind	Motor impairment	Other
Educational attainment						
Males, aged 10+	25 090	4 250	2 400	6 660	7 790	3 990
Illiterate	20 180	3 270	2 220	5 780	5 910	3 000
Read and write	840	90	40	250	260	200
Primary education	2 850	660	100	340	1 220	530
Secondary/professional	100	20	0	20	20	40
Secondary/long	710	150	20	210	210	120
College	80	20	0	30	20	10
Specialist	50	0	0	10	0	40
Not available	280	40	20	20	150	50
Females, aged 10+	15 610	2 450	1 760	5 460	3 660	2 280
Illiterate	14 470	2 290	1 690	5 260	3 230	2 000
Read and write	20	0	0	20	0	0
Primary education	900	100	70	150	380	200
Secondary/professional	20	10	0	0	0	10
Secondary/long	100	20	0	20	40	20
College	20	0	0	0	10	10
Specialist	30	0	0	0	0	30
Not available	50	30	0	10	0	10

Note. Column headings in italics show the national terminology.

Table 6 *(continued)*

Educational characteristics, age and sex	Total disabilities
ZIMBABWE, national survey 1981 a/	
Educational attainment	
Both sexes	
No education	104 200
0-4	9 600
5-15	15 500
16-59	45 600
60+	33 400
1-2 years primary	32 800
0-4	0
5-15	13 400
16-59	12 600
60+	6 700
3 years plus primary	56 100
0-4	0
5-15	10 200
16-59	39 300
60+	6 500
1-2 years secondary	4 300
0-4	0
5-15	400
16-59	3 700
60+	100
2 years plus secondary	1 300
0-4	0
5-15	0
16-59	1 300
60+	0
Post secondary	100
0-4	0
5-15	0
16-59	100
60+	0
Total	198 900

Current school attendance	School attendance before disablement	
		65 000
Attend	Attended	7 400
Attend	Not attended	25 800
Not attend	Attended	2 600
Not attend	Not attended	29 200

a/ Sum of age groups does not necessarily equal total.

Table 7. Employment characteristics of disabled persons, by age, sex and type of impairment or disability

Description of variables

Table 7 provides the number of disabled persons according to their employment characteristics, age, sex and type of impairment or disability. The types of employment characteristics presented in table 7 include economic activity; work status; labour force participation; ability to participate in work before and after a disability. Employment tables included in table 7 use the standard classifications of economic activity regularly employed in population censuses. Employment characteristics of disabled persons according to type of impairment or disability were classified into the ICIDH framework. When numbers of persons were not provided in the published national reports, rates were shown instead, as available. Exceptions to the rule are footnoted at the country level of table 7. All references to ICIDH codes prefaced with an M (for example, M1.1), indicate that the codes are not ICIDH codes, but are devised to accommodate items not readily coded within ICIDH categories.

7. Employment characteristics of disabled persons by age, sex and type of impairment or disability

Employment characteristics, age and sex	Population surveyed	Disabled persons

AUSTRALIA, national survey of handicapped persons 1981

Economic activity

Both sexes, aged 15-64		651 700
Employed		226 200
Unemployed		31 500
Not in the labor force		394 000
Males, aged 15-64	4 829 900	347 700
Employed	4 005 000	153 500
Unemployed	201 800	17 800
Not in the labor force	623 000	176 400
Females, aged 15-64	4 738 300	304 100
Employed	2 292 600	72 800
Unemployed	206 200	13 700
Not in the labor force	2 239 500	217 600

Table 7 *(continued)*

Economic Activity According to Sex	Ocular Impairments	Total Visual: Both Eyes	Near-Total Visual: Both Eyes	Moderate Visual: Both Eyes	Unspecified Moderate Visual: Both Eyes
ICIDH	5	51.0	51.3	53	53.9

AUSTRIA, sample survey on physical disabilities 1976*

	Visual Impairments	*Blind in Both Eyes*	*Partial Sight*	*Farsighted Uncorrect- able*	*Nearsighted Uncorrect- able*
Males, Total	249 000	2 400	3 800	102 200	74 400
Total percent	100.0	100.0	100.0	100.0	100.0
Employed: Own account or family help	9.0	12.3	10.0	9.9	10.1
Employed: Employee	17.6	16.9	..	14.2	26.5
Employed: Worker	14.0	..	12.0	9.9	17.4
Unemployed	0.9	..	..	0.4	1.2
Income recipient	49.9	70.8	72.1	63.1	30.7
Student	7.7	..	5.9	2.2	13.4
Nursing school and kindergarten	0.5	..	..	0.3	0.3
Other dependants	0.4	..	..	..	0.4
Females, Total	369 000	2 500	4 700	167 400	112 500
Total percent	100.0	100.0	100.0	100.0	100.0
Employed: Own account or family help	4.8	..	..	4.5	7.8
Employed: Employee	6.4	10.4	1.0	4.2	11.2
Employed: Worker	5.3	..	5.6	3.8	8.5
Unemployed	0.2	..	..	0.1	0.6
Income recipient	53.2	60.4	78.1	60.4	34.3
Student	4.8	..	0.6	1.3	10.2
Nursing school and kindergarten	0.6	1.2	..	0.4	0.3
Home-maker	24.0	28.0	14.7	24.9	26.5
Other dependants	0.7	..	..	0.4	0.6

----

* Percentage distribution of disabled persons according to economic activity by age, sex and type of impairment or disability.

Note. Column headings in italics show the national terminology.

Table 7 *(continued)*

Employment characteristics, age and sex	Profound visual: one eye	Other visual	Other visual: colour vision	Other: vision
ICIDH	54	57	57.5	57.8

AUSTRIA, sample survey on physical disabilities 1976 * *(cont'd)*

	Blind in one eye	Cataracts or glaucoma	Colour- blind	Other visual
Economic activity				
Males, total number	21 700	21 100	4 400	37 700
Total percent	100.0	100.0	100.0	100.0
Employed: own account or family help	5.8	2.7	9.5	6.5
Employed: employee	11.2	3.5	29.3	18.0
Employed: worker	16.9	3.5	24.4	19.7
Unemployed	2.3	0.2	..	0.7
Income recipient	56.3	87.3	28.5	38.7
Student	6.0	1.8	4.4	14.0
Nursing school and kindergarten	0.6	0.2	..	2.0
Other dependants	0.9	0.8	3.9	0.4
Females, total number	16 800	55 300	1 700	38 300
Total percent	100.0	100.0	100.0	100.0
Employed: own account or family help	0.2	0.3	..	5.8
Employed: employee	3.2	2.0	..	8.2
Employed: worker	10.5	0.4	13.5	5.0
Unemployed	..	..	..	0.1
Income recipient	60.8	81.5	70.3	43.0
Student	0.7	1.0	1.6	9.4
Nursing school and kindergarten	0.4	0.1	..	2.9
Home-maker	20.9	13.7	14.6	25.1
Other dependants	3.3	1.0	..	0.5

* Percentage distribution of disabled persons according to economic activity by age, sex and type of impairment or disability.

Note. Column headings in italics show the national terminology.

Table 7 *(continued)*

Employment characteristics, age and sex	Mental handicap	Total or profound: hearing	Speech and hearing
ICIDH	**M1.1**	**40**	**M40.1**

BAHRAIN, population census 1981

	Total population	*Disabled population*	*Mentally handi- capped*	*Deaf*	*Deaf and mute*
Males, aged 15+	146 514	1 909	304	129	95
Working	123 221	502	20	70	44
Unemployed: looking for work	2 958	34	13	2	4
Unemployed: not looking for work	629	58	31	2	5
Inactive: income recipient	711	36	..	1	1
Inactive: homemaker	..	..	..	..	..
Inactive: student	14 760	88	19	3	15
Inactive: unable to work	3 527	1 012	210	46	23
Activity not stated	708	179	11	5	3
Females, aged 15+	88 822	1 075	138	78	54
Working	14 671	13	2	1	1
Unemployed: looking for work	1 534	2	..	1	..
Unemployed: not looking for work	3 120	36	10	4	7
Inactive: income recipient	160	5	1	..	..
Inactive: homemaker	52 691	302	40	33	23
Inactive: student	12 740	29	3	3	3
Inactive: unable to work	3 644	613	78	36	19
Activity not stated	262	75	4	..	1

	Total visual: both eyes	Unspecified other paralysis of limb	Transverse deficiency unspecified of proximal limb parts	Other impairment
	51.0	73.9	75.9	99
	Blind	*Paralysed*	*Amputee*	*Other*
Males, aged 15+	678	252	228	223
Working	105	44	145	74
Unemployed: looking for work	6	4	4	1
Unemployed: not looking for work	7	3	2	8
Inactive: income recipient	20	6	4	4
Inactive: homemaker	..	..	..	..
Inactive: student	14	26	5	6
Inactive: unable to work	446	152	68	67
Activity not stated	80	17	..	63
Females, aged 15+	472	191	65	77
Working	..	5	2	2
Unemployed: looking for work	..	1	..	..
Unemployed: not looking for work	4	6	..	5
Inactive: income recipient	1	3	..	..
Inactive: homemaker	135	29	32	10
Inactive: student	5	8	4	3
Inactive: unable to work	315	111	26	28
Activity not stated	12	28	1	29

Note. Column headings in italics show the national terminology.

Table 7 *(continued)*

Employment characteristics, age and sex	Disabled persons

CANADA, health and disability survey 1983/84

Economic activity and degree of disability

Both sexes, aged 15-64

Employed: degree of disability	637 000
Some	424 000
Moderate	104 000
Major	24 000
Unknown	86 000

Both sexes, aged 15-64

Unemployed: degree of disability	98 000
Some	57 000
Moderate	21 000
Major	..
Unknown	17 000

Both sexes, aged 15-64

Not in labour force: degree of disability	802 000
Some	405 000
Moderate	190 000
Major	119 000
Unknown	87 000

Both sexes, aged 15-64

Total economically active	1 537 000
Some	886 000
Moderate	316 000
Major	145 000
Unknown	190 000

Table 7 *(continued)*

Employment characteristics, age and sex	Population surveyed	Disabled persons
CANADA, health and disability survey 1983/84 (cont.)		
Economic activity		
Males, employed	6 502 000	400 000
15-24	1 210 000	29 000
25-34	1 830 000	70 000
35-54	2 589 000	169 000
55-64	738 000	103 000
65+	135 000	29 000
Females, employed	4 593 000	275 000
15-24	1 114 000	36 000
25-34	1 338 000	56 000
35-54	1 725 000	123 000
55-64	373 000	50 000
65+	43 000	9 000
Males, unemployed	688 000	57 000
15-24	275 000	15 000
25-34	196 000	13 000
35-54	165 000	19 000
55-64	51 000	10 000
65+	..	..
Females, unemployed	545 000	41 000
15-24	216 000	9 000
25-34	149 000	7 000
35-54	150 000	19 000
55-64	29 000	7 000
65+	..	..
Males, not in labour force	2 167 000	651 000
15-24	705 000	34 000
25-34	120 000	26 000
35-54	164 000	80 000
55-64	297 000	154 000
65+	881 000	357 000
Females, not in labour force	4 641 000	1 024 000
15-24	815 000	43 000
25-34	702 000	59 000
35-54	1 048 000	171 000
55-64	781 000	236 000
65+	1 295 000	516 000
Males, total	9 357 000	1 108 000
15-24	2 190 000	78 000
25-34	2 146 000	108 000
35-54	2 917 000	269 000
55-64	1 086 000	268 000
65+	1 017 000	385 000
Females, total	9 779 000	1 339 000
15-24	2 145 000	87 000
25-34	2 189 000	122 000
35-54	2 922 000	312 000
55-64	1 183 000	293 000
65+	1 339 000	525 000

Table 7 *(continued)*

Employment characteristics, age and sex	Population surveyed	Prevalence per 100 population	
		Generalized, sensory and other impairments	Locomotor disability
ICIDH		9	4

DENMARK, living conditions survey 1976

		Problems with vision or hearing	*Mobility problems*
Economic activity			
Males, aged 20-44		11	5
Total employed		10	5
Self-employed		10	4
Salaried		9	4
Manual worker		12	5
Skilled		11	5
Unskilled		13	6
Without a job		14	12
Unemployed		14	10
Pensioner		..	..
Homemaker		..	..
Other-without job		11	5
Females, aged 20-44		10	5
Total employed		9	4
Self-employed		4	6
Salaried		8	3
Manual worker		13	4
Skilled		..	..
Unskilled		14	4
Without a job		11	8
Unemployed		13	4
Pensioner		..	..
Homemaker		10	9
Other-without job		12	5
Males, aged 45-69		28	20
Total employed		25	14
Self-employed		23	15
Salaried		17	8
Manual worker		33	17
Skilled		36	17
Unskilled		32	17
Without a job		39	45
Unemployed		45	24
Pensioner		39	50
Homemaker		..	..
Other-without job		..	..

Note. Column headings in italics show the national terminology.

Table 7 *(continued)*

Employment characteristics, age and sex	Population surveyed	Prevalence per 100 population	
		Generalized, sensory and other impairments	Locomotor disability
ICIDH		9	4

DENMARK living conditions survey 1976 (cont'd)

		Problems with vision or hearing	*Mobility problems*
Economic avtivity			
Females, aged 45–69		24	23
Total employed		20	11
Self-employed		16	15
Salaried		17	5
Manual worker		24	13
Skilled		..	..
Unskilled		24	13
Without a job		27	33
Unemployed		..	..
Pensioner		32	47
Homemaker		23	20
Other-without job		..	..
Both sexes, aged 20–69	5 166	17	12
Total employed	3 624	15	7
Self-employed	672	15	10
Salaried	1 588	11	5
Manual worker	1 362	19	9
Skilled	352	16	7
Unskilled	1 010	20	9
Without a job	1 542	22	24
Unemployed	180	19	12
Pensioner	525	34	47
Homemaker	618	17	15
Other-without job	219	12	5

Note. Column headings in italics show the national terminology.

Table 7 *(continued)*

Employment characteristics, age and sex	Mental handicap	Severe impairment of communication	Total or profound impairment of hearing	Speech and hearing
ICIDH	**M1.1**	**30**	**40**	**M40.1**

EGYPT, population census 1976

	Disabled population	*Mentally disabled*	*Mute*	*Deaf*	*Deaf and mute*
Economic activity					
Males, aged 5+	81 696	5 679	2 389	3 725	8 334
Self employed	10 319	0	270	604	909
Employers	4 017	0	85	243	299
Paid employees	29 525	12	939	1 757	3 835
Unpaid family workers	1 427	31	145	79	296
Other unpaid workers	13	0	1	0	2
Unemployed (previously employed)	830	0	25	18	89
New unemployed	1 312	31	121	51	209
Students	10 524	113	323	309	1 215
Housewives	0	0	0	0	0
Retired	0	0	0	0	0
Unwilling to work	0	0	0	0	0
Aged persons	5 790	164	38	239	179
Unable to work	16 541	5 308	427	297	941
Not stated	1 398	20	15	128	360
Females, aged 5+	27 827	1 747	837	1 299	3 464
Self employed	319	0	5	14	21
Employers	61	0	4	6	5
Paid employees	2 324	1	99	95	459
Unpaid family workers	64	3	4	0	4
Other unpaid workers	4	0	0	0	0
Unemployed (previously employed)	51	0	2	1	30
New unemployed	327	11	12	12	54
Students	5 241	48	111	343	774
Housewives	0	0	0	0	0
Retired	0	0	0	0	0
Unwilling to work	0	0	0	0	0
Aged persons	5 435	87	36	251	171
Unable to work	13 757	1 597	561	572	1 817
Not stated	244	0	3	5	129

Note. Column headings in italics show the national terminology.

Table 7 *(continued)*

Employment characteristics, age and sex	Total visual impairment of both eyes	Profound visual impairment of one eye	Transverse deficiency of upper arm	Transverse deficiency of lower leg	Other impairment
ICIDH	51.0	54	75.1	75.6	99

EGYPT, population census 1976

	Blind	*Sight loss in one eye*	*Loss of upper limbs*	*Loss of lower limbs*	*Other infirmities*
Economic activity					
Males, aged 5+	19 656	14 435	6 190	5 057	16 231
Self employed	1 734	3 194	1 209	833	1 566
Employers	645	1 312	729	232	472
Paid employees	2 124	7 112	2 784	1 916	9 046
Unpaid family workers	156	125	30	23	542
Other unpaid workers	1	5	0	0	4
Unemployed (previously employed)	206	56	33	68	335
New unemployed	329	80	65	120	306
Students	5 422	1 258	258	369	1 257
Housewives	0	0	0	0	0
Retired	0	0	0	0	0
Unwilling to work	0	0	0	0	0
Aged persons	3 855	529	184	253	349
Unable to work	5 147	578	667	1 211	1 965
Not stated	37	186	231	32	389
Females, aged 5+	12 422	4 156	512	581	2 809
Self employed	26	87	15	20	131
Employers	14	15	7	0	10
Paid employees	139	593	88	28	822
Unpaid family workers	12	4	2	2	33
Other unpaid workers	2	1	0	0	1
Unemployed (previously employed)	7	6	0	0	5
New unemployed	182	25	3	3	25
Students	2 918	503	128	63	353
Housewives	0	0	0	0	0
Retired	0	0	0	0	0
Unwilling to work	0	0	0	0	0
Aged persons	3 920	583	44	76	267
Unable to work	5 200	2 288	215	388	1 119
Not stated	2	51	10	1	43

Note. Column headings in italics show the national terminology.

Table 7 (continued)

Employment characteristics, age and sex	Disabilities	Mental handicap	Severe impairment of communication	Aural impairments	Ocular impairments
ICIDH		M1.1	30	4	5

EGYPT, national survey 1979-81

		Mental	Mutism	Hearing	Vision
Working status according to the presence of a health centre *					
Both sexes, not working	426	54	36	24	86
Both sexes, not working *(With health centre)*	337	21	30	26	97
Both sexes, not working *(Without health centre)*	175	10	10	11	56
Both sexes, *Status not mentioned*	84				
Both sexes, *Status not mentioned (With health centre)*	72				
Both Sexes, *Status not mentioned (Without health centre)*	53				

	Other impairment of cardio-respiratory function	Impairment of posture	Mixed and other upper limb mechanical impairment	Mixed and other mechanical impairment of limb
	61.8	70.5	71.8	71.9
	Debility	*Spine*	*Upper limb*	*Lower limb*
Working status according to the presence of a health centre *				
Both sexes, not working	12	12	60	142
Both sexes, not working *(With health centre)*	13	0	47	103
Both sexes, not working *(Without health centre)*	3	4	26	55

*   Residing in an area with/without access to a health centre.

Note. Column headings in italics show the national terminology.

Table 7 *(continued)*

Employment characteristics, age and sex	Population surveyed	Prevalence per 100 population			
		Aural impairments	Ocular impairments	Impairment of mastication and swallowing	Locomotor disability
ICIDH		4	5	68	4

FINLAND, survey on living conditions 1978

		Diminished hearing ability	*Diminished vision ability*	*Diminished ability to masticate*	*Diminished moving ability*
Economic status					
Both sexes, aged 15+					
Employed	2 268 000	6	2	11	13
Unemployed	153 000	8	3	11	10
Student	400 000	2	1	0	3
Disabled	113 000	23	18	36	84
Household duties	190 000	11	4	18	26
Both sexes, aged 15–64					
Retired	139 000	22	18	35	83
Both sexes, aged 65+					
Retired	432 000	35	15	59	81

Note. Column headings in italics show the national terminology.

Table 7 *(continued)*

Employment characteristics, age and sex	Disabled persons	Intellectual impairments	Other psycho-logical impairments	Total or profound impairment of hearing	Total visual impairment of both eyes
ICIDH		**1**	**2**	**40**	**51.0**

HONG KONG, population census 1981

		Mentally retarded	*Mentally ill*	*Severely deaf*	*Blind*
Labour force participation rate per 100					
Males	42.9	43.3	35.6	51.6	37.1
15–24	47.8	37.4	44.1	66.5	53.8
25–34	63.2	52.7	36.0	93.4	79.3
35–54	60.0	69.1	36.7	86.7	65.3
55+	21.8	40.0	23.6	24.9	18.7
Females	22.1	29.6	25.4	25.3	9.8
15–24	40.5	30.4	38.5	56.8	39.2
25–34	44.0	29.4	39.5	49.5	56.1
35–54	33.4	31.5	28.2	45.0	30.3
55+	7.4	7.2	7.8	8.7	4.0
Unemployment rate per 100					
Both sexes					
15–34	32.9	41.7	58.6	13.7	20.8
35–44	32.6	42.0	56.7	8.9	18.1
45–64	45.5	24.4	62.1	15.2	43.7
15–64	36.7	41.0	59.3	13.5	32.9

Note. Column headings in italics show the national terminology.

Table 7 *(continued)*

Employment characteristics, age and sex	Impairment of posture	Bilateral complete paralysis of lower limbs: paraplegia	Unspecified spastic paralysis of more than one limb	Paralysis of upper and lower limbs on same side	Transverse deficiency unspecified of proximal limb parts
ICIDH	70.5	72.3	72.9	73.5	75.9

HONG KONG, population census 1981 (cont'd)

	Abnormal spine curvature	Polio or lower body paralysed	Spastic	One side of body paralysed	Loss of limb
Labour force participation rate per 100					
Males	60.7	47.7	54.9	25.1	54.7
15–24	44.4	61.5	61.6	73.7	54.7
25–34	95.7	82.0	69.8	68.1	90.4
35–54	95.2	63.2	60.8	54.9	81.5
55+	23.7	16.5	27.1	18.0	29.6
Females	22.1	26.8	34.8	12.2	21.0
15–24	100.0	55.6	35.2	57.9	61.8
25–34	72.6	61.3	65.6	39.4	50.0
35–54	53.5	34.2	29.1	30.9	34.0
55+	10.1	5.2	16.7	7.6	12.2
Unemployment rate per 100					
Both sexes					
15–34	11.0	23.3	47.0	43.0	16.5
35–44	23.1	38.4	34.1	38.7	17.3
45–64	32.3	65.3	45.6	70.8	39.3
15–64	19.5	30.8	45.5	63.1	29.1

Note. Column headings in italics show the national terminology.

Table 7 *(continued)*

Employment characteristics, age and sex	Disabled persons
JAPAN, national survey of handicapped adults 1980	
Both sexes, aged 18+	1 977 000
Employed	638 000
Unemployed	1 320 000
Employment rate	32.3

Table 7 *(continued)*

Employment characteristics, age and sex	Disabled persons	Intellectual	Severe: communication	Total or profound: hearing	Speech and hearing	Total visual: both eyes
ICIDH		1	30	40	M40.1	51.0

KUWAIT, population census 1980

		Mental retardation	*Mute*	*Deaf*	*Deaf and mute*	*Blind*
Economic activity						
Economically active males, aged 15+	789	21	49	31	23	60
Employed	699	..	38	26	20	57
Working student	5	..	..	1	..	1
Unemployed-worked before	27	1	1	2	..	2
New unemployed/first time unemployed	58	20	10	2	3	..
Economically active females, aged 15+	57	1	2	5	2	5
Employed	53	..	2	5	2	4
Working student	..	..	..	..	..	..
Unemployed-worked before	1	..	..	..	..	1
New unemployed/first time unemployed	3	1	..	..	..	..
Economically inactive males, aged 15+	1 914	631	51	68	44	387
Student	370	126	15	13	34	12
Homemaker	..	..	..	..	..	..
Recipient of outside income	375	40	7	26	1	132
Unable to work	1 169	465	29	29	9	243
Economically inactive females, aged 15+	1 165	344	36	36	44	209
Student	166	36	6	8	20	4
Homemaker	327	66	23	13	15	56
Recipient of outside income	44	5	1	1	..	16
Unable to work	628	237	6	14	9	133
Males, total	2 703	652	100	99	67	447
Females, total	1 222	345	38	41	46	214

Note. Column headings in italics show the national terminology.

Table 7 *(continued)*

Employment characteristics, age and sex	Profound visual: one eye	Unspecified other paralysis of limb	Transverse deficiency				
			Upper arm	Upper arms	Lower leg	Lower legs	Other
ICIDH	54	73.9	75.1	M75.11	75.6	75.61	99

KUWAIT, population census 1980 (cont'd)

	Sight in one eye	Paralysis	Loss of arm	Loss of arms	Loss of leg	Loss of legs	Other
Economic activity							
Economically active males, aged 15+	362	39	23	..	33	1	147
Employed	350	22	22	..	29	1	134
Working student	2	..	..	..	..	..	1
Unemployed-worked before	7	9	..	..	2	..	3
New unemployed/first time unemployed	3	8	1	..	2	..	9
Economically active females, aged 15+	25	2	1	..	4	..	10
Employed	25	2	1	..	4	..	8
Working student	..	..	..	..	..	..	..
Unemployed-worked before	..	..	..	..	..	..	..
New unemployed/first time unemployed	..	..	..	..	..	..	2
Economically inactive males, aged 15+	104	438	9	1	24	8	149
Student	10	122	4	..	4	1	29
Homemaker	..	..	..	..	..	..	..
Recipient of outside income	53	65	2	..	9	2	38
Unable to work	41	251	3	1	11	5	82
Economically inactive females, aged 15+	94	292	2	..	12	6	90
Student	6	67	..	..	..	2	17
Homemaker	60	55	2	..	6	1	30
Recipient of outside income	8	7	..	..	1	1	4
Unable to work	20	163	..	..	5	2	39
Males, total	466	477	32	1	57	9	296
Females, total	119	294	3	..	16	6	100

Note. Column headings in italics show the national terminology.

Table 7 (continued)

Employment characteristics, age and sex	Disabled persons

*NEPAL, national survey 1980 ***

Economic activity

Males, total | 100.00

Agriculture	39.51
Household work	10.67
Service	3.63
Schooling	1.64
Trading	0.59
Other activities	1.17
Non-active	42.79

Females, total | 100.00

Agriculture	31.24
Household work	16.89
Service	0.00
Schooling	0.39
Trading	0.20
Other activities	0.59
Non-active	50.69

---

* Percentage distribution of disabled persons according to economic activity and sex.

Table 7 *(continued)*

	Other psycho-logical	Aural	Ocular	Disabilities		
Employment characteristics, age and sex				Occupa-tional role	Loco-motor	Lifting
ICIDH	2	4	5	18	4	48

NORWAY, level of living survey 1983

Economically active in 1982 rate per 100

	Strongly reduced working capacity	*Reduced mobility*
Both sexes, aged 16-79	405	406
Total number economically active in 1982	115	115
Economically active in 1982 (%)	29	29
>1300 hours of employment (%)	46	47
Unemployed (%)	15	8
Long-time unemployed (%)	7	4

Note. Column headings in italics show the national terminology.

Table 7 *(continued)*

Employment characteristics age and sex	Disabled persons	Severe impairment of communica- tion	Aural Impairments	Ocular impairments
ICIDH		30	4	5

PHILIPPINES, national survey 1980

		Communica- tion	*Aural*	*Ocular*
Participation in economic activity				
Males, aged 0-14	163	5	11	15
Able to work independently	18	1	2	4
Able to work but requires assistance	8	1	2	1
Unable to work	2	0	0	0
Not stated	135	3	7	10
Females, aged 0-14	130	5	8	18
Able to work independently	12	0	2	3
Able to work but requires assistance	9	1	2	2
Unable to work	1	0	0	0
Not stated	108	4	4	13
Males, aged 15-64	476	7	24	51
Able to work independently	263	3	18	35
Able to work but requires assistance	80	2	1	8
Unable to work	28	0	1	0
Not stated	105	2	4	8
Females, aged 15-64	323	7	15	42
Able to work independently	151	5	12	25
Able to work but requires assistance	49	1	0	6
Unable to work	18	0	0	1
Not stated	105	1	3	10
Males, aged 65+	134	1	5	13
Able to work independently	44	0	1	6
Able to work but requires assistance	24	1	2	1
Unable to work	26	0	0	2
Not stated	40	0	2	4
Females, aged 65+	111	1	9	12
Able to work independently	25	0	5	0
Able to work but requires assistance	14	0	0	3
Unable to work	24	0	2	0
Not stated	48	1	2	9
Males, total	773	13	40	79
Able to work independently	325	4	21	45
Able to work but requires assistance	112	4	5	10
Unable to work	56	0	1	2
Not stated	280	5	13	22
Females, total	564	13	32	72
Able to work independently	188	5	19	28
Able to work but requires assistance	72	2	2	11
Unable to work	43	0	2	1
Not stated	261	6	9	32

Note. Column headings in italics show the national terminology.

Table 7 *(continued)*

Employment characteristics, age and sex	Visceral impairments	Skeletal impairments	Other and unspecified disfig- urement	And other impairments
ICIDH	**6**	**7**	**87.9**	**9**

PHILIPPINES, national survey 1980 (continued)

	Visceral	*Skeletal*	*Disfiguring*	*Two- category combinations*
Participation in economic activity				
Males, aged 0-14	24	41	10	57
Able to work independently	2	4	1	4
Able to work but requires assistance	1	0	1	2
Unable to work		0	0	1
Not stated	20	37	8	50
Females, aged 0-14	12	43	10	34
Able to work independently	0	6	0	1
Able to work but requires assistance	0	2	1	1
Unable to work	0	1	0	0
Not stated	12	34	9	32
Males, aged 15-64	82	146	14	152
Able to work independently	46	87	9	65
Able to work but requires assistance	13	25	2	29
Unable to work	1	8	1	17
Not stated	22	26	2	41
Females, aged 15-64	66	67	8	118
Able to work independently	30	33	5	41
Able to work but requires assistance	5	12	1	24
Unable to work	7	0	0	10
Not stated	24	22	2	43
Males, aged 65+	19	26	1	69
Able to work independently	5	9	1	22
Able to work but requires assistance	4	9	0	7
Unable to work	2	4	0	18
Not stated	8	4	0	22
Females, aged 65+	11	23	0	55
Able to work independently	2	8	0	10
Able to work but requires assistance	3	4	0	4
Unable to work	3	3	0	16
Not stated	3	8	0	25
Males, total	125	213	25	278
Able to work independently	53	100	11	91
Able to work but requires assistance	18	34	3	38
Unable to work	4	12	1	36
Not stated	50	67	10	113
Females, total	89	133	18	207
Able to work independently	32	47	5	52
Able to work but requires assistance	8	18	2	29
Unable to work	10	4	0	26
Not stated	39	64	11	100

Note. Column headings in italics show the national terminology.

Table 7 *(continued)*

Employment characteristics, age and sex	Disabled persons	Mental handicap	Severe impairment of communication	Aural impairments	Ocular impairments
ICIDH		**M1.1**	**30**	**4**	**5**

PHILIPPINES, national survey 1980 (cont'd)

		Mental impairment	*Communication*	*Aural*	*Ocular*
Ability to work after disability					
Males, aged 0-14	163	18	5	11	15
Continued in same occupation	11	1	0	1	3
Changed occupation	0	0	0	0	0
Stopped working	1	0	0	0	0
Not stated	151	17	5	10	12
Females, aged 0-14	130	13	5	8	18
Continued in same occupation	4	1	0	1	0
Changed occupation	1	0	0	0	0
Stopped working	2	0	0	1	0
Not stated	123	12	5	6	18
Males, aged 15-64	476	45	7	24	51
Continued in same occupation	210	8	3	14	27
Changed occupation	32	0	0	0	2
Stopped working	95	15	1	0	8
Not stated	139	22	3	10	14
Females, aged 15-64	323	55	7	15	42
Continued in same occupation	107	7	2	7	18
Changed occupation	6	1	0	0	0
Stopped working	45	14	0	0	3
Not stated	165	33	5	8	21
Males, aged 65+	134	2	1	5	13
Continued in same occupation	38	0	0	1	5
Changed occupation	4	0	0	0	1
Stopped working	34	2	0	1	3
Not stated	58	0	1	3	4
Females, aged 65+	111	0	1	9	12
Continued in same occupation	12	0	0	0	1
Changed occupation	1	0	0	0	0
Stopped working	21	0	0	0	2
Not stated	77	0	1	9	9
Males, total	773	65	13	40	79
Continued in same occupation	259	9	3	16	35
Changed occupation	36	0	0	0	3
Stopped working	130	17	1	1	11
Not stated	348	39	9	23	30
Females, total	564	68	13	32	72
Continued in same occupation	123	8	2	8	19
Changed occupation	8	1	0	0	0
Stopped working	68	14	0	1	5
Not stated	365	45	11	23	48

Note. Column headings in italics show the national terminology.

Table 7 (continued)

Employment characteristics, age and sex	Visceral impairments	Skeletal impairments	Other and unspecified disfig- urement	And other impairments
ICIDH	6	7	87.9	9

PHILIPPINES, national survey 1980 (cont'd)

	Visceral	Skeletal	Disfiguring	Two- category combinations
Ability to work after disability				
Males, aged 0-14	24	41	10	57
Continued in same occupation	1	3	1	2
Changed occupation	0	0	0	0
Stopped working	1	0	0	0
Not stated	22	38	9	55
Females, aged 0-14	12	43	10	34
Continued in same occupation	0	1	0	2
Changed occupation	0	1	0	0
Stopped working	0	1	0	0
Not stated	12	40	10	32
Males, aged 15-64	82	146	14	152
Continued in same occupation	35	65	7	59
Changed occupation	5	16	0	9
Stopped working	18	24	2	42
Not stated	24	41	5	42
Females, aged 15-64	66	67	8	118
Continued in same occupation	19	24	3	34
Changed occupation	1	2	1	2
Stopped working	17	12	0	13
Not stated	29	29	4	69
Males, aged 65+	19	26	1	69
Continued in same occupation	4	7	1	20
Changed occupation	0	3	0	0
Stopped working	3	2	0	25
Not stated	12	14	0	24
Females, aged 65+	11	23	0	55
Continued in same occupation	2	4	0	5
Changed occupation	0	1	0	0
Stopped working	2	3	0	14
Not stated	7	15	0	36
Males, total	125	213	25	278
Continued in same occupation	40	75	9	81
Changed occupation	5	19	0	9
Stopped working	22	26	2	67
Not stated	58	93	14	121
Females, total	89	133	18	207
Continued in same occupation	21	29	3	41
Changed occupation	1	4	1	2
Stopped working	19	16	0	27
Not stated	48	84	14	137

Note. Column headings in italics show the national terminology.

Table 7 *(continued)*

Employment characteristics, age and sex	Population surveyed	Prevalence per 100 population				
		Aural	Ocular	Occupational role disability	Locomotor disability	Other locomotor disability
ICIDH		4	5	18	4	49

SWEDEN, living conditions survey 1980-81

	Population surveyed	*Reduced hearing*	*Reduced eye sight*	*Reduced work capacity*	*Mobility*	*Serious mobility disability*
Economic activity according to socio-economic group						
Workers aged 16-84	1 969 000	5.8	0.3	5.3	1.9	0.4
Unskilled and semi-skilled	1 328 000	5.3	0.4	5.7	2.1	0.3
Skilled workers	641 000	6.8	0.2	4.5	1.5	0.5
Employees aged 16-84	1 687 000	3.2	0.2	3.1	1.7	0.7
Junior salaried employees	666 000	3.1	0.2	4.2	2.6	1.0
Intermediate salaried employees	597 000	3.8	0.2	3.1	1.3	0.5
Senior salaried employees	424 000	2.5	0.1	1.4	0.9	0.6
Independent aged 16-84						
Farmers	165 000	14.2	0.6	9.6	6.3	2.1
Entrepreneurs	293 000	6.1	0.4	6.1	2.0	0.9
Economically inactive aged 16-84						
Students	454 000	1.6	0.0	2.5	0.4	0.1
Home-makers	366 000	3.5	1.0	9.1	4.1	0.8
Old-age pensioners	1 215 000	17.3	5.8	26.6	29.9	17.5
Old pensioners ex-workers	644 000	18.8	5.6	26.4	30.2	16.6
Old pensioners ex-salaried	239 000	13.4	4.9	17.9	20.8	11.6
Old pensioners ex-farmers	244 000	17.9	7.2	32.5	37.6	24.6
Old pensioners ex-entrepreneurs	65 000	15.3	4.0	33.5	28.9	17.7
Early retirement pensions	210 000	8.2	5.3	83.2	49.1	21.7
Unemployed aged 16-84						
Unemployed for a long time	27 000	3.6	1.7	10.1	5.1	1.7

Note. Column headings in italics show the national terminology.

Table 7 *(continued)*

Employment characteris-tics, age and sex	Disabled persons	Mental handicap	Speech and hearing	Total visual impairment of both eyes	Unspecified other motor impairment of limb	Other impairment
ICIDH		M1.1	M40.1	51.0	74.9	99

TUNISIA, population census 1975

		Mental handicap	*Deaf and mute*	*Blind*	*Motor impairment*	*Other*
Economic activity						
Males aged 15+	22 900	3 780	1 870	6 490	7 220	3 540
Occupied	2 480	180	560	660	840	240
Without work	750	180	70	120	250	130
Without work-first time	310	80	30	50	90	60
Inactive/not available	19 360	3 340	1 210	5 660	6 040	3 110
Females aged 15+	14 210	2 180	1 340	5 330	3 290	2 070
Occupied	360	10	100	90	140	20
Without work	80	10	10	10	30	20
Without work-first time	90	30	30	10	10	10
Inactive/not available	13 680	2 130	1 200	5 220	3 110	2 020

TUNISIA, population census 1984

		Mental handicap	*Deaf and mute*	*Blind*	*Motor impairment*	*Other*
Economic activity						
Both sexes, aged 15+	53 150	11 980	6 410	11 340	19 790	3 630
Economically active-occupied	2 910	230	980	730	890	80
Economically active-without work	1 220	200	330	290	340	60
Unpaid agriculture	3 450	460	290	820	1 630	250
Inactive	45 570	11 090	4 810	9 500	16 930	3 240

Note. Column headings in italics show the national terminology.

Table 7 *(continued)*

Employment characteristics, age and sex	Disabilities

ZIMBABWE, national survey 1981

*Economic activity now, by economic activity
before disablement (both sexes)*

Currently unemployed, seeking job: was

Unemployed-seeking job	2 900
Unemployed-not seeking job	500
Full-time home work	900
Part-time home work	200
Skilled work	1 100
Unskilled work	1 300
Other	100

Currently unemployed, not seeking job: was

Unemployed-seeking job	600
Unemployed-not seeking job	32 800
Full-time home work	12 000
Part-time home work	3 100
Skilled work	12 800
Unskilled work	5 800
Other	4 700

Currently full time home work: was

Unemployed-seeking job	300
Unemployed-not seeking job	400
Full-time home work	8 400
Part-time home work	0
Skilled work	1 100
Unskilled work	500
Other	700

Currently part time home work: was

Unemployed-seeking job	100
Unemployed-not seeking job	300
Full-time home work	7 100
Part-time home work	4 500
Skilled work	1 900
Unskilled work	900
Other	1 000

Note. Column headings in italics show the national terminology.

Table 7 *(continued)*

Employment characteristics, age and sex	Disabilities

ZIMBABWE, national survey 1981 (cont.)

Economic activity now, by economic activity
before disablement (both sexes)

Currently skilled work: was

Unemployed-seeking job	0
Unemployed-not seeking job	100
Full-time home work	100
Part-time home work	0
Skilled work	800
Unskilled work	0
Other	100

Currently unskilled work: was

Unemployed-seeking job	0
Unemployed-not seeking job	200
Full-time home work	100
Part-time home work	0
Skilled work	100
Unskilled work	1 100
Other	100

Currently other: was

Unemployed-seeking job	0
Unemployed-not seeking job	300
Full-time home work	2 500
Part-time home work	1 000
Skilled work	700
Unskilled work	400
Other	2 400
Total	116 400 a/

a/ Sum of causes does not equal total.

Table 8. Marital status of disabled persons, by age, sex and type of impairment or disability

This table provides the numbers of disabled persons according to their marital status, age and sex and type of impairment or disability. If numbers were not available in the published national reports rates were provided e.g., percentage distributions, as available. All references to ICIDH codes prefaced with an M (for example, M1.1), indicate that the codes are not ICIDH codes, but are devised to accommodate items not readily coded within ICIDH categories.

Description of variables

National classifications of marital status usually included distinctions between married or single, widowed, separated or divorced. Sometimes the distinction is between single and cohabitating, or between single and married, or other. Although substantially fewer countries cross-tabulated their results concerning disabled people according to marital status, this table was included because of its importance to policy makers and planners who are concerned with the overall economic and social situation of disabled persons. Irregularities in the data sets are provided in footnotes at the country level, as needed.

8.   Marital status of disabled persons, by age, sex and type of impairment or disability

Marital status, age and sex	Population surveyed	Disabled persons

CANADA, health and disability survey 1983/84

Married

Marital status, age and sex	Population surveyed	Disabled persons
Male, age 15+	6 065 000	786 000
15-34	1 825 000	78 000
35-54	2 521 000	207 000
55-64	937 000	216 000
65+	781 000	285 000
Female, age 15+	6 022 000	698 000
15-34	2 224 000	97 000
35-54	2 371 000	219 000
55-64	848 000	185 000
65+	579 000	197 000

Single (never married)

Male, age 15+	2 788 000	194 000
15-34	2 426 000	102 000
35-54	219 000	34 000
55-64	67 000	26 000
65+	76 000	31 000
Female, age 15+	2 247 000	169 000
15-34	1 908 000	94 000
35-54	175 000	24 000
55-64	65 000	19 000
65+	98 000	33 000

Widowed

Male, age 15+	184 000	71 000
15-34	..	..
35-54	21 000	..
55-64	37 000	12 000
65+	122 000	56 000
Female, age 15+	923 000	350 000
15-34	17 000	..
35-54	103 000	18 000
55-64	197 000	61 000
65+	607 000	271 000

Separated or divorced

Male, 15+	321 000	58 000
15-34	81 000	..
35-54	157 000	25 000
55-64	44 000	14 000
65+	38 000	13 000
Female, 15+	587 000	122 000
15-34	185 000	18 000
35-54	274 000	51 000
55-64	73 000	28 000
65+	55 000	25 000

Table 8 *(continued)*

Marital status, age and sex	Disabled persons	Intellectual impairments	Other psychological impairments	Total or profound impairment of hearing	Total visual impairment of both eyes
ICIDH		1	2	40	51.0

HONG KONG, population census 1981 *

		Mentally retarded	*Mentally ill*	*Severely deaf*	*Blind*
Both sexes, age 15+	100.0	100.0	100.0	100.0	100.0
Never married	41.3	93.6	56.4	25.3	14.0
Married	38.7	5.2	32.2	48.2	49.0
Widowed	18.5	1.1	8.8	24.4	35.8
Divorced/separated	1.5	0.1	2.6	2.1	1.3

	Impairment of posture	Bilateral complete paralysis of lower limbs: paraplegia	Unspecified spastic paralysis of more than one limb	Paralysis of upper and lower limbs on same side	Transverse deficiency unspecified of proximal limb parts
	70.5	72.3	72.9	73.5	75.9

	Abnormal spine curvature	*Polio or lower body paralysed*	*Spastic*	*One side of body paralysed*	*Loss of limb*
Both sexes, age 15+	100.0	100.0	100.0	100.0	100.0
Never married	29.8	43.8	63.2	10.2	24.4
Married	33.7	37.3	27.7	60.3	54.9
Widowed	35.6	18.1	7.3	28.2	18.5
Divorced/separated	1.0	0.8	1.7	1.3	2.2

----

* Percentage distribution of disabled persons, by marital status, age, sex and type of impairment or disability.

Note. Column headings in italics show the national terminology.

Table 8 *(continued)*

Marital status, age and sex	Disabled persons	Aural	Ocular	Visceral	Unspecified other motor impairment of limb	Multiple impairment of all classes
ICIDH		4	5	6	74.9	90.0

JAPAN, national survey of handicapped adults 1980 *

		Auditory	Visual	Internal	Physical	Multiple
Both sexes, age 18+	100.0	100.0	100.0	100.0	100.0	100.0
Single	11.6	12.2	8.8	9.4	12.4	12.4
Married	65.8	63.1	58.3	58.6	69.1	58.6
Other	22.6	24.7	32.9	21.7	18.5	29.0

----

* Percentage distribution of disabled persons by marital status according to age, sex and type of impairment or disability.

Note. Column headings in italics show the national terminology.

Table 8 (continued)

Marital status, age and sex	Impairments			Disabilities		
	Other psychological	Aural	Ocular	Occupational role	Loco-motor	Lifting
ICIDH	2	4	5	18	4	48

NORWAY, level of living survey 1983 *

	Household status	Total number	Disabled	Nervous condition	Reduced hearing	Reduced eye sight	Strongly reduced working capacity	Reduced mobility	Reduced capacity to carry
Total									
16-79		3 929	18	3	4	2	11	10	6
Single									
16-24	Living with parents	393	6	1	1	1	2	2	2
16-24	Other living arrangement	139	6	2	1	1	3	2	2
25-44		176	8	3	1	2	7	3	2
45-66		218	39	7	6	3	27	20	13
67-79		203	53	8	13	10	24	40	23
16-79	With dependants	95	17	4	2	1	12	12	3
Married									
16-44	With no children	273	7	2	1	0	3	3	1
16-79	With youngest child 0-6	713	6	1	1	1	4	2	1
16-79	With youngest child 7-19	829	11	2	3	1	7	5	3
45-66	With no children	603	27	6	4	1	18	16	8
67-79	With no children	287	46	6	12	4	26	32	19

* Percentage of total population that is disabled, according to marital status, type of family situation, age, sex and type of impairment or disability.

Note. Column headings in italics show the national terminology.

Table 8 *(continued)*

Marital status, age and sex	Population surveyed	Mental handicap	Skeletal and/or motor impairments	Multiple impairment of all classes
ICIDH		M1.1	M7.1	90.0

PHILIPPINES, national survey 1980

	Population surveyed	*Mental impairment*	*Physical impairments*	*Mixed impairments*
Both sexes	19 678	102	1 017	27
Single	7 761	84	243	24
Married	10 849	15	603	3
Widow/widower	870	0	154	0
Separated	135	3	15	0
Not stated	63	0	2	0

Note. Column headings in italics show the national terminology.

Table 8 *(continued)*

Marital status, age and sex	Population surveyed	Impairments		Disabilities		
		Aural	Ocular	Occu-pational role	Loco-motor	Other loco-motor
ICIDH		**4**	**5**	**18**	**4**	**49**

SWEDEN, living conditions survey 1980 *

		Reduced hearing	*Reduced eye sight*	*Reduced work capacity*	*Mobility disability*	*Serious mobility disability*
Total						
Aged 16-84	6 464 000	7.1	1.5	11.6	8.9	4.5
Living with parents						
Aged 16-24	556 000	1.2	0.1	2.1	0.6	0.2
Single						
Aged 16-24	201 000	1.3	0.0	1.9	0.2	0.2
Childless aged 25-44	399 000	2.2	0.7	7.9	2.2	1.3
Childless aged 45-64	381 000	7.3	2.2	23.6	14.3	5.2
Pensioners aged 65-74	310 000	13.7	3.3	26.4	24.0	12.1
Pensioners aged 75-84	275 000	20.9	12.1	34.3	48.2	33.7
Parents aged 16-84 with child <7	59 000	1.6	0.0	6.3	0.9	0.0
Parents aged 16-84 with child 7-18	130 000	3.0	0.3	8.6	4.0	1.5
Cohabiting						
Aged 16-24	158 000	0.3	0.0	2.3	1.2	0.3
Childless aged 25-44	320 000	2.0	0.1	5.1	2.0	0.9
Childless aged 45-64	977 000	9.2	1.0	16.1	8.9	3.0
Pensioners aged 65-74	514 000	15.0	1.9	19.7	18.2	7.4
Pensioners aged 75-84	176 000	27.1	9.8	32.1	39.7	26.2
Parents aged 16-84 with child <7	918 000	2.7	0.1	2.6	0.6	0.2
Parents aged 16-84 with child 7-18	1 090 000	5.7	0.3	5.6	2.8	1.0

* Percentage of total population that is disabled, according to marital status, type of family situation, age, sex and type of impairment or disability.

Note. Column headings in italics show the national terminology.

Table 9. Family characteristics of disabled persons, by age, sex and type of impairment or disability

Table 9 provides the numbers of disabled persons, by age and sex and type of impairment or disability, according to their family characteristics. Numbers are provided unless not available. In this circumstance, rates are presented instead, as available. Exceptional cases are footnoted in table 9 at the country level.

Description of variables

Family characteristics provided by national data include such diverse topics as parental status, indicating whether parents are still alive; whether a disabled person has disabled relatives; and with whom the disabled person lives. The classifications used by countries to describe family characteristics in table 9 are self-explanatory. If required, unusual categories are described in footnotes at the country level.

9. Family characteristics of disabled persons by age, sex and type of impairment or disability

Family characteristics, age and sex	Disabled Population

ETHIOPIA, survey of children 1981

Parental status

Total ages 0-14 | 29 631

Both are alive	20 036
Both are dead	1 002
One is alive	3 980
Separated	902
Divorced	970
No response	2 741

With whom children live

Total ages 0-14 | 29 631

Parents	15 119
Father	2 275
Mother	3 479
Relatives	1 412
Institution	42
Others	6 205
Not stated	1 099

Table 9 (continued)

Family characteristics, age and sex	Disabled persons	Intellectual	Severe: commun- ication	Total visual: both eyes	Other and unspecified disfigure- ment	Multiple: all classes	Other
ICIDH		1	30	51.0	87.9	90.0	99

KENYA, national survey of persons 1981

Disabled relatives (of disabled persons, aged 15+)

Total	1 774
None	716
Brother/sister	162
Uncle/cousin/nephew	73
Father/mother	39
Son/daughter	30
Husband/wife	15
Other	54
Missing information	685

Type of impairment of relative (of disabled persons, aged 15+) a/

		Mentally retarded	Mute	Blind	Crippled, lame or deformed	Multiple disability	Other
Total percent		100.0	100.0	100.0	100.0	100.0	100.0
Mentally retarded (1)*	8	62.5	9.7	5.5	3.0	7.7	23.1
Mute (30)	31	25.0	71.0	6.8	6.0	0.0	7.7
Blind (51.0)	73	0.0	3.2	50.7	14.5	0.0	7.7
Crippled, lame or deformed (87.9)	235	12.5	12.9	27.4	66.4	7.7	0.0
Multiple disability (90.0)	13	0.0	0.0	1.4	3.0	69.2	0.0
Other (99)	13	0.0	3.2	8.2	7.2	15.4	61.5

Relationship to disabled relative (of disabled persons, aged 15+) a/

Total number	368	9	33	59	241	13	13
Total percent	100.0	100.0	100.0	100.0	100.0	100.0	100.0
Brother/sister	42.9	44.4	63.6	33.9	42.7	38.5	38.5
Uncle/cousin/nephew	19.8	0.0	6.1	23.7	22.4	23.1	0.0
Father/mother	10.3	11.1	9.1	16.9	8.3	23.1	7.7
Son/daughter	8.2	33.3	9.1	8.5	5.8	15.4	23.1
Husband/wife	4.1	11.1	0.0	6.8	3.3	0.0	15.3
Other	12.5	0.0	9.1	10.2	17.4	0.0	15.4

----

a/ Percentage distribution of disabled persons by family characteristics, age, sex and type of impairment or disability.

* Numbers in parenthesis indicate the approximate ICIDH codes of impairments of relatives.

Note. Column headings in italics show the national terminology.

Table 9 *(continued)*

Family characteristics, age and sex	Disabled persons

NEPAL, national survey 1980 *

	Families with disabled persons
Both sexes	100.0
1	1.7
2–3	13.5
4–5	28.1
6–7	27.7
8–9	15.0
10	3.6
Above 10	10.4

---

* Percentage distribution of families with disabled persons according to family size.

Note. Column headings in italics show the national terminology.

Table 9 (continued)

Family characteristics, age and sex	Population surveyed	Impairments		Disabilities		
		Aural	Ocular	Occu-pational role	Loco-motor	Other loco-motor
ICIDH		4	5	18	4	49

SWEDEN, living conditions survey 1980 *

	Population surveyed	Reduced hearing	Reduced eye sight	Reduced work capacity	Mobility	Serious mobility disability
Family conditions (disabled persons not living in an institution)						
Total number, ages 16-64	5 185 000	235 000	25 000	415 000	205 000	75 000
Total percent	100.0	100.0	100.0	100.0	100.0	100.0
Live with parents	12.7	4.8	4.9	6.3	3.2	3.8
Live with brothers and sisters	0.5	0.6	2.4	1.2	0.8	0.7
Cohabitants with no children	23.9	32.8	34.8	36.0	40.4	37.1
Cohabitants with children	42.8	45.4	19.3	27.2	24.1	24.7
Single persons with children	4.4	2.5	3.1	5.5	5.6	4.0
Living alone	14.8	13.0	35.6	22.8	25.3	29.2
Total number, ages 65-84	1 280 000	225 000	70 000	335	370 000	215 000
Total percent	100.0	100.0	100.0	100.0	100.0	100.0
Live with parents	0.0	0.0	0.0	0.0	0.0	0.0
Live with brothers and sisters	2.7	2.6	2.1	2.0	1.9	2.3
Cohabitants with no children	50.3	51.1	37.1	43.8	40.9	36.9
Cohabitants with children	4.0	4.7	1.2	3.6	3.3	2.6
Single persons with children	2.5	2.1	3.0	2.7	3.6	3.9
Living alone	39.5	38.9	55.6	46.9	48.9	53.5

* Percentage distribution of total population and disabled population according to family situation.

Note. Column headings in italics show the national terminology.

Table 10. Housing characteristics of disabled persons, by age, sex and type of impairment or disability

Description of variables

Housing characteristics, or living arrangements of disabled persons, include descriptions of living quarters of disabled persons; type of occupancy (rental versus ownership of home); institutional care by type of institution; length of residence. To a great extent, the classifications used by countries are self-explanatory. If required, unusual categories are described in footnotes at the country level. All references to ICIDH codes prefaced with an M (for example, M1.1), indicate that the codes are not ICIDH codes, but are devised to accommodate items not readily coded within ICIDH categories.

10. Housing characteristics of disabled persons, by age, sex and type of impairment or disability

Housing characteristics	Disabled persons	Intellectual impairments	Other psychological impairments	Aural impairments
ICIDH		1	2	4

AUSTRALIA, national survey of handicapped persons 1981

		Mental retardation	*Mental disorders*	*Hearing loss*
Areas of handicap, by type of residence				
Self care	544 200	54 900	104 600	116 300
Household	448 300	29 100	62 000	91 100
Institution	95 900	25 800	42 600	25 200
Mobility	921 600	66 700	155 600	19 400
Household	812 800	37 900	109 000	164 900
Institution	108 800	28 800	46 600	29 100
Communication	260 400	48 900	47 100	160 300
Household	204 900	27 400	18 900	142 000
Institution	55 500	21 500	28 300	18 300
Schooling	95 700	37 500	9 100	19 300
Household	90 700	33 300	8 300	18 500
Institution	5 000	4 200	800	800
Employment				
Household	498 300	21 500	101 400	69 600

Note. Column headings in italics show the national terminology.

Table 10 *(continued)*

Housing characteristics	Ocular impairments	Shortness of breath	Other impairment of internal organs	Other impairments of internal organs	Other motor impairment of limb: other	Unspecified other motor impairment of limb
ICIDH	5	61.0	66	66.8	74.8	74.9

AUSTRALIA, national survey of handicapped persons 1981 (cont'd)

Areas, of handicap by type of residence	Sight loss	Respir-atory disease	Circul-atory disease	Nervous system disease	Musculo-skeletal disease	Other physical condition
Self care	78 000	48 600	136 500	82 500	272 100	158 200
Household	52 200	44 500	104 300	59 100	237 500	121 500
Institution	25 800	4 100	32 100	23 400	34 600	36 700
Mobility	124 900	90 400	256 200	108 200	420 900	241 300
Household	96 100	85 300	220 700	83 300	382 800	201 900
Institution	28 800	5 100	35 500	25 000	38 100	39 400
Communication	48 800	10 300	47 000	34 500	57 000	59 000
Household	33 900	8 200	30 000	19 200	41 000	37 900
Institution	14 900	2 100	16 900	15 300	16 000	21 100
Schooling	7 400	13 500	..	15 400	7 100	20 600
Household	6 600	13 400	..	13 100	6 600	19 900
Institution	800	..	..	2 300	..	700
Employment						
Household	27 800	48 500	113 400	54 800	217 400	129 700

Note. Column headings in italics show the national terminology.

Table 10 (continued)

Housing characteristics	Population surveyed	Disabled persons

AUSTRALIA, national survey of handicapped persons 1981 (cont'd)

Nature of housing occupancy

	Population surveyed	Disabled persons
Total	12 685 800	1 129 300
Owner/outright	3 640 900	612 300
Owner/purchasing	5 337 200	243 500
Renter/commission	732 800	85 700
Renter/private	2 293 900	142 900
Other	681 100	44 900

Institutionalized persons, size of institution

	Population surveyed	Disabled persons
Total in institutions		111 100
1-20		700
21-40		18 300
41-60		17 000
61-80		11 100
81-100		9 600
101-150		12 400
151-200		5 900
201-300		8 100
301-400		4 700
401-500		2 900
500+		14 000

Table 10 *(continued)*

Housing characteristics	Disabled population				
	Ages 0-4	Ages 5-14	Ages 15-24	Ages 25-34	Ages 35-44

AUSTRALIA, national survey of handicapped persons 1981 (cont'd)

Type of institution according to age of occupants

	Ages 0-4	Ages 5-14	Ages 15-24	Ages 25-34	Ages 35-44
Total	..	3 600	5 700	4 200	3 200
General hospital	..	..	..	..	..
Nursing homes	..	..	..	..	..
Aged homes	..	..	..	..	..
Psychiatric hospital	..	700	1 900	2 000	1 500
Special homes	..	2 800	3 200	2 000	1 200

	Ages 45-54	Ages 55-64	Ages 65-74	Ages 75+	All ages
Total	4 700	7 800	17 800	63 700	111 100
General hospital	500	600	1 600	5 500	8 800
Nursing homes	1 200	2 900	8 000	34 600	47 700
Aged homes	..	1 100	5 100	20 100	26 700
Psychiatric hospital	1 300	2 200	2 000	2 000	13 600
Special homes	1 400	900	1 000	1 500	14 300

Table 10 *(continued)*

Housing characteristics	Disabled population, time in institution			
	Less than 6 months	6-12 months	1-3 years	3-5 years

AUSTRALIA, national survey of handicapped persons 1981 (cont'd)

Length of time in institution, by type of institution

	Less than 6 months	6-12 months	1-3 years	3-5 years
Total	22 700	10 300	30 600	17 800
General hospital	4 600	1 000	2 000	700
Nursing home	10 400	4 600	14 700	8 600
Aged persons homes	3 600	2 300	8 500	5 000
Psychiatric hospital	1 700	900	2 400	1 600
Special homes/hostels	2 500	1 500	3 000	1 900

	5-10 years	10 years or more	Total
Total	17 900	11 900	111 100
General hospital	..	..	8 800
Nursing home	7 600	1 900	47 700
Aged persons homes	4 800	2 600	26 700
Psychiatric hospital	2 600	4 400	13 600
Special homes/hostels	2 500	2 800	14 300

Table 10 *(continued)*

Housing characteristics	Disabled persons

AUSTRALIA, national survey of handicapped persons 1981 (cont'd)

Institutionalization status according to age

Ages 0-4	..
Permanently	..
Not permanently	..
Ages 5-14	3 600
Permanently	2 800
Not permanently	800
Ages 15-24	5 700
Permanently	3 700
Not permanently	1 900
Ages 25-34	4 200
Permanently	3 000
Not permanently	1 200
Ages 35-44	3 200
Permanently	2 400
Not permanently	800
Ages 45-54	4 700
Permanently	3 300
Not permanently	1 400
Ages 55-64	7 800
Permanently	5 200
Not permanently	2 600
Ages 65-74	17 800
Permanently	11 700
Not permanently	6 200
Ages 75+	63 700
Permanently	47 100
Not permanently	16 600
Total	111 100
Permanently	79 500
Not permanently	31 700

Table 10 *(continued)*

Housing characteristics	Population surveyed	Disabled persons

CANADA, health and disability survey 1983-84

Type of dwelling, within age group

Ages 15-34	8 670 000	395 000
Single detached	5 118 000	205 000
Double	452 000	22 000
Row or terrace	458 000	30 000
Duplex	331 000	17 000
Apartment/flat	2 031 000	107 000
Mobile home	240 000	13 000
Other	41 000	..
Not stated	..	..
Ages 35-54	5 840 000	581 000
Single detached	4 077 000	363 000
Double	277 000	24 000
Row or terrace	250 000	27 000
Duplex	148 000	17 000
Apartment/flat	933 000	126 000
Mobile home	115 000	17 000
Other	38 000	7 000
Not stated	..	..
Ages 55-64	2 270 000	561 000
Single detached	1 561 000	363 000
Double	74 000	16 000
Row or terrace	56 000	14 000
Duplex	77 000	20 000
Apartment/flat	443 000	125 000
Mobile home	38 000	14 000
Other	20 000	7 000
Not stated	..	..
Ages 65+	2 356 000	910 000
Single detached	1 406 000	533 000
Double	66 000	23 000
Row or terrace	44 000	16 000
Duplex	74 000	30 000
Apartment/flat	681 000	269 000
Mobile home	42 000	17 000
Other	43 000	23 000
Not stated	..	..
Total, all ages	19 136 000	2 448 000
Single detached	12 162 000	1 463 000
Double	870 000	85 000
Row or terrace	809 000	86 000
Duplex	630 000	84 000
Apartment/flat	4 089 000	627 000
Mobile home	435 000	62 000
Other	142 000	40 000
Not stated	..	..

Table 10 *(continued)*

Housing characteristics	Population surveyed	Disabled persons	Intellectual	Other psycho-logical	Total or profound: hearing	Total visual: both eyes	Unspecified other motor: limb
ICIDH			1	2	40	51.0	74.9

*HONG KONG, population census 1981 ***

	Mentally retarded	*Mentally ill*	*Severely deaf*	*Blind*	*Physically disabled*
Housing type					
Total	100.0	100.0	100.0	100.0	100.0
Public/aided housing	44.2	46.9	28.7	46.3	49.5	46.6
Private housing	35.9	34.0	20.7	43.7	36.7	39.9
Institutions	13.3	13.8	44.6	2.0	5.8	6.8
Temporary housing	6.7	5.4	6.0	8.0	8.1	6.7
Total (number)	41 463	9 140	6 323	6 316	4 360	15 324

	All domestic households	Domestic households with disabled persons
Domestic household size		
Total	100.0	33 200
1	15.2	3 457
2 – 3	30.8	8 122
4 – 5	31.5	9 413
6 and over	22.5	12 208
Average household size	3.9	4.7

---

* Percentage distribution of disabled persons according to housing status and type of impairment.

Note. Column headings in italics show the national terminology.

Table 10 *(continued)*

Housing characteristics	Occupational role disability	Locomotor disability
ICIDH	18	4

NORWAY, level of living survey 1983

	Strongly reduced working capacity	*Reduced mobility*
Housing condition: type of building and tenure status		
(Ages 16-79): Total surveyed	405	406
(percentage)		
Live in one-dwelling building.	77	76
Own their dwelling	71	71
Tenants without deposit/share or with special leases	17	17
Live without bath or w.c.*	11	11
Live in damp dwelling	7	8
Live in cold dwelling	9	8
Live with bath and w.c.* and without cold/damp room	78	78
Live in crowded dwelling	10	10
Live in spacious dwelling	40	43
Live in old/crowded dwelling	28	29
Noise from road traffic	20	17
Noise from dwelling	30	26
Traffic/industry pollution	29	27
Noise or pollution	40	38

----

* water closet/toilet
Note. Column headings in italics show the national terminology.

Table 10 *(continued)*

Housing characteristics	Severe impairment of commun-ication	Total or profound impairment of hearing	Speech and hearing	Total visual impairment of both eyes	Bilateral complete paralysis of lower limbs: paraplegia	Bilateral paralysis of upper limbs
ICIDH	30	40	M40.1	51.0	72.3	73.0

SRI LANKA, population census 1981

Means of livelihood for disabled persons according to sex and residence

	Mute	Deaf	Deaf and mute	Blind	Paralysis of both legs	Paralysis of both hands
Living in an institution						
Total						
Males	251	221	602	413	332	104
Employment	39	26	52	34	17	2
Supported by family or relatives	55	16	29	21	41	17
Supported by institution or organization	150	177	510	346	258	80
Begging	0	0	0	0	0	0
Other	7	2	11	12	16	5
Females	163	188	474	341	268	86
Employment	13	6	16	13	1	0
Supported by family or relatives	42	14	33	29	35	19
Supported by institution or organization	104	168	417	284	222	65
Begging	0	0	0	0	0	0
Other	4	0	8	15	10	2
Urban						
Males	133	18	304	182	187	75
Employment	10	1	19	12	5	0
Supported by family or relatives	15	5	5	2	8	5
Supported by institution or organization	106	11	279	167	172	69
Begging	0	0	0	0	0	0
Other	2	1	1	1	2	1
Females	78	65	273	184	178	58
Employment	0	0	1	6	0	0
Supported by family or relatives	7	7	8	3	9	3
Supported by institution or organization	69	58	260	168	165	54
Begging	0	0	0	0	0	0
Other	2	0	4	7	4	1

Note. Column headings in italics show the national terminology.

Table 10 *(continued)*

Housing characteristics	Paralysis of dominant upper limb	Other paralysis of lower limb	Transverse deficiency of carpus	Transverse deficiency of carpi	Transverse deficiency of lower leg	Transverse deficiency of lower legs
ICIDH	73.1	73.4	75.3	75.31	75.6	75.61

SRI LANKA, population census 1981 (cont'd)

Means of livelihood for disabled persons according to sex and residence

	Paralysis of one hand	*Paralysis of one leg*	*Loss of one hand*	*Loss of both hands*	*Loss of one leg*	*Loss of both legs*
Living in an institution						
Total						
Males	163	239	55	9	103	32
Employment	26	56	13	0	23	8
Supported by family or relatives	35	33	18	4	28	6
Supported by institution or organization	94	141	22	5	48	17
Begging	0	0	0	0	0	0
Other	8	9	2	0	4	1
Females	88	133	9	3	37	6
Employment	4	17	1	0	0	0
Supported by family or relatives	16	23	0	1	9	0
Supported by institution or organization	63	88	6	2	25	6
Begging	0	0	0	0	0	0
Other	5	5	2	0	3	0
Urban						
Males	54	92	18	3	42	10
Employment	6	14	1	0	4	1
Supported by family or relatives	6	4	8	2	11	0
Supported by institution or organization	39	71	9	1	24	8
Begging	0	0	0	0	0	0
Other	3	3	0	0	3	1
Females	36	58	2	3	26	3
Employment	0	4	0	0	0	0
Supported by family or relatives	5	7	0	1	4	0
Supported by institution or organization	30	43	1	2	19	3
Begging	0	0	0	0	0	0
Other	1	4	1	0	3	0

Note. Column headings in italics show the national terminology.

Table 10 *(continued)*

Housing characteristics	Severe impairment of commun-ication	Total or profound impairment of hearing	Speech and hearing	Total visual impairment of both eyes	Bilateral complete paralysis of lower limbs: paraplegia	Bilateral paralysis of upper limbs
ICIDH	30	40	M40.1	51.0	72.3	73.0

SRI LANKA, population census 1981 (cont.)

Means of livelihood for disabled persons according to sex and residence

	Mute	Deaf	Deaf and mute	Blind	Paralysis of both legs	Paralysis of both hands
Living in an institution						
Rural						
Males	100	194	283	212	127	23
Employment	21	19	21	17	9	1
Supported by family or relatives	32	9	22	13	22	7
Supported by institution or organization	43	166	231	172	82	11
Begging	0	0	0	0	0	0
Other	4	0	9	10	14	4
Females	70	118	191	140	78	23
Employment	3	3	7	3	1	0
Supported by family or relatives	30	5	23	15	17	12
Supported by institution or organization	35	110	157	115	55	10
Begging	0	0	0	0	0	0
Other	2	0	4	7	5	1
Estate sector						
Males	18	9	15	19	18	6
Employment	8	6	12	5	3	1
Supported by family or relatives	8	2	2	6	11	5
Supported by institution or organization	1	0	0	7	4	0
Begging	0	0	0	0	0	0
Other	1	1	1	1	0	0
Females	15	5	10	17	12	5
Employment	10	3	8	4	0	0
Supported by family or relatives	5	2	2	11	9	4
Supported by institution or organization	0	0	0	1	2	1
Begging	0	0	0	0	0	0
Other	0	0	0	1	1	0

Note. Column headings in italics show the national terminology.

Table 10 *(continued)*

Housing characteristics	Paralysis of dominant upper limb	Other paralysis of lower limb	Transverse deficiency of carpus	Transverse deficiency of carpi	Transverse deficiency of lower leg	Transverse deficiency of lower legs
ICIDH	**73.1**	**73.4**	**75.3**	**75.31**	**75.6**	**75.61**

SRI LANKA, population census 1981 (cont'd)

Means of livelihood for disabled persons according to sex and residence

	Paralysis of one hand	*Paralysis of one leg*	*Loss of one hand*	*Loss of both hands*	*Loss of one leg*	*Loss of both legs*
Living in an institution						
Rural						
Males	81	112	28	5	49	22
Employment	10	25	9	0	14	7
Supported by family or relatives	17	21	6	1	13	6
Supported by institution or organization	49	61	11	4	21	9
Begging	0	0	0	0	0	0
Other	5	5	2	0	1	0
Females	45	62	6	0	9	3
Employment	2	6	0	0	0	0
Supported by family or relatives	6	10	0	0	3	0
Supported by institution or organization	33	45	5	0	6	3
Begging	0	0	0	0	0	0
Other	4	1	1	0	0	0
Estate sector						
Males	28	35	9	1	12	0
Employment	10	17	3	0	5	0
Supported by family or relatives	12	8	4	1	4	0
Supported by institution or organization	6	9	2	0	3	0
Begging	0	0	0	0	0	0
Other	0	1	0	0	0	0
Females	7	13	1	0	2	0
Employment	2	7	1	0	0	0
Supported by family or relatives	5	6	0	0	2	0
Supported by institution or organization	0	0	0	0	0	0
Begging	0	0	0	0	0	0
Other	0	0	0	0	0	0

Note. Column headings in italics show the national terminology.

Table 10 *(continued)*

Housing characteristics	Severe impairment of communication	Total or profound impairment of hearing	Speech and hearing	Total visual impairment of both eyes	Bilateral complete paralysis of lower limbs: paraplegia	Bilateral paralysis of upper limbs
ICIDH	30	40	M40.1	51.0	72.3	73.0

SRI LANKA, population census 1981 (cont.)

Means of livelihood for disabled persons according to sex and residence

	Mute	Deaf	Deaf and mute	Blind	Paralysis of both legs	Paralysis of both hands
Not living in an institution						
Total						
Males	6 497	1 648	4 629	4 663	6 118	2 286
Employment	793	503	939	394	302	44
Supported by family or relatives	5 113	931	3 287	3 455	5 239	2 055
Supported by institution or organization	25	16	26	86	78	22
Begging	28	17	19	167	76	26
Other	538	181	358	561	423	139
Females	4 934	1 402	3 636	3 914	4 315	1 605
Employment	168	102	177	102	34	7
Supported by family or relatives	4 323	1 130	3 124	3 271	3 989	1 476
Supported by institution or organization	13	17	23	95	44	23
Begging	10	17	10	50	21	12
Other	420	136	302	396	227	87
Urban						
Males	1 025	180	573	653	867	323
Employment	137	43	120	118	58	5
Supported by family or relatives	784	102	389	393	717	292
Supported by institution or organization	6	9	6	21	9	1
Begging	4	3	3	34	13	9
Other	94	23	55	87	70	16
Females	723	188	531	483	642	217
Employment	14	15	28	29	6	1
Supported by family or relatives	628	146	441	359	579	197
Supported by institution or organization	2	3	9	25	5	1
Begging	2	5	1	7	3	4
Other	77	19	52	63	49	14

Note. Column headings in italics show the national terminology.

Table 10 *(continued)*

Housing characteristics	Paralysis of dominant upper limb	Other paralysis of lower limb	Transverse deficiency of carpus	Transverse deficiency of carpi	Transverse deficiency of lower leg	Transverse deficiency of lower legs
ICIDH	73.1	73.4	75.3	75.31	75.6	75.61

SRI LANKA, population census 1981 (cont'd)

Means of livelihood for disabled persons according to sex and residence

	Paralysis of one hand	Paralysis of one leg	Loss of one hand	Loss of both hands	Loss of one leg	Loss of both legs
Not living in an institution						
Total						
Males	4 740	6 700	1 291	132	2 192	449
Employment	393	986	286	6	439	36
Supported by family or relatives	3 789	4 951	798	109	1 400	320
Supported by institution or organization	52	77	23	3	41	11
Begging	78	94	41	2	86	26
Other	428	592	143	12	226	56
Females	2 580	3 990	353	60	500	159
Employment	36	145	22	0	15	4
Supported by family or relatives	2 312	3 474	294	49	433	142
Supported by institution or organization	21	30	2	1	5	0
Begging	16	34	6	1	3	1
Other	195	307	29	9	44	12
Urban						
Males	761	1 032	194	24	374	107
Employment	53	137	45	1	74	19
Supported by family or relatives	590	756	112	20	222	64
Supported by institution or organization	10	14	4	0	9	2
Begging	19	25	8	0	19	10
Other	89	100	25	3	50	12
Females	360	632	60	15	108	33
Employment	6	26	2	0	3	1
Supported by family or relatives	322	527	49	12	88	30
Supported by institution or organization	2	6	1	1	2	0
Begging	2	6	3	0	0	0
Other	28	67	5	2	15	2

Note. Column headings in italics show the national terminology.

Table 10 *(continued)*

Housing characteristics	Severe impairment of communication	Total or profound impairment of hearing	Speech and hearing	Total visual impairment of both eyes	Bilateral complete paralysis of lower limbs: paraplegia	Bilateral paralysis of upper limbs
ICIDH	30	40	M40.1	51.0	72.3	73.0

SRI LANKA, population census 1981 (cont.)

Means of livelihood for disabled persons according to sex and residence

	Mute	*Deaf*	*Deaf and mute*	*Blind*	*Paralysis of both legs*	*Paralysis of both hands*
Not living in an institution						
Rural						
Males	5 266	1 369	3 884	3 798	4 976	1 867
Employment	613	424	764	250	229	33
Supported by family or relatives	4 197	779	2 796	2 921	4 286	1 684
Supported by institution or organization	19	7	19	63	68	20
Begging	23	13	16	116	57	14
Other	414	146	289	448	336	116
Females	4 024	1 164	2 987	3 164	3 515	1 319
Employment	123	72	118	65	23	3
Supported by family or relatives	3 559	952	2 612	2 695	3 269	1 220
Supported by institution or organization	11	14	14	68	37	21
Begging	5	12	7	40	18	8
Other	326	114	236	296	168	67
Estate sector						
Males	206	99	172	212	275	96
Employment	43	36	55	26	15	6
Supported by family or relatives	132	50	102	141	236	79
Supported by institution or organization	0	0	1	2	1	1
Begging	1	1	0	17	6	3
Other	30	12	14	26	17	7
Females	187	50	118	267	158	69
Employment	31	15	31	8	5	3
Supported by family or relatives	136	32	71	217	141	59
Supported by institution or organization	0	0	0	2	2	1
Begging	3	0	2	3	0	0
Other	17	3	14	37	10	6

Note. Column headings in italics show the national terminology.

Table 10 *(continued)*

Housing characteristics	Paralysis of dominant upper limb	Other paralysis of lower limb	Transverse deficiency of carpus	Transverse deficiency of carpi	Transverse deficiency of lower leg	Transverse deficiency of lower legs
ICIDH	73.1	73.4	75.3	75.31	75.6	75.61

SRI LANKA, population census 1981 (cont'd)

Means of livelihood for disabled persons according to sex and residence

	Paralysis of one hand	*Paralysis of one leg*	*Loss of one hand*	*Loss of both hands*	*Loss of one leg*	*Loss of both legs*
Not living in an institution						
Rural						
Males	3 827	5 412	1 038	101	1 731	324
Employment	320	781	221	5	347	14
Supported by family or relatives	3 082	4 025	654	82	1 119	244
Supported by institution or organization	42	61	18	3	32	9
Begging	58	66	31	2	60	15
Other	325	479	114	9	173	42
Females	2 101	3 164	264	42	371	120
Employment	18	76	11	0	10	2
Supported by family or relatives	1 894	2 810	227	34	329	108
Supported by institution or organization	18	24	1	0	3	0
Begging	12	26	3	1	3	1
Other	159	228	22	7	26	9
Estate sector						
Males	152	256	59	7	87	18
Employment	20	68	20	0	18	3
Supported by family or relatives	117	170	32	7	59	12
Supported by institution or organization	0	2	1	0	0	0
Begging	1	3	2	0	7	1
Other	14	13	4	0	3	2
Females	119	194	29	3	21	6
Employment	12	43	9	0	2	1
Supported by family or relatives	96	137	18	3	16	4
Supported by institution or organization	1	0	0	0	0	0
Begging	2	2	0	0	0	0
Other	8	12	2	0	3	1

Note. Column headings in italics show the national terminology.

Table 10 *(continued)*

Housing characteristics	Mental handicap	Intermittent: consciousness	Speech and hearing	Total visual: both eyes	Cardio-respiratory function	Other and un-specified disfig-urement	Other
ICIDH	M1.1	21	M40.1	51.0	61	87.9	99

St. Helena, national survey 1976

	Disabled persons	Mentally infirm	Epileptic	Deaf and mute	Blind	Cardiac disablement	Crippled	Bed-ridden
Type of residence according to sex								
Males								
Home	31	4	1	4	5	1	14	2
Institution	6	4	0	0	0	0	0	2
Females								
Home	31	6	0	8	3	0	14	0
Institution	15	10	0	0	1	0	0	4
Whether infirmity prevents earnings								
Males								
Home	11							
Institution	2							
Females								
Home	16							
Institution	5							
Whether infirmity does not prevent earnings								
Males								
Home	20							
Institution	4							
Females								
Home	15							
Institution	10							

- -

Note. Column headings in italics show the national terminology.

Table 10 *(continued)*

Housing characteristics	Population surveyed	Aural	Ocular	Occupational role disability	Locomotor disability	Other locomotor disability
ICIDH		4	5	18	4	49

SWEDEN, living conditions survey 1980/81 *

		Reduced hearing	*Reduced eye sight*	*Reduced work capacity*	*Mobility*	*Serious mobility disability*
Type of residence according to age						
Ages 16-64	5 185 000	235 000	25 000	415 000	205 000	75 000
Total	100.0	100.0	100.0	100.0	100.0	100.0
One family house	57.1	61.0	46.2	48.7	47.4	43.7
Apartment house	42.7	38.4	51.8	48.8	50.8	53.9
Institution	0.2	0.6	2.0	2.5	1.8	2.4
Ages 65-84	1 280 000	225 000	70 000	335 000	370 000	215 000
Total	100.0	100.0	100.0	100.0	100.0	100.0
One family house	45.5	49.9	33.9	38.3	36.8	34.9
Apartment house	49.9	47.0	58.5	49.6	51.5	48.0
Institution	4.6	3.1	7.6	12.1	11.7	17.1

Housing characteristics of disabled persons not living in an institution

Ages 16-64 (percentage)						
No lift-not on ground floor		23.8	24.8	24.2	26.4	24.5	20.7
Wheelchair-inaccessible to home		85.7	92.4	86.4	84.8	80.0	68.5
Ages 65-84 (percentage)						
No lift not on ground floor		25.1	23.1	24.2	25.1	25.5	25.1
Wheelchair, inaccessible to home		87.7	89.5	83.5	86.1	85.6	83.7

* Percentage distribution of disabled persons by type of residence, and percentage of non-institutionalized persons according to whether there is a lift on ground floor and according to whether wheelchair is inaccessible to home.

Note. Column headings in italics show the national terminology.

Table 11. Causes of impairments of disabled persons, by age, sex and type of impairment or disability

Table 11 presents the reported causes of impairments of disabled persons, by age, sex and type of impairment or disability. When available, numbers of persons are presented. When not available, priority is given to the presentation of rates, as available, by country.

Description of variables

Data on cause are not standardized. The variation in presentations of causes of impairments is great. National classifications are left intact and presented as given in the published reports of population censuses, national surveys and registration systems. Typical causes reported include accidents (by type of accident), war, injury, abnormal pregnancies, congenital factors or birth defects, and illness (either infectious or chronic). In some cases, different causes were allowed depending upon the specific impairment (e.g., India, 1981). Population censuses generally reported the numbers of disabled persons or numbers of disabilities by cause, whereas surveys generally reported the percentage distribution of causes by type of impairment or disability.

All references to ICIDH codes prefaced with an M (for example, M1.1), indicate that the codes are not ICIDH codes, but are devised to accommodate items not readily coded within ICIDH categories.

11. Causes of impairments of disabled persons by age, sex and type of impairment or disability

Cause of visual impairment	Disabilities	Total visual impairment of both eyes	Near-total visual impairment of both eyes	Moderate visual impairment of both eyes	Unspecified moderate visual impairment of both eyes
ICIDH		51.0	51.3	53	53.9

AUSTRIA, sample survey on physical disabilities 1976 *

	Total visual impairments	*Blind in both eyes*	*Partial sight*	*Farsighted uncorrectable*	*Nearsighted uncorrectable*
Total number	570 600	4 900	7 000	240 800	162 600
Total percent	100.0	100.0	100.0	100.0	100.0
Result of war	5.1	16.8	6.9	..	..
Work accident or work related	9.2	4.8	5.1	9.6	8.3
Traffic accident	1.2	..	..	..	..
Congenital	6.2	28.6	4.6	2.3	8.1
Illness	42.7	39.0	56.4	45.0	36.9
Other accidents	5.3	3.1	8.5	..	..
Unknown	30.3	7.7	18.3	33.7	39.8

	Profound visual impairment of one eye	Other visual impairment	Other visual impairment, colour vision	Other impairment of vision
	54	57	57.5	57.8

	Blind in one eye	*Cataracts or glaucoma*	*Colour blind*	*Other visual*
Total number	28 400	58 000	3 400	65 500
Total percent	100.0	100.0	100.0	100.0
Result of war	14.1	..	..	7.3
Work accident or work related	17.9	..	..	10.3
Traffic accident	4.7	..	..	..
Congenital	9.0	3.6	39.5	14.3
Illness	27.9	61.2	11.4	38.7
Other accidents	13.9	..	..	9.3
Unknown	12.5	16.7	16.1	17.1

* Percentage distribution of disabled persons according to cause of disability and type of impairment or disability.

Note. Column headings in italics show the national terminology.

Table 11 *(continued)*

Cause of impairment, age and sex	Disabled persons	Mental handicap	Total or profound: hearing	Speech and hearing	Total visual: both eyes	Unspecified other paralysis of limb	Transverse deficiency unspecified of proximal limb parts	Other
ICIDH		M1.1	40	M40.1	51.0	73.9	75.9	99

BAHRAIN, *population census 1981*

		Mentally handi-capped	Deaf	Deaf and mute	Blind	Paralysed	Amputee	Other
Males	2 205	392	144	150	704	327	237	251
Infant birth trauma	571	175	46	106	88	80	28	48
Injury	362	50	11	8	111	47	95	40
Disease	1 192	155	71	28	471	200	110	157
Congenital	77	12	16	8	32	0	4	5
Not stated	3	0	0	0	2	0	0	1
Females	1 273	198	85	80	487	243	72	108
Infant birth trauma	301	79	20	54	55	45	14	34
Injury	123	22	3	3	36	25	24	10
Disease	812	85	60	20	382	170	33	62
Congenital	37	12	2	3	14	3	1	2
Not stated	0	0	0	0	0	0	0	0

Note. Column headings in italics show the national terminology.

Table 11 *(continued)*

Cause of disability, age and sex	Disabled persons

CANADA, health and disability survey 1983-84

Both sexes, aged 15+	3 867 000
Congenital	208 000
Disease/illness/stroke	662 000
Disease/illness/treatment after-effect	305 000
Accident	575 000
Aging	623 000
Other	268 000
Don't know	1 226 000

Cause of impairment, age and sex	Disabled persons

ETHIOPIA, survey of children 1981

Both sexes, aged 0-14	29 631
Natural	12 821
Accident	2 644
Illness	10 460
Not stated	3 706

Table 11 (continued)

Cause of disability	Deaf and/ or mute	Ocular	Visceral	Impairment of posture	Impairment of limb
ICIDH	M40.2	5	6	70.5	74.9

FEDERAL REPUBLIC OF GERMANY, biannual survey of 1983
(compilation of state registration system of disabled persons)

	Speech/ hearing/ balance	Blindness/ difficulty seeing	Inner organs	Reduced spine function	Reduction in limb function
Total	201 616	269 074	2 338 143 a/	1 012 334	937 415
Congenital	25 180	15 095	15 746	10 967	43 389
Work accident/related	1 835	5 447	85 598	6 505	53 260
Traffic accident	409	2 591	1 058	3 196	24 211
Home accident	162	1 856	371	1 294	8 330
Other/not specified accident	478	5 488	737	2 961	23 573
Acknowledged war injuries	5 679	17 695	49 425	12 574	133 297
Other: including vaccination reaction	158 232	206 704	2 145 770	904 949	594 093
Other/additional	9 641	14 198	116 438	69 888	57 262

	Transverse deficiency unspecified of proximal limb parts	Other and unspecified disfigurement	Other impairment	Unspecified other impairment
	75.9	87.9	99	99.9

	Limb loss/ partial loss	Dwarfism/ disfigurement	Paraplegia/ mental/addict	Other
Total	142 151	121 009	630 119	842 078
Congenital	3 404	2 221	121 603	11 904
Work accident/related	16 309	181	7 409	11 932
Traffic accident	5 774	144	9 500	2 978
Home accident	1 089	73	1 108	689
Other/not specified accident	4 690	123	4 650	1 774
Acknowledged war injuries	75 848	1 218	25 477	67 854
Other: including vaccination reaction	31 471	111 805	411 296	631 966
Other/additional	3 566	5 244	49 076	112 981

----

a/ Sum of causes does not equal total for inner organs.
Note. Column headings in italics show the national terminology.

Table 11 *(continued)*

Cause of impairment, age and sex	Language impairments	Aural impairments
ICIDH	**3**	**4**

*INDIA, national survey of handicapped 1981 ***

	Speech	*Hearing*
Both sexes, aged 5+		
Urban	100.0	
Voice disorder	3.8	
Cleft palate	1.9	
Illness	17.0	
Injury	1.8	
Medical and surgical intervention	.8	
Others, and not known	74.7	
Rural	100.0	
Voice disorder	3.1	
Cleft palate	1.2	
Illness	11.0	
Injury	.8	
Medical and surgical intervention	.4	
Others, and not known	83.5	
Urban		100.0
German measles		1.0
Noise induced hearing loss		3.0
Ear discharge		13.7
Following illness		24.6
Following injury		5.5
Following medical and surgical intervention		3.0
Others, and not known		49.2
Rural		100.0
German measles		.6
Noise induced hearing loss		2.3
Ear discharge		17.4
Following illness		21.5
Following injury		4.0
Following medical and surgical intervention		1.4
Others, and not known		52.8

---

* Percentage distribution of disabled persons according to cause of impairment, age and residence.
Note. Column headings in italics show the **national terminology**.

Table 11 (continued)

Cause of impairment, age and sex	Total visual impairment of both eyes	Near-total visual impairment of both eyes
ICIDH	51.0	51.3

INDIA, national survey of handicapped 1981 (cont'd) *

	No light perception	*Having light perception*
Both sexes, total		
Urban	100.0	100.0
Cataract	15.6	28.5
Glaucoma	6.4	5.9
Corneal opacity	24.6	4.0
Injuries	5.3	3.0
Eye haemorrhage other than injury	.8	.3
Myopia	0.0	.2
Others, and not known	0.0	..
Not recorded	47.3	58.1
Rural	100.0	100.0
Cataract	19.8	24.3
Glaucoma	7.8	4.6
Corneal opacity	15.2	4.6
Injuries	2.8	2.1
Eye haemorrhage other than injury	.8	.4
Myopia	0.0	.1
Others, and not known	0.0	..
Not recorded	53.6	63.9

---

* Percentage distribution of disabled persons according to cause of impairment, age and residence.
Note. Column headings in italics show the national terminology.

Table 11 *(continued)*

Cause of impairment, age and sex	Unspecified other paralysis of limb	Other motor impairment of limb	Transverse deficiency unspecified of proximal limb parts	Other and unspecified disfigurement
ICIDH	73.9	74	75.9	87.9

INDIA, national survey of handicapped 1981 (cont'd) *

	Paralysis	*Dysfunction of joints*	*Amputation*	*Deformity of limb*
Both sexes (total)				
Urban	100.0	100.0	100.0	100.0
Cerebral palsy	9.9	..	..	3.2
Burns and injury	2.0	41.6	27.9	22.3
Medical/surgical intervention	1.0	2.9	2.3	1.9
Polio	43.6	12.0	..	43.4
Leprosy	.3	1.2	7.7	3.2
Stroke	11.2	2.4	..	1.2
Other illness	16.1	20.2	40.8	13.0
Other cause	15.9	18.7	21.2	11.8
Rural	100.0	100.0	100.0	100.0
Cerebral palsy	15.2	..	..	2.6
Burns and injury	2.1	42.3	21.9	26.7
Medical/surgical intervention	.5	2.0	3.0	1.7
Polio	27.7	8.0	..	29.1
Leprosy	.2	1.2	12.4	7.5
Stroke	12.4	2.0	..	1.5
Other illness	19.1	23.6	27.8	15.9
Other cause	22.8	20.9	34.9	15.0

----

* Percentage distribution of disabled persons according to cause of impairment, age and residence.
Note. Column headings in italics show the national terminology.

Table 11 *(continued)*

Cause of impairment, age and sex	Disabled persons

JAPAN, national survey of handicapped adults 1980

Both sexes, aged 18+　　　　　　　　　　　1 977 000

Traffic accident	92 000
Work accident	177 000
Other accident	119 000
War injury	97 000
Infectious disease	91 000
Toxic disease	8 000
Other disease	841 000
Impairment at birth	70 000
Other (including congenital abnormality)	252 000
Unknown	230 000

Disabling diseases

Both sexes, aged 18+　　　　　　　　　　　1 977 000

Cerebral palsy	59 000
Poliomyelitis	53 000
Spinal cord injury	66 000
Progressive muscular dystrophy	5 000
Cerebro-vascular accident	227 000
Inflammatory joint defect	184 000
Rheumatoid	92 000
Middle ear infection	72 000
Inner ear infection	82 000
Disease of the cornea	74 000
Disease of the lens	65 000
Retino-choroidal and optic nerve disease	118 000
Other disease	880 000

Table 11 *(continued)*

Cause of impairment, age and sex	Disabled persons
KENYA, national survey of persons 1981	
Both sexes, aged 15+	1 774
Poliomyelitis	499
Unspecified diseases	402
Specified diseases	84
Occupational accidents	110
Road accidents	61
Unspecified accidents	22
Congenital defects	110
Medical negligence	54
Measles	53
"Bewitched"	33
Other	14
Don't know	275
Missing information	57

Table 11 *(continued)*

Cause of impairment, age and sex	Disabled persons
	*NEPAL, national survey 1980 **
Males	100.00
Birth defects	29.07
Diseases	50.88
Accidents	20.05
Females	100.00
Birth defects	28.49
Diseases	58.15
Accidents	13.36
Both sexes	100.00
Birth defects	28.85
Diseases	53.60
Accidents	17.55
Both sexes	
Hills	100.00
Birth defects	29.72
Diseases	47.46
Accidents	22.82
Terai region	100.00
Birth defects	27.73
Diseases	61.51
Accidents	10.76

* Percentage distribution of disabled persons by causes of impairments, sex and residence.

Table 11 *(continued)*

Cause of impairment, age and sex	Disabled persons

*NEPAL, national survey 1980 (cont'd) ***

Males

Hills

	100.00
Birth defects	31.42
Diseases	42.04
Accidents	26.54

Terai region

	100.00
Birth defects	26.18
Diseases	61.78
Accidents	12.04

Total

	100.00
Birth defects	29.07
Diseases	50.88
Accidents	20.05

Females

Hills

	100.00
Birth defects	27.03
Diseases	56.08
Accidents	16.89

Terai region

	100.00
Birth defects	30.52
Diseases	61.03
Accidents	8.45

Total

	100.00
Birth defects	28.49
Diseases	58.15
Accidents	13.36

----

* Percentage distribution of disabled persons by causes of impairments, sex and residence.

Table 11 *(continued)*

Cause of impairment, age and sex	Intellectual impairments	Speech and hearing	Total visual impairment of both eyes	Other impairment
ICIDH	1	M40.1	51.0	99

PANAMA, general census of population and housing 1980

	Mentally retarded	*Deaf/Mute*	*Blind*	*Invalid*
Ages 0-39				
Congenital				
Males	2 449	782	111	939
Females	1 906	741	86	721
Acquired (other cause)				
Males	440	135	127	531
Females	308	127	90	277

Note. Column headings in italics show the national terminology.

Table 11 *(continued)*

Cause of impairment	Disabled persons	Language	Severe: communi- cation	Voice production	Voice quality	Speech fluency	Aural
ICIDH		3	30	35	36.6	37.0	4

PHILIPPINES, national survey 1980

	Aphasia	Mutism	Dysarthria	Nasal twang	Stuttering
Total	19	60	49	40	45
Congenital	5	44	11	38	26
Infectious	5	3	1	0	3
Trauma	1	0	1	0	0
New growth	0	0	0	0	0
Vascular	8	0	30	0	1
Degenerative	0	0	0	0	0
Metabolic endocrine	0	0	0	0	0
Not stated	0	2	6	2	15

		Communication	*Aural*
Total	1 292	26	72
Congenital	332	14	4
Infectious	120	0	20
Trauma	87	0	11
New growth	12	0	0
Vascular	8	2	0
Degenerative	46	0	14
Metabolic endocrine	3	0	0
Combination of causes	471	0	4
Not stated	213	10	19

Note. Column headings in italics show the national terminology.

Table 11 *(continued)*

Cause of impairment	Total or profound: hearing	Moderate bilateral hearing	Mild bilateral hearing	Ocular	Total visual: both eyes	Near-total visual both eyes	Profound visual: one eye
ICIDH	40	45.4	45.7	5	51.0	51.3	54

PHILIPPINES, national survey 1980 (cont'd)

	Total hearing loss	Hearing loss severe	Hearing loss mild	Ocular	Blind both eyes	Partial both eyes	Blind one eye
Total	43	57	184	151	63	37	113
Congenital	30	15	24	35	5	0	7
Infectious	4	10	41	28	11	3	27
Trauma	4	6	18	21	4	1	27
New growth	0	1	0	2	2	0	0
Vascular	2	0	1	2	1	0	3
Degenerative	2	18	63	24	25	24	28
Metabolic endocrine	0	0	0	2	1	1	0
Combination of causes				3			
Not stated	1	7	37	34	14	8	21

Note. Column headings in italics show the national terminology.

Table 11 *(continued)*

Cause of impairment	Near-total visually impaired: one eye, other eye not stated	Other visual	Visceral	Skeletal	Mechanical and motor: face	Posture	Un- specified: posture
ICIDH	54.5	57	6	7	70.2	70.5	70.59

PHILIPPINES, national survey 1980 (cont'd)

	Partial one eye	Strabismus	Kyphosis	Weakness or face paralysis	Scoliosis	Others, spine deformity
Total	11	61	33	23	13	6
Congenital	1	42	4	0	7	0
Infectious	1	5	6	0	4	1
Trauma	1	4	4	10	0	2
New growth	0	0	0	0	0	0
Vascular	0	0	0	2	1	0
Degenerative	5	0	3	0	0	0
Metabolic endocrine	0	0	0	0	0	0
Not stated	3	10	16	11	1	3

	Visceral	Skeletal
Total	214	346
Congenital	137	31
Infectious	50	14
Trauma	15	29
New growth	4	0
Vascular	0	4
Degenerative	0	3
Metabolic endocrine	0	1
Combination of causes	8	144
Not stated	0	120

Note. Column headings in italics show the national terminology.

Table 11 *(continued)*

Cause of impairment	Mixed and other mechanical impairment of limb	Bilateral complete paralysis of lower limbs: paraplegia	Unspecified spastic paralysis of more than one limb	Paralysis of upper and lower limbs on same side	Paralysis of all four limbs	Other flaccid paralysis of limb
ICIDH	71.9	72.3	72.9	73.5	73.7	73.85

PHILIPPINES, national survey 1980 (cont'd)

	Fracture	*Paraplegia*	*Spastic*	*Hemiplegia*	*Quadriplegia*	*Flaccid*
Total	43	28	30	62	17	74
Congenital	0	9	0	7	5	0
Infectious	0	5	0	11	5	0
Trauma	43	7	0	2	5	0
New growth	0	0	0	1	4	0
Vascular	0	4	0	40	0	0
Degenerative	0	0	0	0	1	0
Metabolic endocrine	0	0	0	0	0	0
Not stated	0	3	30	1	2	74

	Unspecified other paralysis of limb	Other motor: limb	Other bilateral motor: upper limbs	Other motor impairment of limb: other	Unspecified other motor impairment of limb		
					Impairment of limb	Tremor nos[*]	Limping nos
	73.9	74	74.0	74.8	74.9	74.92	74.97

	1-limb paralysis	*Rigid*	*Athetosis*	*Limb movement abnormal or other*	*Polio*	*Tremors*	*Unequal limb length or other*
Total	114	50	14	6	82	58	29
Congenital	10	0	8	0	0	17	0
Infectious	37	0	2	1	82	17	0
Trauma	40	0	0	3	0	12	0
New growth	0	0	0	2	0	1	0
Vascular	15	0	2	0	0	12	0
Degenerative	5	0	1	0	0	6	0
Metabolic endocrine	0	0	0	0	0	0	0
Not stated	7	50	1	0	0	3	29

---

[*] Not otherwise specified

Note. Column headings in italics show the national terminology.

Table 11 *(continued)*

Cause of impairment	Transverse deficiency of upper arm	Transverse deficiency of lower leg	Transverse deficiency unspecified of proximal limb parts	Deficiency in head region	Other disfigurement of trunk	Congenital deformity: disfigurement of metacarpus and hand
ICIDH	75.1	75.6	75.9	80	83	84.03

PHILIPPINES, national survey 1980 (cont'd)

	Right and left upper	*Right and left lower*	*Less than one extremity*	*Face and head*	*Trunk/Body*	*Claw-hand*
Total	18	17	4	80	15	26
Congenital	1	3	2	54	5	10
Infectious	1	3	2	6	0	6
Trauma	15	9	0	8	4	9
New growth	0	0	0	4	3	0
Vascular	0	1	0	0	0	1
Degenerative	0	0	0	0	0	0
Metabolic endocrine	0	1	0	3	0	0
Not stated	1	0	0	5	3	0

Note. Column headings in italics show the national terminology.

Table 11 *(continued)*

| Cause of impairment | Disfigurement of limb: congenital deformity | | Other disfigurement | Other and unspecified disfigurement | Generalized, sensory and other impairments | Other sensory impairment: pain |
	Of knee and leg	Of ankle, foot and toe				
ICIDH	84.06	84.07	87	87.9	9	98.3

PHILIPPINES, national survey 1980 (cont'd)

	Genu recurvatum	*Club foot*	*Others, limb deformity*	*Extremities*	*Sensory impairment*	*Joint/Muscle pain present*
Total	42	14	84	43	82	
						440
Congenital	12	9	9	16	0	0
Infectious	22	5	29	5	0	0
Trauma	5	0	36	8	0	0
New growth	0	0	0	10	0	0
Vascular	0	0	3	0	0	0
Degenerative	0	0	2	0	0	0
Metabolic endocrine	0	0	0	0	0	0
Not stated	3	0	5	4	82	440

	Disfiguring	*Two-category combinations*
Total		
Congenital	16	95
Infectious	6	2
Trauma	8	3
New growth	6	0
Vascular	0	0
Degenerative	0	5
Metabolic endocrine	0	0
Combination of causes	5	307
Not stated	2	28
	43	440

Note. Column headings in italics show the national terminology.

Table 11 *(continued)*

Cause of impairment, age and sex	Severe: communica- tion	Total or profound: hearing	Speech and hearing	Total visual: of both eyes	Bilateral complete paralysis of lower limbs: paraplegia	Bilateral paralysis of upper limbs
ICIDH	30	40	M40.1	51.0	72.3	73.0

SRI LANKA, population census 1981

	Mute	Deaf	Deaf and mute	Blind	Paralysis of both legs	Paralysis of both hands
Total						
Males	6 748	1 869	5 231	5 076	6 450	2 390
Since birth	5 876	818	4 800	1 638	3 172	1 208
Due to illness	408	393	186	1 587	1 642	574
Due to accident	98	213	61	633	694	142
Due to violence	9	10	1	68	26	18
Unspecified	357	435	183	1 150	916	448
Females	5 097	1 590	4 110	4 255	4 583	1 691
Since birth	4 596	737	3 831	1 438	2 428	925
Due to illness	221	348	121	1 485	1 244	360
Due to accident	34	116	22	278	210	69
Due to violence	1	6	1	8	8	2
Unspecified	245	383	135	1 046	693	335
Urban						
Males	1 158	198	877	835	1 054	398
Since birth	964	72	785	261	491	195
Due to illness	83	44	33	243	276	85
Due to accident	24	20	19	131	127	25
Due to violence	1	1	-	14	5	2
Unspecified	86	61	40	186	155	91
Females	801	253	804	667	820	275
Since birth	709	133	751	231	362	145
Due to illness	36	41	18	217	252	57
Due to accident	9	19	3	46	62	14
Due to violence	-	-	-	-	0	0
Unspecified	47	60	32	173	144	59

Note. Column headings in italics show the national terminology.

Table 11 (continued)

Cause of impairment, age and sex	Paralysis of dominant upper limb	Other paralysis of lower limb	Transverse deficiency of carpus	Transverse deficiency of carpi	Transverse deficiency of lower leg	Transverse deficiency of lower legs
ICIDH	73.1	73.4	75.3	75.31	75.6	75.61

SRI LANKA, population census 1981 (cont'd)

	Paralysis of one hand	Paralysis of one leg	Loss of one hand	Loss of both hands	Loss of one leg	Loss of both legs
Total						
Males	4 903	6 939	1 346	141	2 295	481
Since birth	1 227	1 905	205	54	172	142
Due to illness	1 767	2 480	114	23	641	143
Due to accident	803	1 269	743	29	1 101	111
Due to violence	81	63	74	5	46	4
Unspecified	1 025	1 222	210	30	335	81
Females	2 668	4 123	362	63	537	165
Since birth	805	1 463	133	34	110	83
Due to illness	978	1 530	60	12	195	48
Due to accident	299	463	88	1	134	8
Due to violence	11	12	11	0	4	0
Unspecified	575	655	70	16	94	26
Urban						
Males	815	1 124	212	27	416	117
Since birth	175	279	29	6	27	26
Due to illness	308	424	29	4	152	30
Due to accident	113	180	87	7	158	35
Due to violence	10	3	8	3	8	1
Unspecified	209	238	59	7	71	25
Females	396	690	62	18	134	36
Since birth	98	188	10	7	18	18
Due to illness	129	269	18	4	66	13
Due to accident	41	96	18	1	27	2
Due to violence	0	1	0	0	1	0
Unspecified	128	136	16	6	22	3

Note. Column headings in italics show the national terminology.

Table 11 *(continued)*

Cause of impairment, age and sex	Severe: communica- tion	Total or profound: hearing	Speech and hearing	Total visual: of both eyes	Bilateral complete paralysis of lower limbs: paraplegia	Bilateral paralysis of upper limbs
ICIDH	30	40	M40.1	51.0	72.3	73.0

SRI LANKA, population census 1981 (cont'd)

	Mute	*Deaf*	*Deaf and mute*	*Blind*	*Paralysis of both legs*	*Paralysis of both hands*
Rural						
Males	5 366	1 563	4 167	4 010	5 103	1 890
Since birth	4 723	696	3 841	1 307	2 491	958
Due to illness	314	334	150	1 308	1 323	473
Due to accident	72	185	39	469	549	110
Due to violence	8	9	1	53	21	16
Unspecified	249	339	136	873	719	333
Females	4 094	1 282	3 178	3 304	3 593	1 342
Since birth	3 717	578	2 961	1 139	1 970	749
Due to illness	176	302	100	1 217	962	295
Due to accident	25	95	19	213	137	50
Due to violence	1	5	1	8	7	2
Unspecified	175	302	97	727	517	246
Estate sector						
Males	224	108	187	231	293	102
Since birth	189	50	174	70	190	55
Due to illness	11	15	3	36	43	16
Due to accident	2	8	3	33	18	7
Due to violence	-	-	-	1	0	0
Unspecified	22	35	7	91	42	24
Females	202	55	128	284	170	74
Since birth	170	26	119	68	96	31
Due to illness	9	5	3	51	30	8
Due to accident	-	2	-	19	11	5
Due to violence	-	1	-	-	1	0
Unspecified	23	21	6	146	32	30

Note. Column headings in italics show the national terminology.

Table 11 *(continued)*

Cause of impairment, age and sex	Paralysis of dominant upper limb	Other paralysis of lower limb	Transverse deficiency of carpus	Transverse deficiency of carpi	Transverse deficiency of lower leg	Transverse deficiency of lower legs
ICIDH	73.1	73.4	75.3	75.31	75.6	75.61

SRI LANKA, population census 1981 (cont'd)

	Paralysis of one hand	Paralysis of one leg	Loss of one hand	Loss of both hands	Loss of one leg	Loss of both legs
Rural						
Males	3 908	5 524	1 066	106	1 780	346
Since birth	991	1 504	163	43	133	108
Due to illness	1 424	1 994	83	19	476	113
Due to accident	671	1 054	616	20	899	72
Due to violence	70	59	66	2	37	3
Unspecified	752	913	138	22	235	50
Females	2 146	3 226	270	42	380	123
Since birth	660	1 158	111	25	85	63
Due to illness	815	1 222	39	8	125	35
Due to accident	243	353	64	0	101	6
Due to violence	11	11	11	0	3	0
Unspecified	417	482	45	9	66	19
Estate sector						
Males	180	291	68	8	99	18
Since birth	61	122	13	5	12	8
Due to illness	35	62	2	0	13	0
Due to accident	19	35	40	2	44	4
Due to violence	1	1	0	0	1	0
Unspecified	64	71	13	1	29	6
Females	126	207	30	3	23	6
Since birth	47	117	12	2	7	2
Due to illness	34	39	3	0	4	0
Due to accident	15	14	6	0	6	0
Due to violence	0	0	0	0	0	0
Unspecified	30	37	9	1	6	4

Note. Column headings in italics show the national terminology.

330

Table 11 *(continued)*

Cause of impairment, age and sex	Population surveyed	Disabled persons	Total or profound impairment of hearing	Speech and hearing	Total visual impairment of both eyes	Profound visual impairment of one eye
ICIDH			40	M40.1	51.0	54

TURKEY, population census 1975

			Deaf	Deaf and mute	Blind	Sight loss in one eye
Total						
Males	20 744 730	355 557	28 968	26 034	28 963	51 867
From birth		82 647	6 466	13 873	6 632	10 072
Traffic accident		22 913	693	748	1 758	2 689
Labour-hazard		40 960	1 680	1 092	2 960	9 326
Illness		85 821	9 196	5 464	10 393	15 837
Other		55 458	6 850	3 419	4 743	11 044
Unknown		67 758	4 083	1 438	2 477	2 899
Females	19 602 989	232 710	44 274	20 890	22 489	30 044
From birth		64 981	4 192	10 060	4 357	5 771
Traffic accident		9 101	461	556	1 637	1 233
Labour-hazard		10 621	524	336	875	2 236
Illness		71 470	17 172	5 139	9 467	10 794
Other		41 439	11 214	2 552	3 825	7 039
Unknown		35 098	10 711	2 247	2 328	2 971

Note. Column headings in italics show the national terminology.

Table 11 *(continued)*

Cause of impairment, age and sex	Impairment of posture	Unspecified other paralysis of limb	Unspecified other motor impairment of limb	Other and unspecified disfigurement	Other impairment	Unspecified other impairment
ICIDH	70.5	73.9	74.9	87.9	99	99.9

TURKEY, population census 1975 (cont'd)

	Hunchback	*Paralysed*	*Lame*	*Crippled*	*Other*	*Unknown*
Total						
Males	2 533	10 789	102 329	19 582	35 183	49 309
From birth	785	2 552	28 326	4 196	9 745	
Traffic accident	129	394	12 481	2 024	1 997	
Labour-hazard	275	566	15 884	5 047	4 130	
Illness	644	4 905	27 611	2 469	9 302	
Other	562	1 802	14 662	4 355	8 021	
Unknown	138	570	3 365	1 491	1 988	49 309
Females	1 779	7 498	67 626	10 194	17 888	10 028
From birth	520	1 689	30 470	2 312	5 610	
Traffic accident	60	156	3 765	735	498	
Labour-hazard	99	149	4 811	848	743	
Illness	502	3 908	17 156	1 561	5 771	
Other	477	1 187	9 087	1 976	4 082	
Unknown	121	409	2 337	2 762	1 184	10 028

Note. Column headings in italics show the national terminology.

Table 11 (continued)

Cause of disability, age and sex	Chronically disabled persons

URUGUAY, survey of the chronically ill 1984

Urban

Males, aged 45-54

Cause	
	10
Cardiovascular	4
Cerebrovascular	1
Diabetes	2
Pulmonary	1
Rheumatism	..
Neoplasms	..
Psychiatric	..
Other	2

Females, aged 45-54

Cause	
	12
Cardiovascular	6
Cerebrovascular	..
Diabetes	..
Pulmonary	2
Rheumatism	1
Neoplasms	1
Psychiatric	..
Other	2

Males, aged 55-64

Cause	
	16
Cardiovascular	7
Cerebrovascular	..
Diabetes	..
Pulmonary	3
Rheumatism	1
Neoplasms	2
Psychiatric	1
Other	2

Females, aged 55-64

Cause	
	22
Cardiovascular	13
Cerebrovascular	..
Diabetes	2
Pulmonary	..
Rheumatism	3
Neoplasms	2
Psychiatric	..
Other	2

Table 11 *(continued)*

Cause of disability, age and sex	Chronically disabled persons

URUGUAY, survey of the chronically ill 1984 (cont'd)

Urban

Males, aged 65+

Cardiovascular	11
Cerebrovascular	1
Diabetes	..
Pulmonary	1
Rheumatism	2
Neoplasms	..
Psychiatric	..
Other	1

Total: 16

Females, aged 65+

Cardiovascular	23
Cerebrovascular	..
Diabetes	4
Pulmonary	..
Rheumatism	5
Neoplasms	..
Psychiatric	..
Other	2

Total: 34

Males, aged 45+

Cardiovascular	22
Cerebrovascular	2
Diabetes	2
Pulmonary	5
Rheumatism	3
Neoplasms	2
Psychiatric	1
Other	5

Total: 42

Table 11 *(continued)*

Cause of impairment, age and sex	Disabled persons	Disabilities	Mental handicap	Ocular	Mixed and other upper limb mechanical	Mixed and other mechanical impairment of limb
ICIDH			M1.1	5	71.8	71.9

ZIMBABWE, *national survey 1981*

			Mental handicap	*Visual*	*Upper limb*	*Lower limb*
Disease		40 000				
0-4		3 200	..	..	..	..
5-15		10 700	..	..	..	..
16-59		19 000	..	..	..	..
60+		7 200	..	..	..	..
Accident		26 800				
0-4		500	..	..	..	..
5-15		4 100	..	..	..	..
16-59		16 300	..	..	..	..
60+		5 800	..	..	..	..
War		10 500				
0-4		100	..		..	..
5-15		900	..	..	..	..
16-59		8 100	..	..	..	..
60+		1 300	..	..	..	..
			..	..		
Abnormal pregnancy/birth		4 100				
0-4		800	..	..	..	..
5-15		1 300	..	..	..	..
16-59		1 900	..	..	..	..
60+		200	..	..	..	..
Malnutrition		1 300				
0-4		500	..	..	..	..
5-15		300	..	..	..	..
16-59		400	..	..	..	..
60+		100	..	..	..	..
Hereditary		1 300				
0-4		100	..	..	..	..
5-15		500	..	..	..	..
16-59		600	..	..	..	..
60+		100	..	..	..	..
Total	84 000					
Disease			2 000	12 400	5 400	17 300
Accident			1 200	5 500	9 600	12 200
War			400	1 300	3 600	6 000
Total			3 600	19 200	18 600	35 500

Note. Column headings in italics show the national terminology.

Table 11 *(continued)*

Causes of impairment, age and sex	Total visual impairment of both eyes	Near-total visual impairment of both eyes	Profound visual impairment of one eye	Bilateral complete paralysis of lower limbs: paraplegia
ICIDH	51.0	51.3	54	72.3

ZIMBABWE national survey 1981 (cont'd) a/

	Blind	*Partial blindness*	*Sight loss in one eye*	*Loss of use of legs*
Disease	3 400	5 000	3 900	16 000
Measles	2 100	1 900	2 500	..
Polio	..	..	..	13 400
Leprosy	..	..	..	100
Other	1 300	3 100	1 400	2 600
Accident	700	1 400	3 300	7 800
Traffic	100	200	100	2 000
Domestic	300	600	2 200	3 500
Sport	0	0	0	400
Industry	100	0	100	300
Mining	0	0	100	100
Agriculture	0	300	300	500
Assault	100	100	400	500
Other	0	100	0	500
War	200	600	500	4 400
Military	0	100	100	1 000
Civilian	200	500	400	3 400

	Bilateral paralysis of upper limbs	Transverse deficiency of upper arm	Transverse deficiency of lower leg	Other disfigurement
	73.0	75.1	75.6	87
	Loss of use of arms	*Loss of arm(s)*	*Loss of leg(s)*	*Albinism*
Disease	4 400	900	1 000	0
Measles	..	..	..	0
Polio	4 000	0	0	..
Leprosy	900	600	800	..
Other	500	300	200	0
Accident	4 500	5 200	4 400	0
Traffic	400	900	1 100	0
Domestic	2 500	2 500	1 800	0
Sport	0	0	0	0
Industry	500	500	400	0
Mining	300	100	200	0
Agriculture	300	300	200	0
Assault	600	300	0	0
Other	0	300	300	0
War	2 100	1 500	1 600	..
Military	300	100	300	..
Civilian	1 800	1 400	1 400	..

a/ Sum of causes does not necessarily equal total.

Note. Column headings in italics show the national terminology.

Table 12. Aids used for reducing disabilities of disabled persons, by age, sex and type of impairment or disability

Table 12 presents the special aids used by persons with disabilities or impairments to reduce disablement, by age and sex and type of impairment or disability. Only three countries have asked this question at the present. It is anticipated, however, that this will be a more common survey question in the future.

Special aids were typically classified according to the type of disability or impairment being reduced. In some cases, comparisons were also made between special aids used in households versus special aids used in institutions. Special aids most often mentioned included hearing aids, glasses or contact lenses, braces, sticks and crutches, wheelchairs, rails and bars. There are, as yet, no standards for survey questions on the use of special aids, nor is there any general classification scheme into which they may be coded. Some questions were asked about the availability of aids and also reasons for not using one when needed.

12. Aids used for reducing disabilities of disabled persons, by age, sex and type of impairment or disability

Special aids used age and sex	Total disabilities		
	Household	Institution	Total

AUSTRALIA, national survey of handicapped persons 1981

Special aids used age and sex	Household	Institution	Total
Total disabled persons	405 700	78 300	484 100
Self care disabilities	113 100	67 600	181 100
Eating: special crockery or cutlery	12 200	4 400	16 600
Dressing: zip puller, button-hook	8 200	1 500	9 800
Washing: bath seat, special shower fittings	69 000	58 700	127 700
Conventional toilet use: commode, toilet frames or chairs	10 900	2 200	13 100
Housekeeping: special iron/cutting/cooking/opening	5 400	..	5 700
Other	7 400	800	8 200
Support/mobility disabilities	283 400	70 100	353 700
Artificial leg, foot, hip	7 200	..	7 500
Calipers, splints	9 100	1 700	10 800
Braces, belts, corsets	30 300	500	30 800
Sticks, portable frames, crutches for support	157 400	35 200	192 600
Foot or leg support: built-up shoe, ankle strap	15 400	1 300	16 700
Wheelchair: manual or powered	19 000	26 000	45 000
Special chair: ejector chair, hard-back chair	6 100	700	6 800
Special bed or bedding	5 900	500	6 400
Cane, white cane	3 900	800	4 700
Rails, bars, straps, hooks attached to dwelling	10 100	1 400	11 500
Other aids for support and mobility	19 000	2 000	20 900
Communication disabilities	164 200	14 300	178 500
Hearing aids	129 000	10 100	139 000
Telephone attachment or adaptation	3 300	..	3 400
Glasses, spectacles, contact lenses, magnifying glass	24 100	3 200	27 300
Other aids for communication	7 800	1 000	8 800
Medical care disabilities	18 200	..	18 600
Artificial heart stimulus: pacemaker	3 100	..	3 300
Other aids for medical care	15 100	..	15 300
Other	7 200	..	7 500

Table 12 *(continued)*

Special aids used, age and sex	Disabled persons	Disabilities

CANADA, health and disability survey 1983/84

		Disabling conditions
Male		
Total aids used ages 15+		681 000
Cane		274 000
Back or leg brace		97 000
Orthopaedic footwear		85 000
Wheelchair		75 000
Walker		47 000
Crutches		43 000
Foot or leg prosthesis		18 000
Other (unspecified)		42 000
Total persons using one or more mobility aid	467 000	
Female		
Total aids needed ages 15+		72 000
Cane		10 000
Back or leg brace		13 000
Orthopaedic footwear		16 000
Wheelchair		11 000
Walker		0
Crutches		0
Foot or leg prosthesis		0
Other (unspecified)		14 000
Total persons using one or more mobility aid	68 000	

Note. Column headings in italics show the national terminology.

Table 12 *(continued)*

Special aids used, age and sex	Disabled persons	Aural	Ocular
ICIDH		4	5

CANADA, health and disability survey 1983/84 (cont.)

Special features of aids used for getting around residence

Both sexes, ages 15+   2 448 000

Special features used	186 000
No special features used	2 187 000
Use not stated	75 000

Urban

Both sexes, ages 15+   1 609 000

Special features used	129 000
No special features used	1 427 000
Use not stated	53 000

Rural

Both sexes, ages 15+   839 000

Special features used	57 000
No special features used	760 000
Use not stated	21 000

	Hearing	*Seeing*
Aids used		
Both sexes, ages 15+	634 000	331 000
Aids used	179 000	251 000
No aids used	405 000	55 000
Use not stated	51 000	25 000
Urban		
Both sexes, ages 15+	394 000	216 000
Aids used	120 000	165 000
No aids used	244 000	34 000
Use not stated	30 000	17 000
Rural		
Both sexes, ages 15+	240 000	115 000
Aids used	58 000	86 000
No aids used	161 000	21 000
Use not stated	21 000	8 000

Note. Column headings in italics show the national terminology.

Table 12 *(continued)*

Special aids used, age and sex	Aural
ICIDH	**4**

INDIA, national survey of handicapped 1981*

Hearing

Reason for not acquiring hearing aid (age 5+)

Rural

Both sexes aged 5+	100.0
Aid not available	1.5
Aid too expensive	56.0
Not deemed necessary for economic independence	7.9
Not deemed necessary for personal independence	14.3
Other	20.3
Percentage of treated persons aged 5+ advised to use hearing aid	10

Urban

Both sexes aged 5+	100.0
Aid not available	1.3
Aid too expensive	51.8
Not deemed necessary for economic independence	10.7
Not deemed necessary for personal independence	12.6
Other	23.6
Percentage of treated persons aged 5+ advised to use hearing aid	13

----

* Percentage distribution of hearing impaired population aged 5+ according to reason for not acquiring a hearing aid and residence.

Note. Column headings in italics show the national terminology.

Table 12 *(continued)*

Special aids used, age and sex	Total or profound: hearing	Unspecified other motor: limb	Multiple: all classes	Other
ICIDH	40	74.9	90.0	99

NETHERLANDS ANTILLES, general census of population and housing 1981

	Deaf	*Physical*	*Multiple handicap*	*Unknown*
Hearing aid use				
Males				
Yes	104	325	64	10
0-14	38	27	19	3
15-24	17	36	14	1
25-59	24	117	9	4
60+	25	145	22	2
No	202	970	258	128
0-14	31	125	59	42
15-24	19	161	58	36
25-59	55	397	72	40
60+	97	287	69	10
Females				
Yes	124	289	86	5
0-14	52	34	21	..
15-24	20	15	13	..
25-59	24	74	18	3
60+	28	166	34	2
No	209	695	187	119
0-14	27	94	41	32
15-24	14	73	35	21
25-59	62	260	50	41
60+	106	268	61	25

Note. Column headings in italics show the national terminology.

NATIONAL REFERENCES

Africa

Cape Verde	Secretaría de estado de cooperaçao e planeamento. *Recenseamento geral da populaçao e habitaçao - 1980*. vol. III, *Populaçao activa*.
Central African Republic	Bureau central du recensement. *Recensement général de la population de décembre, 1975*. vol. I, *Résultats globaux*. 1980.
Comoros	Direction de la statistique. *Recensement général de la population et de l'habitat, 15 septembre 1980*. vol. I, *Caractéristiques démographiques et mouvements de la population*. vol. II, *Tableaux statistiques du recensement de la population*. *1984*.
Egypt	Central Agency for Public Mobilization and Statistics. *Population and housing census, 1976*. vol. I, *Total Republic* (No. 93-15111, Arabic and English).
	Ministry of Health. *Health interview survey: results of the first cycle; health profile of Egypt*. Publication No.16. Cairo, 1982.
Ethiopia	Nation Children's Commission. *Report of the survey of disabled children in Ethiopia*. Addis Ababa, March 1983.
Kenya	Ministry of Culture and Social Services. *The condition of disabled persons in Kenya: results of a national survey*. By John A. Nkinyangi and Joseph Mbindyo. Institute for Development Studies, consultancy report No. 5. University of Nairobi, 1982.
Mali	Direction nationale de la statistique et de l'informatique. *Recensement général de la population, décembre 1976: résultats definitifs*. vol. I, *Série population et socio-démographique*.
St. Helena	Information Office. *St. Helena and Ascension Islands, census: 31 October 1976*.
Swaziland	Central Statistical Office. *Survey of the handicapped: 1983 report*. 1984.
Tunisia	Institut national de la statistique. *Recensement général de la population et des logements, 8 mai 1975*. vol. III, *Caractéristiques démographiques, tableaux et analyses des résultats du sondage au 1/10ème*.

------.

Recensement général de la population et de l'habitat, 30 mars 1984, vol. IV, *Caractéristiques démographiques.*

Zimbabwe   Ministry of Labour and Social Services and United Nations Children's Fund. *Report on the National Disability Survey, 1981.* 1982.

Asia

Bahrain   Directorate of Statistics. *Census of population and housing, 1981.*

Burma*   Immigration and Manpower Department. *1983 Population census.* 1986.

China   Bureau of Statistics. *The growing Chinese children: sample survey on children, 1983.*

Hong Kong   Census and Statistics Department. *1981 census: disablement characteristics.*

India   National Sample Survey Organization. *Report on survey of disabled persons.* Thirty-sixth round, No. 305, July-December 1981. New Delhi, 1983.

Indonesia   Central Bureau of Statistics. *Population of Indonesia by province: results of the complete count, 1980 population census.* Series L, No. 3. 1981.

------.

Disabled persons in Indonesia: results of the 1980 population census.

------.

Statistical profile of children and mothers in Indonesia, 1982. 1982.

Japan   Society for Rehabilitation of the Disabled. *Rehabilitation services for disabled persons in Japan.* 1983.

Jordan   Queen Alia Social Welfare Fund. *National Survey of the Handicapped in Jordan, September 1979.*

Department of Statistics. *Statistics of the disabled in Jordan, 1983.*

Kuwait   Department of Social Affairs. *Population census of Kuwait,1980.* 1982.

---

* Now Myanmar

Lebanon	Office of Social Development. *Survey for the enumeration and classification of the handicapped in Lebanon, 1980-81: final report.* (Arabic only.)
Nepal	1981 International Year of Disabled Persons Committee. *Report of the sample survey of disabled persons in Nepal.* 1982.
Pakistan	Population Census Organization. *1981 census report of Pakistan: total population.* Census report No. 69. Islamabad, 1984.
	------. *1981 census report of Baluchistan Province.* Census report No. 66. Islamabad, 1984.
	------. *1981 census report of Northwest Frontier Province.* Census report No. 65. Islamabad, 1984.
	------. *1981 census report of Punjab.* Census report No. 67. Islamabad, 1984.
	------. *1981 census report of Sind.* Census report No. 68. Islamabad, 1984.
Philippines	National Census and Statistics Office. *1980 census of population and housing: Philippines.* vol. 2, *National summary.* Manila, 1983.
	National Commission concerning Disabled Persons. *National disability survey.* 1983.
Singapore	Ministry of Community Development, Disabled People Section. *Central registry of disabled people.* In *Quarterly Newsletter.* vol.I, No. 4. (December 1985).
Sri Lanka	Department of Census and Statistics. *Census of population and housing, 1981: statistics on physically disabled persons.* 1981.
Thailand	National Statistical Office. *Statistical tables of the 1981 health and welfare survey.* 1986.
	------. *The children and youth survey, 1983.* 1985.
Turkey	State Institute of Statistics. *1975 census of population: social and economic characteristics of population.* 1982.

Europe

Austria	Statistische Nachrichten 32: Jahrgang 1977 (neue Folge).

Denmark	Danmarks Statistik, Socialforskningsinstitutet, (Institute for Social Research). *Living conditions, Denmark: Compendium of statistics 1984*. Henning Hansen, ed. 1984.
Finland	Central Statistical Office of Finland. *Survey on living conditions in Finland*. Studies, No. 51. 1979.
Federal Republic of Germany.	Statistisches Bundesamt. *Sozialleistungen, Behinderte 1983*. Fachserie 13, Reihe 5.1. Wiesbaden, 1985.
Ireland	Central Statistics Office. *Census of Population Ireland, 1981*. vol.4, *Principal economic status and industries*. 1985.
Norway	Central Bureau of Statistics, *Survey of living standard, 1983* (ISBN 82-537-2144-7). 1985.
Northern Ireland	Alan Whitehead, Stephen Beyer, Karen Buck. *OUTSET action on handicap survey in Northern Ireland: final report*. 1983. (30 Craven Street, London WC2 5BR.)
Poland	Central Statistical Office, *Disabled persons in Poland*. Janusz Bejnarowicz. *Soc. Sci. Med.*, vol. 19, No. 11, pp. 1141-1149. Warsaw, 1984. (Printed in Great Britain.)
Spain	Instituto Nacional de Estadistica, *Censo de población 1981: Caracteristicas de la Población: Avance de resultados*. Madrid, 1984.
Sweden	Statistics Sweden. *Living conditions: Disabled persons*. Report No. 41. S-11581 Stockholm, 1984.

North America

Belize	Caricom Council of Ministers, Regional Census Co-ordinating Committee. *1980-1981 population census of the Caribbean Commonwealth: Belize*. vol. 1.
Canada	Statistics Canada, Health Division and Department of the Secretary of State. *Social trends analysis directorate, 1986*. Report of the Canadian health and disability survey 1983-1984.
República de Cuba	Comité Estatel de Estadísticas, Oficina Nacional del Censo. *Censo de población y viviendas, 1981*. vol. 16.
Jamaica	Ministry of Education. *The Jamaica survey of handicapped children (age 4-11) in schools*. Prepared by Keith Lowe, Frank Ragbir, Research Section. 1983.
Mexico	Instituto Nacional de Estadística Geografía y Informatica, 1984. *X censo general de población y vivienda, 1980*. Resumen general abreviado. 1984.

Netherlands Antilles	Centraal Bureau voor de Statistiek. *Tweede algemene volks: en woningtelling nederlandse antillen, toestand per 1 February 1981.* Series B, No. 1 *Geselecteerde tabellen.* Curaçao, 1983.
Panama	Controlería General de la República, Dirección de Estadística y Censo. *Censos nacionnales de 1980.* vol. II, *Características generales.*
Trinidad and Tobago	Central Statistical Office, Ministry of Finance. *Population and housing census 1980.* vol. II, *Age structure, religion, ethnic group, education administrative areas.*
	Organization of American States, National Project in Special Education and Rehabilitation of the Handicapped. *Report of the national survey of the handicapped children and youth in Trinidad and Tobago.* Prepared by Michael Marge. 1984.
United States of America	Department of Commerce, Bureau of the Census, *1980 census of population.* vol. I, *United States summary: Characteristics of the population; General social and economic characteristics.* Suitland, Maryland, 1983.
	Department of Health and Human Services, Public Health Service, National Center for Health Statistics, Hyattsville, Maryland. *Current estimates from the national health interview survey: Data from the national health survey* series 10. No.150. 1985.

Oceania

Australia	Australian Bureau of Statistics. *Handicapped persons: Australia, 1981.* Prepared by R.J. Cameron, (ABS Catalogue No.4343.0). Canberra, 1984.
Fiji	Bureau of Statistics. *Fiji employment/unemployment survey 1982.* Suva, 1985.
Kiribati	Ministry of Home Affairs, Bairiki. *Report on the 1978 census of population and housing.* vol. I, *Basic information and tables.* Bairiki, 1980.
New Zealand	Department of Statistics. *Report on the social indicators survey 1980-81* (Cat. No. 04.311). Wellington. December 1984.

South America

| Guyana | Caricom Council of Ministers, Regional Census Coordinating Committee. *1980-1981 population census of the Caribbean Commonwealth: Guyana.* vol. I. |

Peru	Instituto Nacional de Estadística. *Censos nacionales: VIII de población III de vivienda. 12 de Julio de 1981.* vol. A, *Nivel nacional: Resultados definitivos.* Julio 1984.
Uruguay	República Oriental del Uruguay, Ministerio de Salud Pública, Organizatión Mundial de la Salud del Uruguay. *Proyecto amro 1700.* 1985
Venezuela	Presidencia de la República, Oficina Central de Estadística e Informatica. *XI censo general de poblacion y vivienda, 20 de Octubre de 1981: Total nacional.*

Annex II

CONDITIONS OF USE AND ORDER FORMS
FOR THE UNITED NATIONS DISABILITY STATISTICS DATA BASE
ON MICROCOMPUTER DISKETTES (DISTAT)
Version 1 (31 December 1987)

The United Nations Disability Statistics Data Base consists of 34 micro-computer spreadsheet files ranging in size from about 7kb to 314 kb and totalling about 3.3mb. The complete data base may be ordered from the Statistical Office on microcomputer diskettes, using the forms provided below. Version 1 of the data base (as of 31 December 1987) contains (a) information on sources and availability of statistics on disability for 95 countries or areas for various years between 1960 and 1986, and (b) detailed statistics on disabled persons from national censuses, surveys and other data sources from 55 of those countries or areas for the period 1975-1986.

CONDITIONS OF USE

The United Nations Disability Statistics Data Base is fully documented in the *United Nations Disability Statistics Data Base, 1975-1986: Technical Manual*, (ST/ESA/STAT/SER.Y/3), Sales No. E.88.XVII.12. Copies of the manual may be obtained from bookstores and distributors handling United Nations publications throughout the world or through the United Nations Sales Section, New York or Geneva.

At the present time the Disability Statistics Data Base is available on diskettes for use on IBM-XT/AT compatible microcomputers using MS-DOS and Lotus 1-2-3 spreadsheet software.[a]

ORDER FORMS
This form is to be returned to:

Statistical Office
United Nations
New York 10017
U.S.A.

A. Diskette format and type[b]

1. Spreadsheet format: Lotus 1-2-3 (version 2) only.

2. Diskette type: 5 1/4" low-density (360kb) only.

---

[a] IBM, is a registered trademark of International Business Machines, Inc. MS-DOS is a registered trademark of Microsoft Corporation. Lotus and 1-2-3 are registered trademarks of Lotus Development Corporation.

[b] Availability is as of 1 May 1990. Diskettes are available in English only. The *Technical Manual* is available in English, Arabic, French, Spanish and Chinese. Other formats and diskette types may become available at a later date.

B. Ordering office and user registration

Name:	Title:
Organization:	
Shipping address:	
City/state/province/country:	
Special shipping instructions, if any:	
Purchase order number:	
Amount to be billed:	

The charge for the United Nations Disability Statistics Data Base is $200, including shipping, payable in local currency at any United Nations office. Note that up to two copies of the diskettes can be made available per Government at no charge. Additional requests will be charged.

I have read the Conditions of Use set out above and agree not to reproduce, copy or publish by any means, in their original or in any altered form, the diskettes which will be shipped to me, except for back-up and analysis of the statistics within my office, distribution to other users in my Government or organization at the same location (which distribution will be registered by me with the Statistical Office of the United Nations Secretariat on forms provided for that purpose with the diskettes) or as otherwise authorized by the United Nations in writing.

Name	Position:
Date:	Signature: